THE CSM
DEVOTIONAL FOR
CHRISTIAN
SCHOOL LEADERS

THE CSM DEVOTIONAL FOR CHRISTIAN SCHOOL LEADERS

*A Journey of
Challenge, Comfort, and Transformation*

Greg Deja, Simon Jeynes, Stephen Zeal

XULON PRESS

Xulon Press
2301 Lucien Way #415
Maitland, FL 32751
407.339.4217
www.xulonpress.com

© 2019 by Greg Deja, Simon Jeynes, & Stephen Zeal

All rights reserved solely by the author. The author guarantees all contents are original and do not infringe upon the legal rights of any other person or work. No part of this book may be reproduced in any form without the permission of the author. The views expressed in this book are not necessarily those of the publisher.

Unless otherwise indicated, Scripture quotations taken from the Holy Bible, New International Version (NIV). Copyright © 1973, 1978, 1984, 2011 by Biblica, Inc.™. Used by permission. All rights reserved.

Printed in the United States of America.

ISBN-13: 978-1-54566-792-7

CONTENTS

Book Reviews	xiii
Introduction	xvi
The Authors	xvii
The Use of this Devotional: The Journey Begins	xviii
Act 1: Mission and Culture (Fall)	1
The Christian Journey: Creation, Advent, and Christmas	1
1. A Prayer for the Beginning of the School Year	2
2. I Am Light in the World	3
3. A New Start for Every Child	4
4. You Have a Blank Page	5
5. The Spirit Gives Life	6
6. We Are a Christian Community – Part 1	7
7. We Are a Christian Community – Part 2	8
8. We Are a Christian Community – Part 3	9
9. We are a Christian Community – Part 4	10
10. I Have a Holy Vocation	11
11. Faithfulness	12
12. The Unlovely Child	13
13. Patience	14
14. I Don't Like Asking for Money!	15
15. If You Don't Ask for It, Fundraising Is Hard Work!	16
Reflection	17
16. Stop Giving!	18
17. United We Stand; Divided We Fall	19
18. Tell Your Story!	20
19. Choose Your Target – It Affects Your Aim!	21
20. What Are the Desires of My Heart?	22

21. Conscience Development......................................23
22. Listen. Act. Be Patient..24
23. God Thinks I'm Somebody 25
24. I Would Love My Faculty to Be Superstars!.........26
25. A Christian Education? What's Different?...........27
26. I Am Not Good Enough!.......................................28
27. God Is a Big Dreamer..29
28. Work Is Worship Is Service 30
29. Hiring the Best Candidate....................................31
30. I Am a Leader and a Manager 32

Reflection..33
31. Grow Up! Make, and Admit, Your Mistakes!......34
32. Problems Are Forever; Take Heart! 35
33. Who Is Mission-Appropriate? 36
34. The Myth of Power and Leadership....................37
35. The Reality of Leadership 38
36. Failing Upwards with Humility 39
37. Do You Know Too Much? 40
38. It's Not Been a Good Week!...............................41
39. In the Beginning..42
40. How Many Children Do You Have in Your School?.....43
41. A Generations Board of Trustees 44
42. Our Neighbors See Us as a Blessing...................45
43. I Am Called and I Am Equipped 46
44. What Is My Blind Spot? 47
45. Come; Take; Learn..48

Reflection..49
46. Signs from Heaven 50
47. The Joy of Getting Up!...51
48. Leading with Dignity 52
49. Fear Is a Constant...53
50. Social Justice and the Way You Talk....................54

51. Truth in Leadership 55

52. Today Is a Happy Day! 56

53. It Doesn't Have to Be Pretty! 57

54. The Challenge of Family 58

55. Time to Do a House Cleaning 59

56. Stand Firm! 60

57. My School Is for Children 61

58. Managing Time Is Wisdom 62

59. The Lord Has Done Great Things for Them 63

60. Unexpected Heroes 64

61. Thank God for Harvest 65

62. Jesus, Son of God 66

Act 2: Toiling and Tilling (Winter) 67

The Christian Journey: Epiphany, Lent, and Easter 67

63. Epiphany and All the Nations 68

64. What's Your Purpose? 69

65. The Size of the Task 70

66. Where Is God's Home? 71

67. Love! That's All it Takes! 72

68. It's Time to Rest on the Sabbath 73

69. Whom Should We Invite to the Feast? 74

70. January Is a Tough Month 75

71. Knowing My Job as a Leader 76

72. Knowing and Loving God 77

73. Can You Endure the Cross? 78

74. Whose List Do I Have Time For? 79

75. Do Not Envy 80

Reflection 81

76. Where Is My Courage? 82

77. Conflict and Relationship 83

78. Life is Not Fair 84

79. Do Something! It's Better than Nothing 85

80. The Beauty of 'Us' 86
81. Separate the People from the Problem! 87
82. Should You Not Expect Works of Power and Authority? 88
83. Shout, and Then Shout Louder! 89
84. Which Students Should Come to Our School? – Part 1 90
85. Which Students Should Come to Our School? – Part 2 91
86. Which Students Should Come to Our School? – Part 3 92
87. Today I Planted a Flower 93
88. Repent, for the Kingdom of Heaven Is at Hand! 94
89. Let's Come Full Circle! 95
90. Interruption 96

Reflection 97

91. Each Parent Is Precious to Me 98
92. How Can I Reach This Student? 99
93. I Am Called 100
94. I Am Different – That's God's Desire and His Gift! 101
95. My Call to Humility 102
96. Mission and Mission Drift 103
97. Get Off the Beach and Onto the Water! 104
98. When Was the Last Time You Worked Out Spiritually? 105
99. Have Plan: Succeed; Have No Plan: Fail 106
100. Teachers Have Enormous Influence in a Child's Life 107
101. Leadership Is an Exercise in Team 108
102 A Young Person's Lodestar 109
103. You Are a Translator Leader 110
104. I Am Really Angry! 111
105. Today Is a Happy Day! 112
106. I Am Blind 113

Reflection 114

107. I Am a Servant 115
108. It's How You Say It 116
109. The Challenge of Being a Hypocrite 117

- 110. The Challenge of Being New 118
- 111. It's Time to Say Goodbye 119
- 112. There's a Rainbow in the Sky! 120
- 113. The Truth Will Set You Free 121
- 114. I Don't Take my Well-Being from the Media! 122
- 115. What Do You Mean? I Have a Great Attitude! 123
- 116. Satan Is the Accuser 124
- 117. Measuring Success 125
- 118. I Am an Eschatological Leader! 126
- 119. Whom Do I Listen To? 127
- 120. It's Not Your Miracle! 128

Reflection 129

Act 3: Celebration and Anticipation (Spring) 131

    The Christian Journey: Pentecost 131

- 121. Praise God! 132
- 122. Admission Season for All the Nations 133
- 123. Sing Praises to Our God 134
- 124. Spring Is in the Air. 135
- 125. God's Revelation; Man's Planning 136
- 126. Unmerited Favor. 137
- 127. The Problem of Evil – Part 1. 138
- 128. The Problem of Evil – Part 2. 139
- 129. The Problem of Evil – Part 3. 140
- 130. A Resurrection Leader 141
- 131. Today Is a Happy Day! 142
- 132. Tend My Sheep 143
- 133. Identity and Purpose 144
- 134. This is a Day When I Want to Give Up! 145
- 135. Make the World a Better Place 146

Reflection 147

- 136. Preparing for the Challenge! 148
- 137. I Have to Fight a Lion Today 149

138. Looking Back; Understanding the Present; Foreseeing the Future 150
139. Do You Need Success to Be on Fire? 151
140. Are Your Children Going to Become a Statistic? 152
141. When Is a Storm Not a Storm? 153
142. Preparing for Graduation 154
143. Exodus and Baptism 155
144. Pentecost – Part 1 156
145. Pentecost – Part 2 157
146. Pentecost – Part 3 158
147. Whose Side? 159
148. Winning Isn't Anything! 160
149. Which Children Are Honorable? 161
150. I Am a Light 162

Reflection 163

151. I Can Be Angry and Hurt! 164
152. It Doesn't Have to Make Sense 165
153. Healthy or Sick? 166
154. A Triptych: Psalm 7 167
155. A Triptych: Psalm 8 168
156. A Triptych: Psalm 9 169
157. God Honors Me! 170
158. Who Deserves What? 171
159. Wasting People 172
160. The Stars Are Shining – It's Time for a Walk! 173
161. Had a Conversation with Me Recently? 174
162. Do You Have to Shout to Be Noticed? 175
163. Don't Worry – God Loves More than We Do 176
164. Friendship and Being a Friend 177
165. Discipling and Leadership 178

Reflection 179

166. The Summer's About Pruning and Growing – Part 1 180
167. The Summer's About Pruning and Growing – Part 2 181

168. The Summer's About Pruning and Growing – Part 3	182
169. The Summer Is for Re-Creation	183
170. Final Reflections on Excellence	184
171. I Give Thanks to the Lord for His Unfailing Love	185

Where Is My Journey Headed Now? 186

Conclusion 187

Appendix 1: Governance – The Cord Principle 189

Appendix 2: The Christian School – The Child Principle 195

Appendix 3: Christian Management / Leadership – The Servant Leader Principle 199

Appendix 4: The Christian School – The Kingdom Principle 203

Appendix 5: Christian Teachers: The Love Principle 207

Appendix 6: Christian Philanthropy – The Mary Principle 211

Appendix 7: Christian Finances – The Ox Principle 215

Appendix 8: The Church Year 219

Appendix 9: The Marketing Page 221

Appendix 10: Index of Bible Passages 223

BOOK REVIEWS

Amanda Jones
Director of Curriculum & Instruction
Legacy Preparatory Christian Academy
The Woodlands, TX

CSM's Christian School Leader's Devotional attempts to challenge and cultivate the soul of Christian school leaders. This devotional is unique and refreshing in many ways. It follows the school and church calendar hitting on various topics and/or tasks pertinent to that season (hiring, fundraising, training teachers and parents, working with the board, etc.), while pushing administrators to think biblically about leading the school and shepherding the teachers. In true devotional style, it prompts school leaders to reflect on their strengths and weaknesses by continually pointing them to the Scriptures. The authors' hearts for true and meaningful Christian education and its leadership are evident in each devotional. To my knowledge, they are the first to create and publish a devotional for Christian school leaders in this manner. This book is a much-needed charge for administrators to create and sustain a Godly culture among the staff, parents, and leaders of their school. Any school would be blessed to have its leaders read and implement the spiritual guidance in this devotional.

Glenn Holzman
Adjunct Professor
Graduate School of Education
Liberty University

In my twenty plus years of Christian school administration, Ecclesiastes 4:9-12 (NIV) was a great source of comfort and encouragement.

> Two are better than one,
>   because they have a good return for their labor:
> [10] If either of them falls down,
>   one can help the other up.
> But pity anyone who falls
>   and has no one to help them up.
> [11] Also, if two lie down together, they will keep warm.
>   But how can one keep warm alone?
> [12] Though one may be overpowered,

two can defend themselves.
A cord of three strands is not quickly broken.

In those times of great challenge, and yes discouragement, that all administers face at some time in their tenures, I found comfort and courage from my Christian colleagues, in my schools, and at sister schools. Tapping into the successes and failures of my colleagues, thus their wisdom, helped me overcome the challenges that I faced. In this day-by-day devotion, you will find the candid and humble wisdom of fellow Christian administrators as they share their wisdom learned and earned in the crucible of school administration. You will find practical strategies for day-to-day issues that are presented with care for Christian schools and a commitment to Christ-centered servant leadership. It is a strand that you will want to add to your cord!

Sheryl L. Jo
Director of School Improvement
Christian Schools International
Grand Rapids, MI

Through their intentional use of the Gospels, Psalms, and the seasons of both the school and church year calendars, the authors of *CSM's First Christian School Leaders' Devotional* speak directly to the reader's heart – to the fears, dreams, challenges, joys, and celebrations of Christian school leaders everywhere. Each devotion offers meditative reflection, thought-provoking questions, and a prayer of desire for forward action. It is clear that authors Deja, Jeynes, and Zeal understand the realities of our Christian school communities, fully anchored in Christ and yet mired in the brokenness of sin. Written in a deeply personal and innovative communicative style, CSM's devotions are thought-provoking, brutally honest, and echo the voice of Jesus. I highly recommend this book to all individuals who are seeking spiritual growth as Christian school leaders and are looking for a powerful resource to fuel their daily commitment to walking with Christ.

H. Lothar Thoelke, *pastor emeritus*
Trinity Evangelical Lutheran Church & School,
Crown Point, Indiana

Devotions are much like the food we eat. They may be nourishing or not, attractive or plain, spicy or bland. The writers of the Christian School Leader's Devotional want to be spiritual neighbors along our journey as Christian educators and succeed in doing that. These spiritual exercises, not quite devotions in the traditional sense of simply nurturing our personal relationship with Christ, focus on Christ's purpose for us as administrators and teachers in our schools, opening up our minds and hearts to his will for us in our vocation.

These are not comfortable or particularly pious devotions. They confront, are honest and frank, question, lead, encourage and help the reader to see both problems and solutions in a fresh light, usually accompanied by a couple of prodding questions to explore. These devotions are what they were intended to be: "real." There's real meat, real food for thought — invitingly prepared.

The framework of the liturgical year into which the devotions are placed is very helpful, not only to those of us who belong in this tradition. The choice of texts only from the Psalms and the Gospels I find less compelling. Those using these devotions will certainly benefit. They will be challenged to become better disciples, explore new ways of seeing things, and find encouragement and help in their task.

INTRODUCTION

Welcome to this devotional! We, the authors, hope and pray that this will be a great journey for you. CSM is committed to reversing the decline in Christian education and has already, since its humble beginnings in August 2017, published books for the Christian School Trustee, and for the Board President / Principal.

Why now a devotional? It is clear to us that we not only need key technical advice, but spiritual neighbors along the pilgrim way who understand our schools, the issues they face, the questions they tussle with, and the glorious outcomes we seek.

Thus, this is a devotional which is part Scripture study, part emotional dive, part intellectual interrogation, and part personal stirrings. We have tried to leave issues open-ended so that the devotions remain thoughtful rather than didactic. At the same time, we also hope to provide enough intellectual and spiritual and emotional meat that you are quickly weaned from milk and taken on a journey with stronger stuff.

Allow us to pray Philippians 1 with and for you:

"I thank my God every time I remember you. In all my prayers for all of you, I always pray with joy because of your partnership in the Gospel from the first day until now, being confident of this, that he who began a good work in you will carry it on to completion until the day of Christ Jesus. It is right for me to feel this way about all of you, since I have you in my heart and, whether I am in chains or defending and confirming the Gospel, all of you share in God's grace with me. God can testify how I long for all of you with the affection of Christ Jesus. And this is my prayer: that your love may abound more and more in knowledge and depth of insight, so that you may be able to discern what is best and may be pure and blameless for the day of Christ, filled with the fruit of righteousness that comes through Jesus Christ—to the glory and praise of God."

Amen. Hallelujah. Amen.

In his service,

Greg, Simon, and Steve

THE AUTHORS

Greg Deja

Greg is the Principal / CEO of Catholic Central High School, the nation's oldest Catholic, coed, diocesan high school and the largest school in the Diocese of Grand Rapids, MI. As an educator, Greg is passionate about schools that are faith-based and desire excellence. He believes schools must know their purpose, have high expectations, and offer relentless support to students.

Simon Jeynes

Simon has been Executive Director of CSM since founding the organization in August 2017. He consults directly with Christian schools, provides association- and school-hosted workshops, writes Entheos (the CSM weekly advice and counsel letter), and works to extend God's kingdom by training and coaching other Christian school leaders to work with CSM. Simon is passionate about reversing the decline in Christian education that has happened during the 21st century. He works to ensure that Christian schools are healthy and full of joy. Simon currently worships at The Gathering Place, an evangelical non-denominational church in his hometown of Ridgetown, Ontario, Canada.

Stephen Zeal

Originally from Wales, Steve has over 30 years of PK-12 independent school education experience and teaching prowess in Wales, Scotland, and the Unites States. Steve has served as the District Representative for the Association of Christian Schools International (ACSI) since 2006. In that capacity, he has led workshops and served on several accreditation teams. In 2002, Steve was the founding Headmaster of a successful classical, Christian school in Houston, TX. He is an ordained Presbyterian elder.

THE USE OF THIS DEVOTIONAL: THE JOURNEY BEGINS

The book is laid out in 3 acts corresponding to the 3 seasons of the school year. The use of the church year to mark the story of Creation through Incarnation to Resurrection and Pentecost is a marvelous way to give your school year a rhythm that is Christian, rather than secular. And each Festival, as it comes, is an opportunity to think deeply about the transformative nature of our faith. The 3 acts correspond to August to December, January to March, April to June.

There are no dates in the book and the contents do not have to be used consecutively unless there are devotion collections that are numbered together.

The Bible passages are taken from 2 places only – the Gospels and the Psalms. Sometimes the meditation invites us to pray a Psalm. This is intentional. CSM's mission is For Jesus; Through Mission; With Students, and we wanted the focus of this devotional to constantly echo the voice of Jesus, our Redeemer, our Brother, and our Friend. And the New Testament quotes the Hebrew Scripture 287 times, with 116 of them being from Psalms. Jesus went to the Mount of Olives singing a Psalm of Ascent. It is impossible to separate Jesus from the Psalms. They are also the most human of interactions with the divine, full of rage and fear and love and submission and humility and raw emotion. This is a template for what we want to do.

The meditations are in a lot of different voices and come from a variety of places. We have not attempted to be entertaining with *Reader's Digest*-style stories – not that we have anything against that. It's just that schools are difficult communities to lead and we neither wanted to be miserable or Pollyanna but, rather, real. We want to recognize real challenges and offer real ways of thinking about them from our own faithfulness and experience.

The prayers are not intended to be final statements of theology or finely wrought literary pieces. They are intended to be cries of the heart, fragments of incomplete thought that look to Christ, the perfecter of our faith (Hebrews 12:2). Some of them may feel incomplete. We want you to be co-creators in allowing your spirit to groan before the throne of God. Praying is not a neat, tidy thing. It's messy, beginning where we are, and never truly completed as we move forward.

There are pages left deliberately blank for you to reflect in yourself. There is a margin down each page for you to use as you reflect. There is a final page for each act for you to write down your reflections. Use these devotions with a pencil or pen and make sure each is well scribbled on before you are finished with it. May it be a blessing for you.

ACT 1: MISSION AND CULTURE (FALL)

THE CHRISTIAN JOURNEY: CREATION, ADVENT, AND CHRISTMAS

My personal mission statement
_____
_____
_____

My current top 5 leadership gifts
1. _____
2. _____
3. _____
4. _____
5. _____

What I hope to get from using this devotional this year
_____
_____
_____
_____
_____
_____

Who will I meet with this year to reflect on my journey?
_____
_____
_____

1. A PRAYER FOR THE BEGINNING OF THE SCHOOL YEAR

Bible Reference: "By day the Lord directs his love, at night his song is with me – a prayer to the God of my life" (Psalm 42:8).

Meditation: You have been rescued by God and set on the path of salvation. You now lead in your school and call upon the name of the Lord. He is your flame by night and your cloud by day. He is your light and your protection. Do not be downcast but rejoice because the Lord himself is your hope and your Savior.

Can I come to God as a Child at the beginning of this new year?

Is this a new beginning for me as well?

"Loving God, let me be strong today as I meet new people in new places. Make me brave when I am worried. Show me how to learn from everyone around me. Help me to do my very best. Amen." (Church of England)

"Gracious God, we come to you at the beginning of this academic year with our many feelings, expectations, fears and hopes. Help us to remember, however, we have the comforting assurance from you: 'I will always be with you.' Loving God, for all of us this is a time of transition. It is transition from the work and leisure of summer back to the classroom. It is transition from time spent with family and friends. Give us patience with ourselves as we transition as well as patience with one another. Give to each member of my school the seven gifts of the Spirit: wisdom, understanding, right judgment, courage, knowledge, reverence, and awe and wonder. Amen." (Marquette University)

"Father, I want you to be right beside me at school this year, almost like you're my best friend. If you were really walking beside me, maybe I'd be more concerned about pleasing you than pleasing others. If you were there beside me, maybe I'd realize I could talk to you anytime I wanted and lean on you when I'm feeling sad or dumb. Help me know you really will be right beside me each day of this school year. Amen." (*Christianity Today*)

2. I AM LIGHT IN THE WORLD

Bible Reference: "A town built on a hill cannot be hidden" (Matthew 5:14).

Meditation: Many of the criticisms of Christian schools unfairly, in my opinion, view them merely as a refuge from a rapidly changing and sometimes frightening world. They accuse Christian parents of running from the "real world." I totally reject this argument. Choosing a Christian school is not running or hiding *from* the world, it is running *toward* the truth and embracing it!

Earlier in the above scripture, Jesus tells us that: "**YOU** are the salt of the earth ... **YOU** are the light of the world." Jesus himself is telling us that society is to be guided and influenced by Christians. Unfortunately, if we look at today's society, it would be fair to ask, "Where exactly is this Christian influence and guidance?"

A cursory glance at the evening news reminds us that war is an ever-present reality, crime rates make us nervous, the family is harder and harder to define, and it looks as though the church has lost much of its ability to be salt and light to the world. The world can be a dark place, but darkness is simply the absence of light, and Jesus makes it clear that we are the light of the world.

If we are to have a positive impact on this world for the kingdom of Jesus Christ, one of the major means of doing so will be found in how we choose to educate our precious children. Plainly stated, the future of this great nation and the world is being shaped right now in the classrooms of your school!

Your school is where children learn how to think, how to communicate, and how to work with others. Without a Christian worldview during these formative years, our Christian witness can wither as it becomes accustomed to being silent, confined to church and Bible study, and never growing beyond elementary school level. Our lamp is hidden and becomes dim, and our salt is no longer good for anything.

You were made in God's image and likeness; you are filled with his Spirit, presence, and light. God needs you to be acting on his behalf. He needs you to shine his light into the darkness of the world. You are called to shine in this dark world because when you do, his powerful and brilliant light, shining through you, can illuminate the darkness and change the world.

How much light are you taking in each day? How much light are you giving out?

Lord, help us to be people who bring light to others; to all those around us. Every day may we be light to the world. And as we let our light shine, may others see our light and praise our Father in heaven. Amen.

3. A NEW START FOR EVERY CHILD

Bible Reference: "But it was not this way from the beginning" (Matthew 19:8).

Meditation: Leading a faculty retreat at the beginning of the school year can be an amazing experience. To worship together again after the summer break; to learn new skills to share with the children; even to deal with the humdrum of technical information that we have to go over every year tells us that the doors are about to open for another year of studying God's world.

Maybe take a pause – 90% of your children are returning from last year. Will it be a new year for them? Jesus is telling his hearers that the rules they are following are not the ones that were intended for humankind. They need to think of them as a last resort kind of law but not ideal. In fact, Jesus really wants them to go back to the way it should have been.

Maybe ask your faculty to take a pause – 90% of your children are returning from last year. Will it be a new year for them? Ask your faculty if each child can return to the beginning, to hope for it to be the way it should have turned out. That student who was struggling last year, can that student experience a new beginning? The student who had issues with self-control, can that student be seen as a new creation? That class that has been difficult since 1st grade, can that class experience new life?

The answer is, only if we give the child, the children, the class, the spiritual space to do it. Our assumptions are amplified because of the child's own lack of belief in new beginnings. We have to believe ourselves, and we have to believe for the child as well!

Ask your faculty to take a pause. Ask them to pray over each child. Ask God to change our assumptions for bad behavior, poor academic progress, challenging social skills to a belief in new beginnings. You're saying BUT, BUT, BUT! I can hear you.

God didn't say but. He believed in new beginnings for you – YOU. He believed so hard that he sent his Son to demonstrate that love changes everything. Don't let even one child suffer because of your hardness of heart. Take a pause. Pray and work for new beginnings.

Which children just don't fit my picture?
Where can we as a community find hope for each child?

Dear Jesus: It's too easy to say "that's the way it is." You never said that. You said, but to you who are listening I say love your enemies, do good to those who hate you. You believed in new beginnings and new ways of doing things. Forgive me all my negative "buts" that would leave the child where she or he is. Help me to see only possibility and hope. Thank you for your belief in me and my possibility by coming here on earth. Amen.

4. YOU HAVE A BLANK PAGE

Bible Reference: "He put a new song in my mouth, a hymn of praise to our God. Many will see and fear the Lord and put their trust in him" (Psalm 40:3).

Meditation: A new song describes a new experience, and the start of the new school year is always a time for fresh starts and new hope. It's a new song! There is a certain energy that accompanies the start of a new school year. I believe there's something deep in our spirit that naturally draws us toward new things and fresh beginnings. New beginnings often feel great because we get to leave the past behind as we anticipate a new season of hope and promise.

As you prepare to symbolically turn the page from the last school year, you will notice that there is nothing yet written on the next one. It's blank! The blank page is an exciting concept. From this day forward, you can write anything that you want on that blank page. But with the blank page comes responsibility. Going forward, you are responsible for what goes on your blank page. What will you write? What story will your school tell this year?

You can see the life of your school as a part of God's novel, and you are a leading character ... so let him write it. To look at it another way, God is the writer, you and your school are his book, and together you can write something magnificent that will light not only this world, but also eternity.

On your life journey this year, this new school year, strive to remain conscious of the unfolding grace within you and ask the Lord to give you a new song. A song of thanksgiving and praise to God for what Christ has done and will continue to do for your school.

What story will you write this year?

How will you ensure that God is the author?

Lord, be with me as I begin this year. Give me faith and eager expectancy as I look to You and begin to write another chapter. Help my heart and my mind to be open to what you will reveal through your loving presence. Fill me with love and grace so that I radiate hope. Teach me to sing a new song of thanksgiving and praise for all that Christ has done for me. Thank you. Amen.

5. THE SPIRIT GIVES LIFE

Bible Reference: "It is the spirit that gives life. The flesh is useless" (John 6:63).

Meditation: When does a conversation have life in it, and when is it dead? What does that even mean? The simple answer for our schools is: when the mission is at the center of it. Should we take this 5-year-old boy into our school? He has parents who would be strong donors, he is talented in music, he is strong for his age, I like him. These are all answers that are full of the flesh. They are all answers that speak to how the child and his family can benefit the school.

The spirit of a school is in its mission. It's about what we can do for the child. When we put the mission into the conversation, it changes and becomes full of life. *Trinity Christian School exists to educate students to the glory of God by pursuing excellence for mind and heart.* Should we take this 5-year-old into our school? Does the family want us to educate the child to the glory of God? Are they willing to pay the price for pursuing excellence? Are they as interested in the heart as the mind? Do they understand what we will do? Are they enthusiastic? All of a sudden, the conversation is forward-looking and visionary.

The difference between the spirit and the flesh can be illustrated in every area of leadership. In our schools, the spirit conversation has to come back to the mission, while the flesh conversation ignores it. You are a leader who is called to your school's mission and dedicated to seeing it manifested in your area of responsibility. Give life! Your modeling of mission-centered conversations is powerful in your leadership, centering those around you and attracting the right families and the right staff to the school.

Do I know the mission of my school, and could I tell somebody what it is if asked?

Am I convicted by the mission of my school?

Dear Jesus: I admit that sometimes I think very fleshly thoughts. I admit that what people can do for me and for the school sometimes overwhelms what I and the school can do for them. Please help me keep the foundation of my conversations clearly centered on my school's mission. Help me be a life-giving leader, pointing to the mission and, through that, pointing to you. Amen.

6. WE ARE A CHRISTIAN COMMUNITY – PART 1

Bible Reference: "But with you there is forgiveness, so that we can, with reverence, serve you" (Psalm 130:4).

Meditation: Community is not a word that should come up only when the school is in crisis. There is, God forbid, a school shooting and we use phrases like "gather around," "come together." If that is the only time the word community is used, your school has no community. Nor is community a family. The school is not a family. Parents come and go based on their self-interest expressed through their children's lives. That's not family.

No, community is something else. When our school is a Christian community, it embodies the presence of Jesus on earth. That clearly means a life committed to serving, forgiving, healing, suffering, and resurrection. Here, I ask you to focus on forgiveness, seen and unseen. The unseen forgiveness is where we forgive without the other even knowing about it. We feel wronged; we feel resentful; we take it to the Lord in prayer and he leads us to understand how we have been forgiven ourselves – and then to forgiveness for the other.

Community is where the seen forgiveness happens. In community, we are called to truly appreciate and stand in awe of the wonders God has wrought in other people, some of whom we genuinely like. But if liking is necessary to community, we are in troubled waters. Rather, let us praise God for the gifts, talents, and strengths of others that, if we are honest, complement those we have ourselves. It is in this attitude that community can exist and can experience forgiveness. Why is forgiveness so important?

The Psalmist suggests that only when we have been forgiven can we truly serve the living God. Only when we can forgive each other, can we serve each other – there is no community without forgiveness. If you, Lord, kept a record of sins, Lord, who could stand? (vse. 3). If we want to identify and attack the darkness in others, we can indeed rip each other to shreds. But to find the light, ah, there's the beauty of community! My brothers and sisters are also forgiven by God – the barrier of sin is destroyed, and growth is possible.

In what ways am I acting as a forgiven person?

How can I lead my community to greater forgiveness?

Dear Jesus: You taught us to pray that we should forgive others as we have been ourselves forgiven. Take away my fear and pain and replace it with your love and compassion. Help me lead a community of forgiveness. Thank you for dying so that we might be forgiven. Amen.

7. WE ARE A CHRISTIAN COMMUNITY – PART 2

Bible Reference: "He heals the brokenhearted and binds up their wounds" (Psalm 147:3).

Meditation: Are we in a community that recognizes its wounds? I served a school that had gone through 4 Principals in 7 years. That school had deep wounds of distrust and loss of faith. Another school had a Principal who led without listening – the faculty banded together, not in a community, but in an armed camp. Yet another school had two teachers who were toxic and who infected the entire group with their gossip, bad-mouthing, negativity, and selfishness. These were all schools that had no community. Their wounds were deep and just festered below the surface.

In community, we are accountable to and for each other. That is hard to do. Community does not mean glossing over issues. In fact, community is the opposite of that. It is being willing to hear when someone speaks of the ways in which we are impacting others. It is being willing to be that person who can with kindness ask someone to look in the mirror and see what he or she is doing. Accountability means, sometimes and unhappily, letting people go who cannot face up to the wounds they are creating.

In community, we can be vulnerable and therefore grow. Jean Vanier writes in *Community and Growth*: "Each one of us carries within us wounds and fragilities; we can be quickly frightened by other people and their ideas; we all have difficulty truly listening to others and appreciating them. However, we must all work on our emotional life and deepen our spiritual life in order to be more centred in truth, in love, in God, and in order to speak and act out of that centre and not to judge others" (pg. 36). Letting go of our wounds is necessary for us to be able to move forward in and with the community.

There is much research that supports, from a secular point of view, what we know from a spiritual point of view. Phrases like "emotional contagion" and "cognitive resonance" connote the reality that we are not silos, mere individuals who operate in isolation. Forming intentional community is critical to build relationships that support growth and health rather than disease and decay.

Are there any wounds in your community that have not been dealt with?

What do you need to lead with both accountability and vulnerability?

Dear Jesus: Your disciples laid it all on the line. Not always perfectly, they held each other accountable, recognized each other's wounds, were vulnerable offering themselves up in service. Help me to follow their example and lay my own wounds at the foot of the cross. Thank you for the wounds with which you saved me. Amen.

8. WE ARE A CHRISTIAN COMMUNITY – PART 3

Bible Reference: "The Lord is near to all who call on him, to all who call on him in truth" (Psalm 145:18).

Meditation: Current mythologies of truth include the idea that it is the expert who "knows" and that we should listen well because we are all amateurs. This reminds me of the brilliant essay by G. K. Chesterton titled "The Twelve Men." I commend it to you! The last paragraph reads:

"Our civilization has decided, and very justly decided, that determining the guilt or innocence of men is a thing too important to be trusted to trained men … When it wants a library catalogued, or the solar system discovered, or any trifle of that kind it uses up its specialists. But when it wishes anything done which is really serious, it collects twelve of the ordinary men standing round. The same thing was done, if I remember right, by the Founder of Christianity."

Our Christian schools are not profound places if they are filled with mere experts. Our Christian schools are profound places if they are committed as a community of truth. And truth is not a list of propositions identified by the experts and repeated by the child. As Parker Palmer puts it in *The Courage to Teach*: "The community of truth, far from being linear and static and hierarchical, is circular, interactive and dynamic." If you as a leader are the expert, the school will be the poorer for it. If you are part of a community, the school will be messy, but alive.

Only Christian community allows us to pursue truth through a common conversation. In that way, it is a dangerous place. Truth is not always easy to be in touch with. But the Psalmist points us to God's joy: he feeds – all living (vse. 16); he is close – to all who call him (vse. 18); he does the desire – of those who revere him (vse. 19); and preserves – all who love him (vse. 20). The truth conversation in community draws us closer and closer to God himself. In such a community, children can truly live.

In what ways are we afraid of the truth conversation?

How does our community talk?

Dear Jesus: You fearlessly proclaimed the truth, and you created a community of disciples where the truth could be touched, lived, and proclaimed. Help me to lead a community where we find truth in each other and are led to the ultimate truth of a God who wants us to live with him in community. Let me not be scared of the truth. Let this community not be scared of the truth. Thank you that you are the truth, the way and the life. Thank you that you are Emmanuel, God with us, in our conversation, in our community. Amen.

9. WE ARE A CHRISTIAN COMMUNITY – PART 4

Bible Reference: "For I tell you that unless your righteousness surpasses that of the Pharisees and the teachers of the law, you will certainly not enter the kingdom of heaven" (Matthew 5: 20).

Meditation: When I am working with a Board of Trustees, I will sometimes get to a point in the facilitation where I tell them that I don't trust any of them individually, but I definitely trust them as a group of wise, committed, God-loving people, i.e., as a community with a shared meaning and purpose. This is a power of community. Collectively, where it is operating with forgiveness at its heart, vulnerable in its wounds, in the truth conversation, it will lead in a direction that is positive and in which God can bless it. I don't say here that the community is "right." I do say that it will move in a way that God can bless. I think that there is an obsession with being right and it is often destructive of our meaning and purpose. Community does not seek to be right but to be faithful.

Think about the numbers of times you were personally right and it all went wrong. I can be justified in many actions that I should never take. I've experienced this with my children, with my wife, and certainly in all my work situations. Think. Being right is just not enough. Communities that focus on being right become self-righteous, dogmatic, and lose faith, hope, and love as they descend into the "law." It's where the term Pharisaical comes from. Jesus speaks directly to that in Matthew.

Being faithful is something entirely different. There's a fascinating story in Acts 15 where the early Christian community debated a tough issue and made a decision with these words: "It seemed good to the Holy Spirit and to us" (vse. 28). There is a seemly humility in the words "and to us"! Faithfulness, I think, is deeply connected with wisdom. As Timothy Keller puts it in *Every Good Endeavor*: "(the Spirit makes) Jesus Christ a living, bright reality, transforming our character, giving us new inner poise, clarity, humility, boldness, contentment and courage. All of this leads to increasing wisdom as the years go by, and to better and better professional and personal decisions" (p. 218). I add – in Christian community.

Are you trying to be right or faithful?

How would you know that your community is committed to faithfulness and wisdom?

Dear Jesus: It's a challenge being a leader. Leading myself is hard enough. Leading a community as a servant is way harder. Help me not to become Pharisaical. Help me to become wise. Help me to be faithful. Thank you for the many examples of Christian community that inspire me. Amen.

10. I HAVE A HOLY VOCATION

Bible Reference: "Blessed are all who take refuge in him" (Psalm 2:12).

Meditation: Do you doubt your vocation? Even as the year begins, are there doubts in your mind about whether you are the person for the job, whether your school has truly been given to you by God? Often, those doubts come because of the obstacles that exist for you. Maybe you are short a couple of students. Maybe the new teacher you hired isn't working out or a veteran teacher is suddenly struck ill. Maybe you yourself are facing troubles in your own family. Or maybe everything is going just fine and the obstacle is understanding the long game, how this will eventually work out, whether you are made for the 8-year journey it will take to impact the health of your school.

Psalm 2 tells us that God knows all about obstacles. The Psalmist is filled with the same doubts. "The kings of the earth rise up and the rulers band together against the Lord and his anointed" (vse. 2). There is no doubt that the Exile from the Garden of Eden is still alive and well in the time of Israel and it is alive and well in our own time. The Psalmist, though, knew of a certain hope that the Exile would come to an end. "I have installed my king on Zion, the holy mountain… I will make the nations your inheritance, the ends of the earth your possession" (vse. 6, 8).

The Psalmist hoped, but we have something better. We know the hope is fulfilled. "Today, the Scripture is fulfilled in your hearing" (Luke 4:21). The doubts in your mind are real. The tension that you feel about your strengths and weaknesses is real. The accuser is real and tries to get into your mind and heart and tell you that your doubts are reality. But there is a difference between real and a reality. The reality is that God's king has come who will "break them with a rod of iron" (vse. 9). Your doubts can be shattered as you worship the King; your doubts can turn into certainty that your King will make, in some tiny temporal way, your school God's possession and your children God's inheritance.

What doubts do you have? Write them down! They are real!

What confidence do you have? Write them down! They are resurrection reality!

Dear Jesus: You made me to honor and praise you – to be your image. You gave me my vocation of tending the Garden of Eden. Take away my doubts and the sin that Satan desires to turn to his advantage. Replace them with your saving love and the confidence that you have given me my vocation and will hold me with your strong hand in it. Amen.

11. FAITHFULNESS

Bible Reference: "... and Boaz, the father of Obed by Ruth" (Matthew 1:5).

Meditation: It's probably been a long time since you read the beginning of the 1st chapter of Matthew. Most of us start at verse 18: "Now the birth of Jesus the Messiah took place in this way." The first 17 verses, however, provide us with spiritual insight and much fodder for thought. This verse 5 is one of them. When was the last time you celebrated Christmas and thought about Ruth? She was a foreigner, a Moabite. She was female. She had married into a Jewish family, forbidden by the Law. Her husband had died. She was childless. Her Jewish mother-in-law was bitter about her lot in life. They were poor. They were unknown.

Yet here she is in the story of Jesus. She, a Moabite, widow, foreigner, is an ancestor of Jesus. If you ever doubt your importance or the impact you can have, think of Ruth. Not because she became important. Not because she was an ancestor of Jesus. Not because she eventually ended up in the wealthy house of Boaz. But because she was faithful to her mother-in-law Naomi when it would have been easier to go back to her homeland. It is in the faithfulness through what seem to be the most difficult times, times that can you make you bitter, that Jesus can work in and through you.

As a leader in your school, you are the "ancestor" of so many lives. Through your faithfulness, lives are impacted and transformed. Often, you don't even know that your kind word or even look, your touch on the shoulder, the time you spent in conference, the listening you did with the family – you don't know that your actions have eternal significance. Trust the story of Ruth. Your faithfulness, unknown, unsung, unheard, nonetheless sings in the hallways of heaven.

What does faithfulness look like for me?

How do I model faithfulness as a Christian leader?

Dear Jesus: I have to admit that I didn't think I was that important. I don't realize that I have eternal impact on children's lives. It is you that takes my faithfulness and blesses it and makes it miraculous in the lives of children. Oh, give me faithfulness like that of Ruth. Help me to trust you not for prestige or reputation but for blessing. I don't need to know what happens. I trust that you will use me for good. Thank you for giving me Ruth as an example. Let me follow that example of faithfulness better each day. Amen.

12. THE UNLOVELY CHILD

Bible Reference: "If you then, who are evil, know how to give good gifts to your children, how much more will the heavenly Father give the Holy Spirit to those who ask him!" (Luke 11: 13).

Meditation: It's a week into school and you have found the unlovely child. It's the boy or girl that is hard to like. These children don't quite fit in. They're not traditionally beautiful. They don't have easy communication. They are awkward. They offend others, sometimes easily. They are already in trouble. It looks as if, for them, it's going to be a long year.

It's actually predictable. It happens every or almost every year. Even at the interview, you wondered. Or maybe the parent wasn't entirely transparent about the child's social skills. Or there is an odd habit that the other children are already teasing them about. But Jesus is on the ball. He doesn't pull punches. When you think about that child, he says, or when you are praying for that child, remember that *you* are evil. You give good things to your own children because they are members of your family and you love them. But you don't smell so good to God. Even so, when you pray to him, he will give you the Holy Spirit, the greatest gift.

Ask God how you can love this child and ensure that every teacher and administrator and staff member that comes into contact with this child loves her or him. Reach out to God.

Seek the wisdom to know how to ask for your own heart to be touched in such a way that this child can meet the love of God in you. Seek for yourself.

Knock on the door of the child's heart. You have looked to the arms of Jesus. You have sought the Father's gift of the Spirit in your own heart. Now you can knock on the door of the child's mind and spirit and uncover the uniqueness of God's creation in her or him.

What is making this child unlovely?

What is my own relationship with God, Father, Son, and Holy Spirit?

Dear Jesus: Because of your own boundless love, you were able to knock on the heart of everyone you met. You have knocked on the door of my unlovely heart. Again, Lord, I respond with eagerness to your invitation. Give me love and wisdom and courage to trust your gifts to me in reaching out to the unlovely child. She is precious in your sight. Let her be precious in mine as well. Thank you for the power to make a difference in a child's life. Amen.

13. PATIENCE

Bible Reference: "I waited patiently for the Lord; he turned to me and heard my cry" (Psalm 40: 1).

Meditation: The famous marshmallow test was run by Walter Mischel and his associates from the 1960s through to their famous paper in 1990, "Predicting adolescent cognitive and self-regulatory competencies from preschool delay of gratification: identifying diagnostic conditions." You can buy it online for $11.95! The paper suggested that delay of gratification ability as a preschooler (the ability to not eat the marshmallow in the hope of more than 1) was a significant predictor of academic success and the ability to manage stress as a teenager. The importance of self-control is well attested. As one paper puts it: "Self-control—typically understood to be an umbrella construct that includes gratification delay but also impulsivity, conscientiousness, self-regulation, and executive function – averaged across early and middle childhood, predicted outcomes across a host of adult domains" (http://journals.sagepub.com/doi/pdf/10.1177/0956797618761661).

So how many marshmallows are there in your life? What is sitting on your desk, on your email, in your inbox, daring you to take a bite or even eat the whole thing? Or what are you waiting patiently for, not just for a moment or two but for days, months, years, and even generations? Are you an instant gratification leader, always needing new initiatives, greater stimulation, bigger annual fund, more and more buildings? How do you distinguish when these things are actually good to want, and when these things are marshmallows?

David had to search his own heart. He was anointed by Samuel but had to wait patiently for his kingship. He prepared for the Temple but had to accept that his son would build it. He waited for the Messiah but it would be generations before Jesus would come. It might be helpful to think of it this way: Is the marshmallow a person or a thing? Does it lead to relationship or to acquisition? Is its root the desire for personal success for each child or is its root prestige seeking and social acceptance?

What's your current "marshmallow"?

How can you build up your own ability to wait patiently?

Dear Jesus: You were patient for 30 years before you began your ministry. You were patient with your disciples as they struggled to understand who you are and how they should respond to Good News. Please help me to be patient as well. I don't have to achieve everything today. I am a leader under your sovereignty. I trust your Word that you will turn and hear my cry. Thank you. Amen.

14. I DON'T LIKE ASKING FOR MONEY!

Bible Reference: "After this, Jesus traveled about from one town and village to another, proclaiming the good news of the kingdom of God. The Twelve were with him, and also some women who had been cured of evil spirits and diseases: Mary (called Magdalene) from whom seven demons had come out; Joanna the wife of Chuza, the manager of Herod's household; Susanna; and many others. These women were helping to support them out of their own means" (Luke 8:1-3).

Meditation: A former colleague used to ask Board members if they would prefer to be run over by a car or ask somebody for money in person. Many chose the car! There is something odd about how we think about money. We are deeply conscious that the love of money is the root of many evils (1 Timothy 6:10). We are convinced that we should live by faith (Romans 1:17). There is somehow something sordid about talking about money, let alone asking for it. An article about an evangelist who recently bought a new luxury jet suggests everyone doesn't feel the same way!

The good news is that neither the idolatry of loving money rather than God, nor the ascetic John the Baptist "desert model" is how we are supposed to think about asking for money. Jesus provides us with a straightforward example — he and the group that was travelling with him needed a place to stay, food and drink, new sandals occasionally; generous women provided these things by offering their own money; one at least of these women moved in wealthy circles — Joanna. Do not fear to do what Jesus did.

Luke seems pretty interested in this idea. Later, in Chapter 11, Jesus tells a story finishing with "I tell you, even though he will not get up and give you the bread because of friendship, yet because of your shameless audacity he will surely get up and give you as much as you need." I know he's not talking about fundraising, but the idea of shameless audacity fits right in, I think. Christian school leaders must be shameless in what they ask for on behalf of the kingdom!

When was the last time you asked someone to help the children at the school and enjoyed it?

How can you make enjoyment a part of inviting others into the mission of the school through their gifts?

Dear Jesus: You were both flesh and spirit as we are. You know our needs before we ask them. Still, you want us to pray for what we need and to ask those around us to support the children we serve. Give me shameless audacity on behalf of the Gospel. Thank you for your own gift of yourself. Amen.

Christian School Leader's Devotional

15. IF YOU DON'T ASK FOR IT, FUNDRAISING IS HARD WORK!

Bible Reference: "All you need to say is simply 'Yes' or 'No'; anything beyond this comes from the evil one" (Matthew 5:37).

Meditation: Here is an extract from an actual Christian school's website: "Throughout the school year, families from [this] School take part in 4 fundraisers. The money raised from these sales allows us to purchase books for our school library and accelerated reader prizes, helps off-set transportation costs for field trips…"

Have you done fundraisers? The long meetings of preparation, the hours of implementation, the bookwork, cleaning up. This particular school wants parents to make pizzas for sale twice a year and sells Dairy Queen certificates and candy bars.

How long does it take you to make a pizza? How much does it cost you to make a pizza – they're not cheap! What food regulations do you have to contend with? Where do you bring them? How do you get orders? Who organizes all the money coming from every direction? How do you know everyone is being honest? CSM worked with a school that had just experienced an embezzlement. I wish I could say it was incredibly rare.

What Jesus says has absolutely nothing to do with sales or fundraising or one technique against another. He's actually talking about oaths and being trustworthy. But let's take a little liberty here. What if there's another way to think about fundraising that is so much simpler, so much cleaner, so much more honest? How many pizzas do you really want?

All you need to say is the following: "I'm a parent at the school. I give a donation each year that I plan for in my budget. I love the school because of what it has done for my children – this year, we are going to buy more books for the school library and new uniforms for the bell choir. Will you join me?"

Make more money; spend less time; enjoy the process. Keep it simple. Just say yes.

How many fundraising events do we have this year?

What are the obstacles in my school to just asking for money?

Dear Jesus: Thank you for your wisdom that you put in words even a child can understand. Thank you for your own recognition of the need to satisfy physical wants. Help me to see money as a gift from the Father and the words to ask for it as an inspiration of the Spirit. Give me courage to make it simple and just ask for it. Thank you for being a generous God. Amen.

REFLECTION

It is time to take a break and think about the journey you are on. Use this page to reflect on how you can accelerate your impact as a Christian school leader.

16. STOP GIVING!

Bible Reference: "You should have practiced the latter, without neglecting the former" (Matthew 23:23).

Meditation: In a disquisition on hypocrisy, Jesus berates the Pharisees for obeying the law but not obeying the law of the heart – they gave a 10th of their spices but did not practice justice, mercy, and faithfulness. Your school has givers like that. It's hard to rejoice about such giving.

What happens to giving when a people (a person) practices justice, mercy, and faithfulness? Giving radically increases. What does it look like to be a Christian school leader where you tell people to stop giving because you've already got too much? Scripture tells us that as the people brought gifts to build the Tabernacle, there were some who did what was required but there were also some who did much more than was required. Eventually, Moses had to say to them "Stop!" "So the people were restrained from bringing any more for the materials were more than enough for them to do all the work" (Exodus 36:6-7). Wow!

What happens when leaders in the school community give inspirationally? Everyone is inspired! The reason we need leaders to give is to do that very thing – inspire followers. Not everyone is capable of giving $100,000. But everyone is capable of giving enthusiastically, whatever the amount. But leaders have to go out front. David was as good at inspiring as Moses. He wanted to give his son Solomon a real head start on building the Temple so he gave first, then inspired the other leaders of Israel to give, then went to the people. "The people rejoiced at the willing response of their leaders, for they had given freely and wholeheartedly to the Lord. David the king also rejoiced greatly" (1 Chronicles 29:9).

What do you do? Give yourself. Then ask the Board to give. Then ask everyone employed by the school to give. Then the philanthropic leaders by dollar amount. Then the people – everyone else. Leaders lead by example. Who knows? You may have to tell them to stop!

Where is philanthropic leadership in your school?

How do you inspire giving through leadership?

Dear Jesus: You gave me everything. You gave me yourself. Everything that I have is from you. Help me to know that when I give, I only give what you first gave me, my talents, my time, my money, my family, my students, my school. Help me to practice justice, mercy, and faithfulness. Help me to give as a leader. Let me inspire everyone in my community so that I have to cry STOP! Thank you for the abundance surrounding me. Thank you for the riches you want me to have. Amen.

17. UNITED WE STAND; DIVIDED WE FALL

Bible Reference: "If Satan is divided against himself, how can his kingdom stand?" (Luke 11:18)

Meditation: I can't help but think of schools I have visited or know of where the Board and the Principal are at loggerheads, or the church and the school are in conflict. I think of the Head who was fired while he was at a workshop I was leading. I think of Principals who are weary of the unending struggle to gain alignment within governance. Disunity is the evidence of a culture in turmoil.

Jesus is, as always, so interesting. He says that unity is critical to evil as well as to good and that disunity leads to the failure of good. In John 17:21, Jesus notes the unity of the Creator and the Word, between him and his Father, the Father and the Son. The familial speaks to the unity of the human family when man and woman become one (Genesis 2:24). If the devil cannot stand unless the forces of evil are united, even more so do the forces of God fail when they allow disunity in their midst.

But how is unity possible in a school? How do you lead so many disparate people and contrasting interests? There are certain things we cannot be united on, so let's be realistic. We can't all be required to love playing golf as some Board members do; we can't all be required to love eating sushi as you and your spouse do; we can't all be required to attend the same church, even if we are all the same denomination. Unity in a school does not require conformity.

You are a unifying leader when you call every Board member and every school employee to the mission. You are a unifying leader when you foresee / anticipate where the school will be going and articulate a clear vision as to where you want to lead. You are a unifying leader when you and the Board create the plan to get there and keep to it. Call, foresee, plan. For God and to his glory and as his image. That's unity that will bring godly benefit (Hebrews 13:17).

In what ways is your school divided? Are you calling, foreseeing, planning?

Do you have the strength to let people go who divide the house contentiously?

Dear Jesus: You called people to yourself, you pointed the disciples towards Jerusalem and to the coming of God's kingdom on earth, and you carried out the plan, the will of your Father in heaven. Bless my leadership that I can also call, foresee, and plan for my community. You have called us to unity. Even though I don't do these things perfectly, for only you are perfect, nonetheless bless them so that the school I lead has unity. Amen.

18. TELL YOUR STORY!

Bible Reference: "In reply, Jesus said" (Luke 10:30).

Meditation: What do you say when someone asks you where you work, or what you do, or about your school? The reality for most people is that they answer the question literally. I work at this school, I sit in my office all day, my school is on Yardland Avenue. It's true of the people around you as well. That wasn't Jesus' style at all. When he was asked a question or when he was faced by a crowd, he often told a story. Jesus told stories, allegories, parables, metaphors, fiction and non-fiction all combined together, all designed to encourage the listener to enter the kingdom of heaven.

Think about the reference above. Jesus said. You know what comes next. It's the story of the Good Samaritan. Was it true? That's not the point. It was intended to engage, make the listener come back for more, teach something important, point to the storyteller. It was done so well, people would literally walk around the Sea of Galilee to listen to Jesus.

By and large, people don't want facts because they're not interesting. Don't get me wrong. Facts are critical – God IS the Creator of the Universe; Jesus rose from the dead. But the outcome of those facts is what convicts and makes people act. "Go and do likewise" (Luke 10:37) is not the reaction to encyclopedic knowledge but to an emotional connection.

When people ask you what you do, go for the heart. "I do God's work with children. There was a boy named Josiah …" Or about the school: "We've been doing God's work for 33 years. One of our alumnae, Sarah, was telling me at a gathering …" Let people see you and the school in which you lead through the eyes of those you serve. This has the added advantage of taking away the ego. It's no longer about you. The story might not even be about a person you personally taught or advised. It's about the child or child-become-adult. We are in the resurrection business. Let me tell you a story …

How can you train yourself to move from fact giving to engaging the emotions?

What stories do you remember about your own journey that still have incredible impact?

Dear Jesus: You were the greatest storyteller. Thank you for your modeling of this. You remind me continually of the importance of making it personal. You died for me personally. You rose for me personally. You know each hair on my head. Help me to make my testimony more personal. Help me to really work at my story techniques. I know that this will help build your kingdom. Amen.

19. CHOOSE YOUR TARGET – IT AFFECTS YOUR AIM!

Bible Reference: "But seek first his kingdom and his righteousness, and all these things will be given to you as well" (Matthew 6:33).

Meditation: One of the biggest challenges on the enrollment front is to persuade parents of the value of our schools. The quip "You can't beat free" applies to a large percentage of our secular society. And, if we believe all schools have the same purpose and strive for the same outcomes, people are right. But we don't believe that, of course. We believe that children are made up of a body, mind, and soul. And all require attention.

Sometimes we may get caught up in the secular concept of education as we compete in the market, which may result in using the wrong measuring stick for our success. In doing so, the foundation of the school can become weak and we can impact students in unsatisfying ways. We must take caution that if we lead our schools for external achievement, we are probably missing our intended targets. The scripture above could not be clearer in reminding us of the ultimate target. In the most meaningful way, our success will be assessed in the Lord's eyes when he considers how Jesus' messages of faith, hope, and love manifest in the hearts and minds of our young people.

This is a good time in the school year to reflect on the school's mission, vision, and goals, and finely calibrate our messages to students, parents, and staff. These messages should be shared with conviction and inspiration as we strive for excellence not because we seek recognition or reward, but rather because in striving for excellence – casting a vision, praying together, aligning efforts, synergizing talents, clarifying expectations, creating opportunities – our school can become a tool in making the world a more grace-filled place that better reflects the kingdom of God.

How can I best rally the school for this awesome task?

As the school year unfolds, how can I feed and renew this focus?

Heavenly Father, guide my thoughts, words, and actions so that I lead the school community not in being *first*, but in being *good*. Help me to always remember that I am a small and capable instrument in how You will build your kingdom on earth. Thank you that you always knew what the target was. Thank you for your saving grace. Amen.

20. WHAT ARE THE DESIRES OF MY HEART?

Bible Reference: "The eyes of all look hopefully to you, and you give them their food in due season … You fulfill the desire of those who fear you" (Psalms 145:15-19).

Meditation: The Bible is full of stories about human desires. While some of these desires were honorable, most were selfish, if not wicked. Abraham desired to make it to the Promised Land. Moses desired to see the Lord in the burning bush. But a great majority of God's people simply desired worldly things such as Aaron's golden calf or Naboth's vineyard.

You may notice that the scripture starts with a fully inclusive "all" and concludes with the more selective "those." All God's people know, however deep in their hearts, their desires both come from him and must be fulfilled in him. And yet most of us are too impatient to wait for our "due season." It took the people of God more than 40 years to search for the right directions before they made it to the Promised Land. The first generation didn't get there because they failed to 'fear God'.

People in our time continue to feel lost and unsure where to turn in pursuit of their desires. Different techniques, schools of thought, and practices – some even based in research – have become commonplace in our society to help aid people in becoming happier and more fulfilled. It is suggested we practice mindfulness. Practice gratitude. Discover your big why. But when – and where – can we say, confidently and calmly, with reasonableness and charity, that the key to having our desires met is through Jesus Christ? Our path to happiness, fulfillment, and heaven is through him, the way, the truth, and the life. The "when" is always, I'd bet Jesus would say; and the "where" sure ought to be a Christian school.

Do I turn to prayer when I become overwhelmed by my desires?

Do I counsel others to do the same?

Do I truly believe spending a brief moment with the Lord can bring peace, joy, and other blessings to a weary soul?

Lord Jesus, hold my hand so that I may not stray too far from you as we walk together in this life. Help me to avoid harmful wishes and only desire you and the kingdom of heaven above all else. Feed my soul that I may have the patience and focus to rely on you in my daily challenges. Thank you for wishing with all your heart to give me the right food in the right season. Thank you for giving me yourself as a living sacrifice. Amen.

21. CONSCIENCE DEVELOPMENT

Bible Reference: Knowing their thoughts, Jesus said, "Why do you entertain evil thoughts in your hearts?" (Matthew 9:4).

Meditation: We have all been given a conscience. It is something that separates us from every other species on the planet. Some would say it is more important than our spirit, mind, and body combined. Our conscience serves as a moral compass that helps us know right from wrong and guides us through some of the tough decisions of our daily lives. Like any tool, it must be understood and then developed with great deliberation and care to function optimally. It is vital we give our conscience a good formatting and careful update with the right teachings and ethical standards. "The testimony of our conscience is that we have conducted ourselves in the world with simplicity and sincerity of God, not by human wisdom but by the grace of God" (2 Corinthians 1:12).

My wife and I were taking our children to see a relative, so, as good parents do, we coached them in advance about making a good impression. Asking them what they should *not* do at the house, we expected to hear "tease each other," "jump on the couch," or "interrupt adult conversation." My 4-year-old daughter, however, did not hesitate in proudly stating, "Steal anything!" To my surprise and in good humor, I could only reply "Yes, dear, that's true." Out of the mouths of babes!

The 10 Commandments is a tremendous foundational piece for our consciences to be developed initially. But as children grow into early adulthood and accumulate more nuanced experiences, they need support and assistance in the formatting and updating of their consciences. It's quite sobering to think about the number of hours we invest in students' minds and bodies compared to the time devoted to developing their consciences. The dichotomy of right and wrong can serve as a convenient scapegoat in the minds of adults when dealing with students. But we should take an honest look at the practices within our school community to inform how young people conduct themselves with simplicity and sincerity before God, and how we provide support in helping them develop their conscience.

What teachings and standards have I used to inform my conscience?

How long has it been since my school community considered how to develop conscience?

Lord Jesus, source of good teachings and right conduct, you have helped clean my conscience through your Passion and my Baptism. Give me the wisdom and courage to find the right teachings to update my conscience and keep it from endangering me and others with wrongful thoughts and actions. I pray that I will have a contrite spirit and see the value of your words so that I can live life fully in your presence. Amen.

22. LISTEN. ACT. BE PATIENT.

Bible Reference: "When Joseph woke up, he did what the angel of the Lord had commanded him and took Mary home as his wife. But he did not consummate their marriage until she gave birth to a son. And he gave him the name Jesus" (Matthew 1: 24-25).

Meditation: Think about the sequence! A dream – an angel. An impossible message – the baby is from the Holy Spirit. An action of integrity – marrying a pregnant girl. Great self-restraint – no sex. Follow-through – named the baby Jesus. So many ways for Joseph to fall down!

The story of your school is also a sequence of miracles. Founding families. Provision of resources. The gift of children year after year. The transformation of lives. The witness of alumni. God is good. Note, though, the actions of Joseph. He listens to the voice of God through a messenger. Are you listening to the voice of God through the messengers around you? Scripture says that we meet angels without knowing it (Hebrews 13:2). Joseph acts on that voice with courage and determination and integrity. Where is your courage as a leader? Jesus says to us: "Take courage!" (Mark 6:50). Joseph is self-controlled, one of the gifts of the Spirit (Galatians 5:23). Do you show restraint and patience in seeing your school move on its journey?

Your school is God's miracle. To him be the glory! But it only brings glory to God if it is led in the Joseph way. It seems obvious that Joseph and Mary were attracted to each other because their characters were aligned. They both listened to God's voice through messengers. They both acted on their convictions. They both acted with patience. God blessed them. Schools are patient places. Schools are places that require a lot of listening. Schools are also places of action, but squeezed between listening and patience.

I am a person of action. Do I listen? Am I patient?

I am a person of faith. How will that play out in my future Christian leadership?

Dear Jesus: The story of your birth is so amazing. It is even more amazing that it happened in the lives of ordinary and yet extraordinary human beings. Let me take the example of Joseph to heart and help me to listen better to the messengers in my life. Let me follow in Joseph's footsteps and be patient in action. I too want to be extraordinary like ordinary Joseph. Through your grace, I can be. Thank you. Amen.

23. GOD THINKS I'M SOMEBODY

Bible Reference: "Once when he was serving as priest before God and his section was on duty, he was chosen by lot, according to the custom of the priesthood, to enter the sanctuary of the Lord and offer incense" (Luke 1:8-9).

Meditation: It may not have occurred to you – the impact of this service of Zechariah's. Zechariah was a nobody, except that he was of the priestly order through Abijah. He lived in Judea, which was not a major center and not in the least important from a priest's point of view. But here he was, up in Jerusalem, carrying out a task that a priest was only allowed to do once in his life – burn incense in the Holy Place. This was a task that had to be done with exacting accuracy or face the possibility of death. Pretty nerve-wracking and amazing all at the same time!

So, reflect on that a moment from your point of view. There are some meaningful parallels with Zechariah. You are a priest in the priesthood of all believers. You toil in a place that probably has no great reputation or importance. Yet you are called to perform the most amazing task of all. You are called to "Let the little children come to me, and do not hinder them, for the kingdom of heaven belongs to such as these" (Matthew 19:14). Just as with Zechariah's task, this is accompanied by a warning: "If anyone causes one of these little ones – those who believe in me – to stumble, it would be better for them to have a large millstone hung around their neck and to be drowned in the depths of the sea" (Matthew 18:6). Pretty nerve-wracking and amazing all at the same time.

Be encouraged. The angel says to you as to Zechariah: "Do not be afraid for your prayer has been heard" (vse. 13). Your task matters. You matter. Your leadership matters. You need not be afraid because God himself has heard you, his ministering angels, his servants here on earth, are intent on your success.

It is human to fear. What are you afraid of? Make a list.

It is God's pleasure to love us and cast out fear. How has he done that for you in the past?

Dear Jesus: I thank you for blessing Zechariah and Elizabeth. It is a great encouragement to know that you love me personally, whether the world thinks I am important or not. You think I am important. You came to earth yourself to make that obvious. I worship you. I praise you. Love me so that I do not fear. Help me love these little children you have given me in turn. Amen.

24. I WOULD LOVE MY FACULTY TO BE SUPERSTARS!

Bible Reference: "These are the twelve he appointed: Simon (to whom he gave the name Peter), James son of Zebedee and his brother John (to them he gave the name Boanerges, which means 'sons of thunder'), Andrew, Philip, Bartholomew, Matthew, Thomas, James son of Alphaeus, Thaddaeus, Simon the Zealot and Judas Iscariot, who betrayed him" (Mark 3:16-18).

Meditation: Peter is mentioned 191 times in the Gospels. John is mentioned 48 times. James is mentioned 27 times. Nathanael is mentioned 19 times. "And his brother Andrew" is mentioned 12 times. Thomas is mentioned 10 times. Matthew is mentioned 5 times. Bartholomew is mentioned 3 times and only in a list of the disciples. Several are not mentioned again.

How many times do you mention your teachers? Would it be good if they were all superstars? Did Jesus make a mistake when he didn't pick 12 "Peters"? Indeed, did he make a mistake by choosing disbelieving Thomas or treacherous Judas? Obviously not, so what might we glean from this in our own leadership of faculty?

Think about your faculty for a moment. Don't try to put them into neat groups and create a hierarchy of worst to best. Just think about them as individuals. What does each bring to the table? A Peter might bring enthusiasm and impetuosity. A Nathanael brings complete integrity. Each brings gifts, given them by God and developed by them as human beings. Imagine Peter trying to console an introvert? Now imagine James doing it. But, on the other side, imagine Peter with the cheerleading squad! That might work!

If there is a leadership message in Jesus' choice of the 12, it is that we need faculty of many different kinds in order to bring God's kingdom on earth as it is in heaven. Sure, Peter got the headlines. But each one of the disciples died a violent death except John, and he certainly suffered for his faith – they were all witnesses to the ends of the earth and the church today is here because of them. In the same way, each teacher brings a piece of the puzzle for your school to thrive. Love them all equally.

Are there teachers who are hard to love?

Where should we be looking to see the call of God in each teacher's life?

Dear Jesus: You love each of us equally. You suffered and died to take away the sins of the world. That includes me. Help me to see with your eyes of love as I work with each teacher. Help me to nurture and teach so that each teacher can grow in faith and knowledge and skill and become more effective in the lives of children day by day. Thank you for choosing the 12 superstars – thank you for the teachers you have given me. Amen.

25. A CHRISTIAN EDUCATION? WHAT'S DIFFERENT?

Bible Reference: "Then I shall not be put to shame, having my eyes fixed on all your commandments" (Psalm 119:6).

Meditation: As a Christian school Principal, I was often asked to explain how a Christian education is different from any other education. The reason I gave is found in Old Testament scripture. "Fix these words of mine in our hearts and minds ... teach them to your children" (Deuteronomy 11:18). This verse of scripture captures succinctly what I consider to be the very purpose and essence of all educational endeavors.

I continue to be amazed at the number of Christian parents who believe that where their children go to school has little or no influence on their faith development. "After all," they argue, "math is still math and history is still history, isn't it?" They further contend that they can always "counter" any anti-Christian teachings from school at home. I see this as flawed logic. How can a few hours every evening at home truly counter, or even balance, over 35 hours a week of school influence? But perhaps what disturbs me even more is the mistaken belief implicit in this comment that education can somehow be neutral.

Dr. James Carper, professor of American education history at the University of South Carolina, wrote, "Education by its very nature is a value laden enterprise. It will, either implicitly or explicitly, express some worldview." Paulo Freire, a Brazilian educator and philosopher who wrote *Pedagogy of the Oppressed*, expressed it this way: "Education is never a neutral process, it is a political process. This political act can never be divorced from pedagogy. Education is specifically designed and taught to serve a political agenda." To state it plainly, educational neutrality is an oxymoron.

Education results in a worldview. This worldview will be their all-encompassing perspective on everything that matters to them. It will be the driving force in their life and will influence *every* decision they make in life. Your leadership is key to ensuring that the education you provide actually results in the worldview you espouse.

What are the elements that give an education its Christian worldview?

How do you know if faculty, staff, and leadership have the skills to carry out a Christian education?

Lord, I pray that you would give us opportunities to speak truth into our students' lives. I pray that our students' families and homes would be strengthened. Keep our students from sin and its deception, and give us boldness to speak the truth and love to share it effectively. Amen.

26. I AM NOT GOOD ENOUGH!

Bible Reference: "When he had received the drink, Jesus said, 'It is finished.' With that, he bowed his head and gave up his spirit" (John 19:30).

As a school leader, you will be criticized, often unfairly. When you're in a leadership position, it's just part of the job description. You can be an easy target for parents and staff who want to vent their anger and frustration. Intellectually you know this, and you try not to take unfair criticism to heart. But criticism can wear you down like drips of water over time erode rock.

We all struggle because we tie our worth and significance to our abilities and the opinions of others. We exhaust ourselves as we strive to constantly measure up to implicit or explicit expectations. Pause and remember that your worth is not determined by extrinsic measures like recognition and success that are fleeting. Your worth is intrinsic to who you are as a follower of Christ. It is not bought or earned, but simply uncovered. You are already complete in Christ. "For in Christ all the fullness of the Deity lives in bodily form, and in Christ you have been brought to fullness. He is the head over every power and authority" (Colossians 2:9-10).

Don't let the enemy use critics to steal your identity. Let me briefly remind you of exactly who you are.

- You are loved – 1 John 3:3
- You are a child of God – John 1:12
- You are complete in Jesus Christ – Colossians 2:10
- You are free from condemnation – Romans 8:1
- You are a new creation because you are in Christ – 2 Corinthians 5:17
- You do not have a spirit of fear, but of love, power, and a sound mind – 2 Timothy 1:7

Now that's who you are ... that's how God sees you ... remember it ... and don't let anyone tell you anything different. Being complete in Christ doesn't mean that you need to stop trying, but it does mean that you can stop trying out. It is finished!

What unrealistic and unattainable expectations are you striving after?

Who can help you accept who and what you are in Christ?

Lord, criticism is often hard to hear. Too often I find my identity and worth tied up in the opinions of others. Forgive me, Lord, and remind me anew that my worth is in you alone. Through the blood of Jesus, I am loved, accepted, and complete. It is finished! Amen.

27. GOD IS A BIG DREAMER

Bible Reference: "May he grant you your heart's desire and fulfill all your plans!" (Psalm 20:4).

Meditation: Time is a very precious commodity that stands still for no one. It's a currency you never get back once it's been spent. With all you need to accomplish every day, you perhaps know this truth better than most. Just for a moment I'd like you to do something. Look at your calendar for this week – how much time have you have set aside to dream big dreams?

Harriet Tubman, the great American abolitionist and humanitarian, once wrote, "Every great dream begins with a dreamer. Always remember, you have within you the strength, the patience, and the passion to reach for the stars to change the world."

The school you lead has come about because someone had a dream. Dreaming is a God-given tool, and God in his Word has utilized dreams from Genesis to Revelation. So why are more Christians leaders not dreamers? Are they afraid? Or are they so consumed with their everyday lives that they don't take – or think they don't have – time to dream? By his design, God desires to fill your heart with big dreams for your school.

Why does God give us such big dreams? I think there are 2 reasons. First, when we consider what God is asking us to do, we usually let our circumstances and limitations defeat us, and the dream dies. And that's exactly the point. He has put a God-sized dream in your heart that only He can accomplish.

Second, God is far less interested in what we accomplish as we work toward achieving the dream than in who we are becoming in the process. As we struggle and overcome the circumstances we encounter in pursuit of God's dream, he is at work shaping and molding us into the likeness of Christ.

So let me ask you, what are your dreams for your school? What is the far-off, seemingly impossible vision that will demand your best each and every day? Let me encourage you to think about it, pray about it, then work toward achieving it. C.S Lewis put it best when he wrote, "If we only have the will to walk, then God is pleased with our stumbles."

Are you letting your perceived smallness stop you from dreaming big for God?

What makes it safe to dream?

Lord, your Word tells me that you are able to do more than I could ask or imagine. Forgive me, Lord, for thinking and playing small too often. I pray now that you would let me dream big dreams for this school, dreams way beyond my ability. Equip and guide me, Lord, so that you alone may receive all the honor and glory. Amen.

28. WORK IS WORSHIP IS SERVICE

Bible Reference: "May the favor of the Lord our God rest on us; establish the work of our hands for us – yes, establish the work of our hands" (Psalm 90:17).

Meditation: When you hear the word "worship," what comes to mind? Many people see an image of something taking place within a church. In Psalm 90 (attributed to Moses), the word has a much deeper and broader perspective. Did you know that the Hebrew word "avodah" is translated as both work and worship? In fact, throughout the Old Testament "avodah" is used to describe work, worship, service, and cultivation. To put it simply, your work is worship. Is that how you see what you do every day?

Work and the workplace were important to Jesus during his ministry on earth. Os Hillman did a study of work in the Gospels and found "… that of Jesus' 132 public appearances in the New Testament, 122 were in the workplace. Of the 52 parables Jesus told, 45 had a workplace context."

In the scripture passage above, "establish" means to cause something to become significant, widely known, or last for a long time. Moses is asking God to establish the work of our lives, to make it strong and enduring.

As educators, I believe we share a deep longing for "the work of our hands" to be something of value, something that will outlive us and make the world a better place. The opportunity every day to help shape young hearts and minds fulfills for us this longing. The work you do is a daily offering of praise and thanksgiving to God. The manner in which you go about your daily work is a reflection of your relationship to your God.

Just as Moses did, ask God to value, honor, and expand the important work you are doing so that everything you do, from the significant to the everyday, will be a part of God's eternal purposes.

Is the way in which you perform your duties every day a positive reflection of your relationship with God?

In what ways can your work be a paean of praise and worship?

Lord, I am the clay and you are the potter. I thank you for the gifts you have blessed me with. I commit to using them for your honor alone. I ask for your favor to be upon my projects, ideas, and energy so that even my smallest accomplishment may bring you glory. Lord, establish and prosper the work of my hands. Amen.

29. HIRING THE BEST CANDIDATE

Bible Reference: "But seek first his kingdom and his righteousness, and all these things will be given to you as well" (Matthew 6:33).

Meditation: One of the Principal's most important responsibilities is to hire competent, effective teachers and other staff members. And if you're a Principal who has ever had to fill a teaching vacancy, you know how hard it can be. As the time to look at staffing for next year rolls around, Principals usually begin to feel an enormous amount of pressure building. This is understandable; we all want to hire great teachers because great teachers equal great teaching … right? So let's think about this well in advance!

As Jim Collins wrote in *Good to Great*, one of your primary responsibilities is to "start by getting the right people on the bus, the wrong people off the bus, and the right people in the right seats." So, what can you do to ensure great teachers?

First, don't ignore what God has already given you. Look for ways to maximize your existing faculty and staff. Surprisingly, that isn't always about salary. Make a point of recognizing them when they do an outstanding job; provide leadership and professional development opportunities; be receptive to new ideas and willing to collaborate. If you intentionally focus on these 3 factors, you'll likely see an increase in not only retention, but also engagement and overall job satisfaction from your faculty and staff.

Second, wait on the Lord. He is faithful and his timing is perfect. As Psalm 27:14 exhorts, "Wait for the Lord; be strong and take heart and wait for the Lord!" As the days pass and vacancies remain unfilled, we often find ourselves not hiring the best candidate but rather settling for the best available candidate. As difficult as it may be, this needs to stop! If you're not sure in any way, the answer is always unequivocally "no." You'll never be able to get the right people on the bus and in the right seats if you simply select the best available candidate.

Think about a time when perhaps you hired in too much haste. What did you ignore? Upon reflection, what would you have done differently?

What process will lead to "best candidates"?

Lord, hiring and retaining staff is challenging. I pray for wisdom and objective insight as I strive to grow and develop the faculty and staff. Through the power of your Holy Spirit help me "not be anxious about anything, but in everything, by prayer and petition, with thanksgiving, present my requests to God" (Philippians 4:6). Let me trust in you for the best candidate. Amen.

30. I AM A LEADER AND A MANAGER

Bible Reference: "And David shepherded them with integrity of heart; with skillful hands he led them" (Psalm 78:72).

Meditation: Let me ask you a simple question with a follow-up. Are you a manager or a leader? How do you know? There is a difference. The main difference between leaders and managers (or administrators, as we are traditionally called in the school environment), is that people *follow* leaders but *work* for managers. Tom Peters, author of *In Search of Excellence*, wrote, "Management is about arranging and telling. Leadership is about nurturing and enhancing." John Maxwell put it this way, "All leadership is influence."

All true, and you have to do both. A successful school leader needs to be both a strong leader and a manager. As a leader, your job is to get your school community on board with the school's God-given vision. You will need to get the community excited about where he is taking you, while at the same time helping each person to see the roles that each has and the contribution each makes. As Warren Bennis, a pioneer in the field of leadership studies, once said, "Leadership is the capacity to translate vision into reality."

Leadership and management bring vision and execution together. The challenge lies in making sure you are doing both – leading your school as well as effectively managing day-to-day activities. Those who are able to balance these two demands create a vibrant and dynamic environment that gives the school a competitive advantage.

Psalm 78 contains some very important insights into the Lord's requirement for leaders / managers. It also serves as a reminder of the type of leaders God is looking for. David was a man after God's own heart. He wasn't perfect by any stretch of the imagination, but he was a man who passionately pursued knowing the Lord with all his heart, "the integrity of his heart." He also pointed to the example of God himself, a God who had the vision of the Promised Land but who also pointed the way forward with a pillar of smoke, struck the rock to provide water, provided manna to eat. Leadership and management!

What would your colleagues point to as your strengths in leadership and management?

How will you chart a path forward to ensure you can be both?

Lord, as I continue to undertake the role of leader that you have called me to, let me be affirmed by the servant leadership I witness in your Son, Jesus. Teach me to walk in the path he has set. In leading let me never fail to follow you. Amen.

REFLECTION

It is time to take a break and think about the journey you are on. Use this page to reflect on how you can accelerate your impact as a Christian school leader.

31. GROW UP! MAKE, AND ADMIT, YOUR MISTAKES!

Bible Reference: "Though he may stumble, he will not fall, for the Lord upholds him with his hand" (Psalm 37:24).

Meditation: Let me let you in on a secret! Despite your best intentions and efforts, it is inevitable: at some point in your life, you will be wrong. You will say, do, or think things that you shouldn't. That's because we are human and imperfect! "We all stumble in many ways. Anyone who is never at fault in what they say is perfect, able to keep their whole body in check" (James 3:2).

Mistakes can be hard to digest, so sometimes we try to rationalize them or, even worse, double down rather than face them. Why do we instinctively deny our failures rather than admit them? You would think we would eventually learn that covering up our mistakes never works. But that doesn't keep us from trying, does it?

I have come across many people in leadership who believe that admitting they were wrong shows weakness or ineptness. I don't know exactly why so many in the world carry the false belief that admitting their mistakes makes them weak, but I believe that the opposite is almost always true.

Admitting your mistakes doesn't make you a lesser person, or a weak, ineffective leader, but defending them blindly does. Great leaders learn from their mistakes and improve their leadership by avoiding similar errors in the future. They learn from the experience and move forward with a renewed commitment. They don't make excuses or blame others. They take ownership of the issues.

How we react when we are wrong or make mistakes helps define our character. If you want to be genuinely successful in both your professional and personal life, you have to be willing to set aside your pride, your fears, and your insecurities, and really come to recognize that to be *a true leader* that is deserving of your position of authority, you must earn – not demand – the respect of your colleagues. "A man who refuses to admit his mistakes can never be successful. But if he confesses and forsakes them, he gets another chance" (Proverbs 28:13).

Do I make mistakes?

How can I admit them?

Lord, I accept responsibility for the mistakes I make in pursuing my goals. I humbly ask your forgiveness. Lord, help me to understand so I can grow. Give me the wisdom and strength to avoid repeating mistakes in the future. Amen.

32. PROBLEMS ARE FOREVER; TAKE HEART!

Bible Reference: "Wait for the Lord; BE STRONG AND TAKE HEART AND WAIT FOR THE LORD" (Psalm 27:14).

Meditation: The school year is now well underway. You are getting used to waking up early again and the students, and hopefully your faculty and staff, are growing accustomed to the routines … or are they? After the 3rd or 4th week, many of you may be asking anxiously, "Shouldn't they be getting this by now?" How many times have you modeled, reinforced, and reminded the members of your faculty and staff why we don't do things a certain way – and yet, they still do?

Relax. This is a normal part of being a school administrator. I guarantee you'll still have someone running in the hall in June (hopefully only an excited student!), as well as one or two faculty members who still don't get it! It's important not to blame yourself or question your competency as an administrator – and don't give up!

Working with people is much like our Christian walk – we never get to a point where we can put our feet up and say, "Okay, done. I've officially got this down. No need to do anymore because I won't experience any more problems. It's all downhill from here!"

Teaching, handling school administration, and being focused on Jesus are all ongoing processes of learning and trial and error, and they always present challenges. You continue to experience highs and lows, success and failure. Sometimes you feel discouraged and ask yourself, "Am I really making a difference?" or "Am I the right person for the job?"

Be encouraged. You are making a difference. When the tough times come in your ministry and you question your effectiveness or the difference you make, hold on tightly to that thought. You make a difference because God is making a difference in you and through you. "Always give yourselves fully to the work of the Lord, because you know that your labor in the Lord is not in vain." (1 Cor. 15:58)

Before asking whether you are making a difference in others' lives, is God making a difference in your life?

What are common problems that are so common that you can stop calling them problems?

Lord, forgive me for the many times that I focus on my problems instead of focusing upon you. Help me to focus upon all that you are and all that you do. Lord, there are problems. Let me see them as opportunities. Amen.

33. WHO IS MISSION-APPROPRIATE?

Bible Reference: "The Lord reigns, let the earth be glad; let the distant shores rejoice" (Psalm 97:1).

Meditation: It's a tough question for us today! I go into many schools where they define mission-appropriate as Bible-believing. Other schools want the parents to be faithful members of a Bible-believing church. Others again say you have to belong to a particular denomination. Others say at least one parent has to be a believer.

The Psalmist reminds us of many things, but this verse tells us again, as hundreds of verses tell us, that God is the Lord of the earth. This is part of a group of Psalms (93-100) which all have a similar theme of kingship over the whole earth: "He has established the world" (Psalm 93); "He who disciplines the nations, he who teaches knowledge to humankind" (Psalm 94); "In his hand are the depths of the earth" (Psalm 95); "declare his glory among the nations, his marvelous works among all peoples" (Psalm 96); "make a joyful noise to the Lord all the earth" (Psalm 98); "The Lord is king, let the nations tremble" (Psalm 99); "make a joyful noise to the Lord, all the earth" (Psalm 100).

Reflect on your current student body. Is it who you wanted? Is it who God sent? Sometimes we are confused by these 2 different questions. Just because the students came, does it mean that God sent them? Did you miss anybody? Who was invited to the feast? Whom did God invite?

There's still time to reflect on who should be in your school. We must continually question whether we came to those who are well or to those who need a doctor. Are Christian schools Psalm 93-100 schools, attempting to reach out to the whole earth over whom God is sovereign?

I don't pretend there are easy answers. But maybe there is an easier way to consider it. If the child is mission-appropriate, willing and eager to submit to the school's mission / beliefs / values, does it matter what the child's background is or who the parent is?

Who is in your school and is that your intent?

When will be the next time you consider your admission criteria in the light of Scripture?

Dear Jesus: I know you were sent to the lost sheep. I know that you sent out your disciples to tell the good news to all nations. I know the Psalmist thinks of you as sovereign over the whole earth. Help me and those I lead to examine what that means for us in terms of the children we serve. Help us to understand what you would have us do. Thank you for your generosity to me as a sinner. Amen.

34. THE MYTH OF POWER AND LEADERSHIP

Bible Reference: "So the last will be first, and the first will be last" (Matthew 20:16).

Meditation: Sometimes as a leader, it feels as if you have less power than ever. At least, when you were a "follower," you had control over your own classroom and the daily routines. Now it seems as if you have little control, that this parent or that donor or that teacher constantly disrupts your day, making it impossible to accomplish anything. You certainly have power if you want to use it. But the paradox of power is that the more you use it, the less you have of it. Teaching is a classic example – if I believe that my students will learn because I have the power to make them do it, I am sadly mistaken! My students will learn if they love me as their teacher. It's all about the relationship, not about the power.

I think this passage of Matthew is usually interpreted incorrectly. As I was growing up, I was told that I should go to the back of the line because that was the humble thing to do. And, of course, Jesus' story of the feast might support that idea (Luke 14), although the point is subtly different there. Here in Matthew, it seems to me that everyone got the same prize, i.e., at the end of the day, there is no first or last, it's about us all making it. And not being resentful of the latecomers but being glad that everyone made the train.

I remember being on the London Underground and the doors were about to close when a young fellow came leaping down the stairs, dashed across the platform, and slid neatly between the sliding doors. He happily looked around with a big smile as if to say, "Wasn't that well done?" Many people smiled back at him. They were happy he had made it too, even though he was the last one on the train. Maybe he had an appointment to keep or an errand to run or a girlfriend to meet, or maybe he was just full of life that morning. He made us all happy.

So it is with leadership. We lead not through control but through relationship, being as happy with the latecomer – to understanding / to the team – as we are with the one we have worked with for several years in perfect harmony. The first is the last and the last is the first. With that understanding, joyful leadership becomes possible.

Do any of your team members (including yourself) think they are owed special privileges?

How do you integrate the newcomer or the new idea?

Dear Jesus: It's so amazing that you show no partiality. You are just glad when today we will be with you in Paradise. Help me to know that leading in that kind of love and acceptance is so much more powerful and long-lasting and transformative than leading through control. Thank you for not using your power in a controlling way but using it to serve us. Thank you. Amen.

35. THE REALITY OF LEADERSHIP

Bible Reference: "let all the trees of the forest sing for joy" (Psalm 96:12).

Meditation: The beauty of the fall / autumn time is represented in the beauty of the trees as the colors of their leaves change. Maybe you've taken a tour where you were amazed at the browns and yellows and reds and all the colors in between. It's an amazing thing to look down a valley and see a quilt of sensational shades and hues and just to feel awe. God gave us trees for many reasons, but one I am convinced was to convey his peace and allow us to stand in awe of him. Are you feeling oppressed by the daily grind? Walk for 15 minutes beneath a canopy of trees. Are you preparing for a difficult conversation with a parent? Walk among the trees and breathe deeply, allowing your thoughts to rest on the sounds of wind and leaves and branches. Are you feeling grief over a decision that you had to make? Take it to the Lord in prayer – walking in the trees, leaning back against a sturdy trunk, or climbing onto a low-hanging bough.

One Jewish commentary suggests that the forests represent the rulers of the world. This is an interesting way for you as a Christian school leader to read the Psalm. Hashem is coming! *IS* coming! We can count on it. Jesus has come. Jesus will come again. As leaders in particular, we are to sing for joy. Christ our Savior, Yeshua, has already gained the victory for us. We lead our school singing for joy. Another commentator suggested that the word "sing" is better thought of as "ululate," a continuous song of joy that voices our deep thanks for his "marvelous works" over and over again. Being a leader in the footsteps of Yeshua is to be a leader anointed to point the way to him. Being a leader in the footsteps of Yeshua is to be in reality (not false idols or mirages), to be a follower of the Creator of the Universe.

This singing, this pointing, this reality of leadership, this is yours as an inheritance.

Can you see the trees in your neighborhood and hear them proclaim the coming of the Lord?

In what ways does your team still need to be grounded in the reality of leadership?

Dear Jesus: Rejoicing always feels like being happy in my mind. It's often hard to rejoice if that is what it means. I thank you that rejoicing is not about me but in response to your salvation, your righteousness, your truth, your creation. Thank you for the trees that you created to sing continuously for joy. Help me lead my team and my school in such a way that we can sing for joy, we can point to you, we can do both of those in the reality of each day. You are doing marvelous works among our students and parents and staff. I praise you for them. Amen.

36. FAILING UPWARDS WITH HUMILITY

Bible Reference: "But when Jesus turned and looked at his disciples, he rebuked Peter. 'Get behind me, Satan!' he said. 'You do not have in mind the concerns of God, but merely human concerns'" (Mark 8:33).

Meditation: How close success and failure are! Only a couple of verses before this, Peter confesses Jesus as the Messiah. He is a devoted follower of Jesus. Now he is the Satan, the accuser, placing his own human concerns about Jesus' welfare in front of God's redemptive plans for all the nations. Talk about whiplash!

You may be a new leader or someone with a decade or more of experience. This close proximity of success and failure is, interestingly enough, common to all leaders. Not being a leader means being largely responsible for your own expertise and actions. Being a leader means being responsible for many people's expertise and actions. Jesus is demonstrating so many leadership lessons in this verse – your mission as a Christian school is actually more important than an individual experience or need; there is no favoritism; to those to whom much is given, much is expected; don't hesitate to state the truth; and more.

Six days later, Jesus takes Peter, James, and John to the top of the mountain with him for what we know as the Transfiguration. Here's an amazing leadership lesson: Holding someone accountable doesn't change the relationship! Jesus holds Peter accountable, but the relationship is still secure.

How do you grow? I often hear people talk about the importance of humility. I'm often not quite sure what they mean. This passage makes one aspect of humility really clear. We will not grow as leaders except through failure. Now, I'm not humble because I'm not perfect and fail. No, I'm humble so that I can listen to others and learn from my failure. Although it doesn't say so, Peter's journey clearly shows that, like Mary, he pondered all these things in his heart. That allows you to fail upwards. Humble listening allows you to take failure, understand it, and be transfigured.

In what ways have you failed in the last 3 months?

What did you hear people tell you about those failures? Did you listen?

Dear Jesus: You are indeed the great teacher! Thank you for the simple way in which you share with us the most profound lessons. Thank you for the evangelists who made sure that we would have those lessons to contemplate. Help me be a leader who can humbly fail upwards. Amen.

37. DO YOU KNOW TOO MUCH?

Bible Reference: "Whoever has ears to hear, let them hear" (Luke 14:34 cf. Revelation 2:7, 11, 7, 29; 3:6, 13, 22).

Meditation: A student came out of her room one evening when I was supervising study. She asked me a question and it happened to be about the history that I was teaching her. I thought about the question, gave some background as to how to think about it, did a short analysis of the issue, offered possible ways to resolve issues, and waited for the applause. She looked at me for a moment, having waited patiently for about 15 minutes while I talked. Then she said: "I just needed a yes or no" and went back to her room, slamming the door quite hard behind her to display her displeasure!

If we are leaders, it is 98% likely that we are talkers. As I visit schools month in and month out, it is clear that Christian school leaders are strong talkers, even inspirational. We are not necessarily good listeners. Maybe not so oddly, our followers don't want us to show off our knowledge, but to do other things. They are not interested in our technical competence. Principals and division leaders often teach, saying that their faculty like to think they are part of the group. Nothing is further from the truth. Teaching is a waste of the leader's time. Again, the follower doesn't want us to know that kind of stuff.

Followers actually want us to carry out 6 important tasks: be good people and committed to the mission of the school; have a vision for where the school is going; listen to them, really listen, and take their advice on occasion; be a coach and mentor when asked; get resources so they can do their jobs; get rid of obstacles that impede them. Jesus is constantly saying to his disciples and the crowds who follow him, "Listen! Listen and learn!" It's good leadership advice.

What percentage of the time do you talk in various conversations?

Have you ever asked your followers what about you most frustrates them?

Dear Jesus: Your voice is constantly in my head as I go about my day. But listening is really hard. I know that listening means putting my own ego, my own voice, on hold. Help me to learn to listen with intensity so I can truly hear what you are saying to me. Help me to listen to what people around me are saying. Then give me your voice of power and your skill in action. Thank you that God listens to our cries, that the Spirit speaks for us, that you teach and lead us. Amen.

38. IT'S NOT BEEN A GOOD WEEK!

Bible Reference: "In this world you will have trouble. But take heart! I have overcome the world" (John 16:33).

Meditation: "You aren't kidding! Trouble! It's not been a good week. What a list of trouble I've had. The fire marshal told me I have to upgrade the chemistry lab at a cost of hundreds of dollars – that is not in the budget. I had to suspend 2 students for fighting and now one of the parents is threatening to sue the other one. My little boy's goldfish died and we had to have a funeral. Yes, I know it sounds trivial but not to my son and so not to me! And then one of the bathrooms was out of order for 3 days. Did I really sign up for this? Will next week be any better?"

We've all been there. And yes, you did sign up for it. Even if you didn't realize it would be on your shoulders. Of course, Jesus isn't talking about goldfish or even lawsuits. He's talking about the trouble the disciples will have in spreading the good news. He was right. Of the 12 disciples, 11 died violent and often agonizing deaths. Let us pray that we are not put to the test in that way!

Nonetheless, we should not minimize the difficulties you face each day. Satan seeks to devour you because you are doing God's work with the little children whom Jesus hugged and talked to whenever he had the chance. Now you get to do the hugging and talking – and Satan is not happy about that. He wants us stressed and feeling overwhelmed and throws obstacles in our way continuously to discourage and defeat us. Don't deny the realities in front of you, from angry parents to disobedient children to dead goldfish. They all contribute to you not having a good week.

And Jesus tells his disciples that he has already overcome Satan and the world. Remember, that didn't stop them dying and suffering for him. But it did mean that in the midst of troubles, Jesus comes to us and says that he loves us and is with us and will call us to himself – and that his perfect love can cast out our fear. Don't deny it. The week was terrible. And Jesus is still good.

What gives you the most heartburn, and what is your plan for when it happens again and again?

In what ways do you need to strengthen the spiritual fibers of your soul?

Dear Jesus: Life is often not easy, and there's no point pretending that everything will go great because I believe in you. If it didn't for the disciples, I have no right to think it will for me. But you have said that you already have won the victory and will be by my side and in my heart as I lead my team and work with the children. Thank you. Thank you. Amen.

39. IN THE BEGINNING.

Bible Reference: "The beginning of the good news of Jesus Christ, the Son of God" (Mark 1:1).

Meditation: Everything has a beginning. The Bible even begins with "In the beginning" (Genesis 1:1). It is fair to assume that Mark is consciously echoing the moment of creation. And you are at the beginning of a new year, new month, new day. Think about that a bit. Beginning. The etymology of begin includes ideas like to open, to originate, to take the first step. Beginning. Genesis, Luke, Mark, John, and Acts all start with "beginning" and Matthew begins with genealogy.

It's not the same as last year. It's not last year repeated. It's a beginning. Almost unnecessarily, we might say a new beginning. The leadership team is maturing under your coaching. The teachers are learning more and more as you urge and lead them through processes of growth. The Board is taking the next step in its strategic plan and you are leading the school within the context of that plan.

What's the alternative? If this is not a "beginning", there is paralysis on the Board, complacency among the teachers, decline in the school. If it's not a beginning, where are you leading? If it's not a beginning, then find out where to begin! If you aren't sure where to begin, lean on the reality that it begins with "the good news of Jesus Christ, the Son of God" (Mark 1:1). Jesus, on earth as it is in heaven, preparing for 30 years, carrying out the plan for three years, strategically oriented, down-to-earth realism, your model for leading. There's no alternative to "in the beginning." Out of in the beginning came creation, came resurrection. Out of in the beginning came the birth of your school, each resurrection phase of development, each step to where you are now.

"In the beginning" is an exciting phrase. It's a Bible phrase. It's a new day phrase. Embrace it.

Who is "in the beginning" this year among your leadership team, your faculty, your staff, your Board?

Every child is starting a new year. How will it be "in the beginning" for them from creation to resurrection?

Dear Jesus: Thank you that we are at the beginning. It is exciting to be an "in the beginning" kind of school. It can feel exhausting, too. Help me embrace the creation energy and resurrection hope of "in the beginning." Help me inspire those around me to be thankful for the opportunity each beginning provides. Bless us in this new year. Amen.

40. HOW MANY CHILDREN DO YOU HAVE IN YOUR SCHOOL?

Bible Reference: "In those days a decree went out from Emperor Augustus that all the world should be registered" (Luke 2:1).

Meditation: The first day of the school year has come and gone and you now have counted all the students in your school. How many do you have: 75? 100? 150? 300? 1,200? What does that number mean? Of course, you are interested to know whether your budget will work this year. But what about beyond that? Mary and Joseph are in the throes of preparing for their baby. They do the calculation. When the census is to be taken, Mary will be in her 9th month. That's not good timing! But they have no choice. They have to go. And they do.

Did Caesar Augustus know that he was part of God's plan to fulfill the prophecy that the baby was to be born in Bethlehem (Micah 5:2)? Certainly not! Were Mary and Joseph deeply aware that their journey was of historical and eternal significance? Maybe! They certainly knew that their journey was not to be avoided but had to be taken in obedience as they had taken so many obedient steps over the previous year.

You have counted your children. What now? You act as Mary and Joseph did. It's simple though not easy. You just have to be obedient and teach your children "so the next generation would know (the law), even the children yet to be born, and they in turn would tell their children. Then they would put their trust in God and would not forget his deeds but would keep his commands" (Psalm 78:6-7). Don't make it complicated. God will take care of Caesar Augustus. You just have to get to Bethlehem, 3 months away.

Your staff need you to be out front pointing the way. Pointing the way to each child, not to a number or an abstraction. Make it real. We are going to travel on a "donkey." We are going to need supplies for the road. We are going to be fearful of robbers. We are going to trust in our community and God for safety. You are in the real world. Be a real-world leader!

If there were a census today, and you had to take your children to Bethlehem, would you rejoice?

What planning do you still need to do to lead your staff over the next 3 months?

Dear Jesus: You were a number for the Roman Empire, a number that could be taxed. But Caesar Augustus didn't realize that his earthly plan could be used by your Father to do great things for the entire world. Help me to think about each child, not as a number, but as a creation for whom you have already done and still plan for great things. And help me to lead my staff as a real-world leader, in obedience, to Bethlehem. Amen.

41. A GENERATIONS BOARD OF TRUSTEES

Bible Reference: "Posterity will serve him; future generations will be told about the Lord, and proclaim his deliverance to a people yet unborn, saying that he has done it" (Psalm 22:30-31).

Meditation: You are about to go to your next Board meeting. The Board is a group of dedicated and wonderful faith-filled people. It is also possible that the Board is dedicated but not necessarily supportive in the right way, maybe interfering with how you run the school. Another possibility is that the members show up for meetings and are very enthusiastic, but don't do much outside that. Whichever is true for you, from what place do you lead them?

Focus the Board on its mission. "Our Board of Trustees holds the school's mission in trust to Jesus and makes strategic decisions that will ensure our mission will be a blessing to the next generation." Note the word generation. Your leadership of the Board is a "generations" leadership. Remind Trustees that they are a Christian Board, not just any old Board. Being a Christian Board doesn't primarily mean that they pray and use Christian language. It primarily means that they are focused on the future of the school, not the present. They are a "generations" Board.

Psalm 22 is a prophetic Psalm. It is interpreted as being about Jesus – he speaks the first verse (why have you forsaken me) from the cross; actions of the Passion are foreshadowed, e.g., hurling insults, casting lots for his clothing, piercing his hands and feet. When the prophecy was fulfilled, Jesus looked backward but also looked forward – I go to prepare a place for you (cf. John 14). The early church took its lead from him and was deeply concerned to pass on his "deliverance" to the next generation, the people yet unborn.

On the way to your Board meeting and praying for your Board members, memorize these verses from Psalm 22. Our God is returning "soon." Jesus pointed forward – to Jerusalem, to the coming of the Comforter, to the joys of heaven on earth, to the end of time. Our Boards must spend their time considering how "future generations will be told about the Lord."

Is your Board a Christian Board with its orientation on future generations?

If your Board called itself a "generations" Board, what would change?

Dear Jesus: You described yourself as Alpha and Omega (Revelation 22:13). I thank you that in your time on earth, you thought about me today and loved me. I praise you that I have a future in this world and an eternal future in you. Help me lead the Board to be a generations Board, focused on a people yet unborn. Help them to take on that responsibility with great energy, as you demonstrated when you were here on earth. Amen.

42. OUR NEIGHBORS SEE US AS A BLESSING

Bible Reference: "Our mouths were filled with laughter, our tongues with songs of joy. Then it was said among the nations, the Lord has done great things for them" (Psalm 126:2).

Meditation: Just think about it for a moment. Solomon had just built the first Temple, the Ark of the Covenant had been given a permanent home, the 12 tribes were united and at peace, the tribe of Aaron were the priests, and there was prosperity in the land. These were great things indeed! The Psalmist records that those were heady days when the children of Israel laughed a lot and praised God a lot.

What do your neighbors stop and say about your school? Do they look at you and say, "The Lord has done great things for them"? Solomon's Temple was the place where God dwelt – an incredible light shone from the Temple (1 Kings 8:1-11). Is your school a light shiner in your families, your neighborhood, your county, your town, your city, your region? It's not that you intend it to be a light shiner. It's just that because you are a Christian school, you shine light.

This isn't about your children being neatly dressed and polite. Of course, they are those things. It's about each one of them following Jesus in such a way that the school glows. The 1st chapter of John talks about this a lot: "In him was life, and that life was the light of all mankind. The light shines in the darkness, and the darkness has not overcome it" (vse. 4-55).

What about your leadership? Fill your mouth filled with laughter and your tongue with songs of joy! Be a light shiner! Sometimes it doesn't take much. Maybe it's a kind word or a hug. But usually it's harder than that. Leadership laughter and joy is the product of thinking, praying, sleeping, executing the plan, being brave, being open to being vulnerable, being right. It comes from a different place than the laughter of jokes. It comes from the soul, from knowing deeply, from acting with faith over long periods of time. It is an outcome of building a school just as Solomon built the Temple, using the best materials and unstinting in the desire for excellence.

In what ways does your neighborhood have no choice but to acknowledge that you are a Christian school?

What steps can you take in your leadership to experience deep laughter and deep joy?

Dear Jesus: You told us to pray that your kingdom come (Matthew 6:10). Let me be a leader that brings your kingdom here on earth through the school you have given me. Let it be a light shiner because of who we are. I want us to impact the world for you. Let it begin right here with my leadership that results in laughter and joy. Amen.

43. I AM CALLED AND I AM EQUIPPED

Bible Reference: "With God we will gain the victory, and he will trample down our enemies" (Psalm 60:12).

Meditation: On a trip to Normandy, I visited Omaha Beach or "Bloody Omaha," as it is better known. It was difficult to comprehend how on this now tranquil stretch of sandy French beach over 2,000 young men were killed or wounded as D-Day, the liberation of Europe, began and marked the beginning of the end of a brutal worldwide conflict that took the lives of so many.

Like those brave men that came ashore at Normandy in 1944, you and I are also engaged in a mighty war. We are warriors for Jesus Christ! At stake in this battle is every one of the students in your school today. You can storm the beaches because "the Spirit God gave us does not make us timid, but gives us power, love and self-discipline" (2 Timothy 1:7).

Unlike those brave men on D-Day, we are not doing battle against an enemy we can always see. As Ephesians 6:12 reminds us all, "For our struggle is not against flesh and blood, but against the rulers, against the authorities, against the powers of this dark world and against the spiritual forces of evil in the heavenly realms." We are at war with the devil and his forces. It is not a physical war with physical weapons, but a war of the mind and the heart. It is a war to win the souls of our students and to overcome evil. Paul referred to it as "the good fight of faith." We are at war and we need to take serious steps.

Paul continually impresses upon every follower of Christ the importance of being properly equipped for battle. He described that equipment as he wrote to the church at Ephesus. He wrote, "Finally, my brethren, be strong in the Lord and in the power of his might. Put on the whole armor of God, that you may be able to stand against the wiles of the devil." You are where you are as a faithful response to God's calling on your life, and those he calls he equips. At this very moment you have at your disposal all the resources you need to accomplish all that God has planned. The creator of the universe has been patiently preparing and equipping you "for such a time as this."

What beaches do you need to storm?

What equipment do you still need to get?

Dear Lord, I recognize my enemy is at work all around me. I need your supernatural power to stand strong and not surrender. Give me courage, so that I can stand and fight the spiritual battles in my life. Lord, give me the victory that you have already won. Amen.

44. WHAT IS MY BLIND SPOT?

Bible Reference: "Do not judge, or you too will be judged. For in the same way you judge others, you will be judged, and with the measure you use, it will be measured to you. Why do you look at the speck of sawdust in your brother's eye and pay no attention to the plank in your own eye?" (Matthew 7:1-3).

I'm sure other cities can make the claim of worst traffic in America, but I can't imagine anyplace worse than Houston, Texas. To complicate the problem, I wouldn't describe myself as a particularly patient person. In fact, my wife describes me as downright impatient—and she is absolutely right. When in traffic, there have been a few instances when I've not been diligent in checking my blind spot when shifting lanes. Since my blind spot has nearly caused my demise several times, I now pay extra attention to it. I double and triple confirm no cars are there before I merge into another lane.

Jon Maxwell wrote, "Most every leader has a blind spot, in fact, all probably do." He goes on to define blind spot: "An area in the lives of people in which they continually do not see themselves or their situation realistically. This unawareness often causes great damage to the people and those around them."

As Christian leaders, we need to try and avoid these blind spots by always examining ourselves before looking at others. We must take care to understand clearly what Jesus means when he talks about judging. He obviously did not mean you should not judge at all. What Jesus is telling us is that we need to always examine our own motives and conduct before judging others.

Too often we find that the traits that bother us in others are often the habits we dislike in ourselves. Our bad habits and behavior patterns are too often the very ones we want to change most in others. My friends, Jesus is holding up a mirror to us and saying, "Do you find it easy to magnify others' faults while excusing your own? If you are ready to criticize someone, check to see if perhaps you deserve the same criticism. Judge yourself first and then lovingly forgive and help your neighbor."

What are the blind spots in my leadership style?

How can I develop skills to compensate for my blind spots?

Lord, forgive me for the times that I magnify the faults of others while excusing my own. I pray that your Word will be a mirror that shows me who I really am. I want to look at myself as you do, through the eyes of truth. Amen.

45. COME; TAKE; LEARN

Bible Reference: "Come to me, all you who are weary and burdened, and I will give you rest. Take my yoke upon you and learn from me, for I am gentle and humble in heart, and you will find rest for your souls. For my yoke is easy and my burden is light" (Matthew 11:28-30).

Meditation: Let's be honest. The life of a school administrator can be hectic! It is very easy to feel overwhelmed by all the problems that came across your desk. There never seem to be enough hours in the day for you to accomplish all you think you have to do. You instinctively know that something has to change, but you can't always envision a clear strategy.

Jesus' words in Matthew's Gospel are a 3-word antidote for overload and stress: "come," "take," and "learn."

When Jesus tells us to take come to him and take his yoke, he wants us to do something that we instinctively fight against as leaders – he asks us to give up control to him. Jesus understands each of us better than we understand ourselves. Sadly, we often forget this and continue to stubbornly operate in our own strength and understanding and find ourselves trying to carry a yoke not designed to fit us. It chafes and becomes heavy, yet we continue to try and do everything our own way and in our own time. It doesn't have to be that way. When we are yoked with Christ, we move together in the same direction and at the same pace. Proverbs 20:24 reminds us that "Since the Lord is directing our steps, why try to understand everything that happens along the way."

This year, when multitudes of demands clamor for your attention and you begin to feel overwhelmed, be still and claim the inner peace that is your spiritual birthright: the peace of Jesus Christ that passes all understanding. It is offered freely; it has been paid for in full; and, as his precious child, it is yours if you simply ask. What is weighing on you right now? Give it to Jesus.

Am I a control freak?

How can my team help me be more centered on Jesus' yoke?

Lord, I often live in anxiety because I don't place my burdens upon you. In the midst of my busyness, enable me to stop and remember that you are right here with me. I know it is you who directs my steps. I ask now that you share your yolk with me and take my burdens so that my soul finds rest and peace. Amen.

REFLECTION

It is time to take a break and think about the journey you are on. Use this page to reflect on how you can accelerate your impact as a Christian school leader.

46. SIGNS FROM HEAVEN

Bible Reference: "The Pharisees and Sadducees came to Jesus and tested him by asking him to show them a sign from heaven" (Matthew 16:1).

Meditation: It's interesting, isn't it, that the word test used here is the same as the word test used earlier in Matthew to speak of Satan's tempting of Jesus. We're always looking for signs that "we are on the right path" or that "it's working." In some ways, that makes sense. We are looking for evidence of success.

But that's problematic in education. How will we know what has happened until decades later, once the child has become an adult? How do we measure success anyway? Judging by most entranceways in schools, through athletic prowess and fundraising stamina! These are the outward and spectacular visions of success seen in cheering crowds and magnificent buildings. They surely are not where your heart is. And MUST we have this kind of success for us to think that God is on our side? Surely not!

Our signs from heaven are far more potent and not from the devil at all. One teacher was telling me about a little boy who was in a conversation with her when he suddenly broke away because another child had fallen. He wanted to help and give comfort. A student told me of a soccer championship trip to New Orleans; his memory was not of winning the championship, but of the reconstruction he helped with and the people he met in that experience. A Principal told me of the donor who struggled with giving enough to actually meet the campaign goal – hours of walking up and down his bedroom floor brought him to an act of exceptional generosity.

Our signs from heaven are the evidence of hearts that are turned to the Lord, turned to goodness, turned to the light. They are usually tiny acts or words. There are hundreds of them every day in your school. Don't look for the foolish signs of something that doesn't matter. Look and listen for the signs that show your school is moving the heart.

How many signs can I notice in a single day?

Why is it so important to me to think of success in grandiose terms and how can I change that?

Dear Jesus: Success lies with the repentant heart turning to you and living the way of the cross. Thank you that the children you have given to us show the beauty of love freely shared on a daily basis. Help me to see that and be fully satisfied. Grant me wisdom not to chase after success that connects to prestige and praise. Amen.

47. THE JOY OF GETTING UP!

Bible Reference: "For his anger lasts only a moment, but his favor lasts a lifetime; weeping may stay for the night, but rejoicing comes in the morning" (Psalm 30:5).

Meditation: I find it challenging to read Scripture both literally and figuratively. As an English teacher, the joy of "discovering" meaning behind the meaning is exquisite fun. There is, of course, truth in such an endeavor. But just to read on the surface can also uncover deep insights. In fact, that's one of the ways in which we can identify the great writer. So, the Psalmist challenges us beneath the surface to repent and discover God's abiding and eternal love for us. Above the surface, he notices how the evening is a time of reflection when the realities of the day and the difficulties we face can't be hidden by the action of the day. They rush to the surface and confront us, often with unhappy results – self-doubt, depression, physical sickness, greater pain, spiritual struggle.

In the morning though, it's resurrection time! Instead of darkness, there is light; instead of lying down, we stand upright; instead of thoughts about what has already happened, we focus on what will happen; instead of being tired, all of our body systems are stronger – overnight we are physically healing; instead of lack of clarity, we have become smarter. These are all physically true.

How do we respond? Often, we respond with "just wait till" or "yes, but" or even "I'm just kidding myself"! What is a leader's response?

You are a Christian leader because you respond with the heart of thankfulness, the hands of faithful action, the feet of purpose, the brain of insight, and the clothing of joy! Rejoicing comes in the morning! God has "turned my wailing into dancing; removed my sackcloth and clothed me with joy, that my heart may sing your praises and not be silent. Lord my God, I will praise you forever" (vse. 11-12).

What is my routine in the morning?

What are ways in which I can truly rejoice in the morning without artifice?

Dear Jesus: It's true that there are times when rejoicing is tough. I face problems that are insoluble. I have relationships that seem to go nowhere. I am pulled in so many different directions. It's not as if you don't know about that! Help me live in the real world and still rejoice in the morning. Help me acknowledge my true situation and my true emotions and still rejoice. Thank you that you teach me to rejoice. Thank you for telling me that my grief will turn to joy. Amen.

48. LEADING WITH DIGNITY

Bible Reference: "Because Joseph her husband was faithful to the law, and yet did not want to expose her to public disgrace, he had in mind to divorce her quietly" (Matthew 1:19).

Meditation: Of course, we know that public shaming is a bad thing. Now let's remember that it has a strong Christian tradition and a strong historical record in many cultures. Jesus himself was spat on, a sign of public shame. When I was growing up, students were still shamed by being made to stand in the corner, or wear signs in the schoolyard, or stand on chairs. Recently, some jurisdictions forced convicted people to hold signs on public thoroughfares proclaiming their guilt. The internet has allowed vitriolic shaming to occur, sometimes aided and abetted by some news media. It's not new, and it hasn't gone away.

But we're no longer comfortable with it, not because of Christian teaching but because of the insights gained through psychology. To our shame. Gershen Kaufman, a scholar who studies the phenomenon of shame, writes, "Shame is the most disturbing experience individuals ever have about themselves; no other emotion feels more deeply disturbing because in the moment of shame the self feels wounded from within." Of course, we feel shame when our conscience speaks to us. But inflicting shame on someone else is different. It strips dignity from the other, it demeans self-image, it separates the other from everyone else and makes that person a foreigner. It's the putdown, the snide comment, the desire to belittle, the vicious attack, the moral sneer, the arrogant self-justification. It's everything that Joseph did not do.

I challenge you to get through today without shaming anyone. Let's make it tougher. I challenge you to get through today without wanting to shame anyone. Let's call it the Joseph challenge. I don't speak from a position of strength. Alas, my sin is greater. I am inspired by Joseph's example and will take this challenge for myself. Will you join me?

In what ways can you hear shaming as you walk through your day?

Can your community name the issue and talk about it?

Dear Jesus: They tried to shame you, too, and you responded with love. They spat on you, too, and you looked on them with love. They sneered and they mocked you, too, and you responded with love. And you commanded us to love one another just as you loved us. Help me to stop shaming the people around me. Help me to respond with love. Thank you for Joseph, who gives us hope that we can act in the right way. Amen.

49. FEAR IS A CONSTANT.

Bible Reference: "I will not fear though tens of thousands assail me on every side" (Psalm 3:6).

Meditation: Fear is so ubiquitous we stop thinking about it. It just sits bubbling under the surface, barely even recognizable as fear, covered with other language such as fright, alarm, panic, trepidation, anxiety, angst, uneasiness.

Then there are times when it rises to a crescendo due to a tornado, a strange person approaching on a dark street, the lights going out, a dog growling and baring its teeth, my child crossing the street without looking. It has a physical component that goes along with it – increased heart rate, rapid breathing, the adrenal gland putting out adrenaline, changed brain activity, stimulation of the amygdala, pupil dilation. We mutter the 23rd Psalm like some kind of charm until the perceived danger is past, and then feel suitably foolish.

As Christian school leaders, we are not immune to fear. We are scared of our own shadow half the time: fear of enrollment decline, fear we won't be able to make payroll, fear we will lose a great teacher, fear we won't get a great teacher, fear that the campaign will fail, fear that I won't get my work done. It goes on and on.

Fear is good. It attunes us to reality (at its best) and helps us take action. It is pretty unlikely that David did not experience fear as he was on the run from Absalom, so desperate and unsure of his friends that he even left the walls of Jerusalem and headed into the wilderness. It is more likely that, in his fear, he nonetheless was able to put his trust in God to protect and sustain him.

Don't pretend that you are not afraid. Since death came, we have been afraid. With David, though, express your confidence that death has been defeated, that fear is no longer triumphant, that our God is trustworthy. Because of this, you can sleep well at night (vse. 5), not incapacitated by your anxiety. Because of this, you can call on the Lord and find answers to all your fears (vse. 4). In the midst of fear, the valley of the shadow, the Lord is your shield, the One who lifts your head high (vse. 3). What an amazing image! Yes, it is God himself who lifts your head and gives you the victory!

In what ways does fear stop you being a successful leader?

In what ways can you set fear aside and replace it with confidence?

Dear Jesus: You know that I am afraid. Help me not to fear. You know that I lack confidence in you. Help my unbelief. You know that I lack confidence in myself. Help me to seek wisdom. Thank you for your unswerving love for me anyway. Amen.

50. SOCIAL JUSTICE AND THE WAY YOU TALK

Bible Reference: "You have the words of eternal life" (John 6:68).

Meditation: Words are not neutral. Jesus' words both attracted and repelled people, including his own disciples. This passage in John recounts how many of Jesus' disciples stopped following him because his words were too hard to accept. On the other hand, Simon Peter recognizes the hard message but also pays homage to the One who has the words of eternal life. Where else is there to go? he asks.

The power to speak truth and to speak righteousness and to speak salvation is hard for us to emulate. It's easier to be nice and to be holy. Who wants to rock the boat? Well, apparently Jesus did. What might that mean for you as a leader?

I was in a Christian high school that had a very diverse population, but when they sat down for lunch, there was no diversity at all. Each group of people sat with people who looked just like they did. What would be the words of life for those students?

I was at another school where many of the football players were African Americans. Parents questioned their academic credentials and suggested that they had got into the school just to make the football team look good. What would be the words of life for those parents?

At yet another school, the science department got much more time to teach than any other department with the result that there was great antagonism between departments. What would be the words of life for those faculty?

It's not easy to see our social structures in our schools, to look at power dynamics in our schools, and then to be willing to name them. It's easier to accept racism, sexism, gossip, hazing, and other forms of social injustice and think of them as normal. It's what people do. As a leader, you are called to challenge what's wrong – the words of salvation call everyone in the school to a community of forgiveness, suffering, and love; to put ourselves second and the other first; to go the extra mile in all areas.

Am I willing to 'see' injustice in my school?

How can we as a community continually strive for justice, mercy, and peace?

Dear Jesus: You were never content to let things be. It was uncomfortable to walk with you along the roads of Galilee and Judea. Help me to see with your eyes of love and compassion but also with your eyes of discernment and understanding. Give me the words of eternal life. Let me be compelled to follow you and speak your justice and truth in my school. Thank you that you stand up for each person, die for each person, save each person. Amen.

51. TRUTH IN LEADERSHIP

Bible Reference: "Lord, who may dwell in your sacred tent? Who may live on your holy mountain? The one whose walk is blameless, who does what is righteous, who speaks the truth from their heart; whose tongue utters no slander, who does no wrong to a neighbor, and casts no slur on others" (Psalm 15:1-3).

Meditation: Is "truth" in the Christian school what works, what you make it, what authority tells us? Is it even some kind of tyranny that forces intolerance and hatred? Frederick Nietzsche said that were no facts, only interpretations. That's why we don't teach him in our schools! But, unpleasant as his opinion might be, he nonetheless challenges us.

How do we lead in our school? Truthfully?

I was consulting at a Christian school where there were two marketing people. One worked for admission and the other for development. This arrangement had grown up over the years (all 4 staff members had been at the school at least 6 years) due to the strained relationship between the Directors of Admission and Development. I asked to meet with the two marketers, and it was the first time they had been in a room together for months. They sat apart from each other and looked at me. For the first five minutes, the conversation was strained. Finally, I remarked to them about their body language, which I interpreted as dislike for each other, asking whether I was correct. I said that for the school to go forward we had to work together, and I needed to know whether that was possible for them. The conversation became animated, warmed up, and we were able to articulate common genuine enthusiasm for the school's work.

Truth is not a holy abstraction – "I am the Way, the Truth, and the Life." Such holy talk means nothing if we can't make it life-giving in our internal relationships and conversations. It's hard to speak the truth in love as if we believe they are in tension with each other. Not interrogating and finding the truth is where the true tension lies. Lead in truth. Lead with truth. Lead through truth.

Where is truth not happening at your school?

Why do we need courage to be truthful but no courage to be false?

Dear Jesus: You are love and you spoke truth, sometimes in anger, sometimes in sorrow. Yet your relationships with your disciples only deepened until they went out to the whole world to tell others about you. Let my leadership be the same. Let me speak truth and deepen relationships until anything is possible. Thank you for the opportunity to be truth in my community. Amen.

52. TODAY IS A HAPPY DAY!

Bible Reference: "Praise the Lord!" (Psalm 148:1).

Meditation: The power has gone out and the storm is raging. The heavens are gloomy with cloud, only now and then illuminated by the flashes of lightning bolt striking the earth with power.

It doesn't matter – God is love and God loves me! "Praise the LORD from the heavens; praise him in the heights above. Praise him, sun and moon; praise him, all you shining stars. Let them praise the name of the LORD, for at his command they were created" (Psalm 148:1, 3, 5).

My garden is full of weeds that I can never seem to get ahead of. My bedding plants have mostly died from the drought. I have harvested 2 tomatoes so far, and that might be it. My gutters need fixing. The chipmunks are eating the bird feed, and I had to take the dog to the vet.

It doesn't matter – God is love and God loves me! "Praise the Lord from the earth, you great sea creatures and all ocean depths, lightning and hail, snow and clouds, stormy winds that do his bidding, young men and women, old men and children" (Psalm 148:7, 8, 12).

I forgot an important meeting yesterday. I am meeting with the bank today. Tomorrow, I meet with an angry parent and a happy one. After lunch, a donor is coming for a tour. Tonight, it's my turn to take my daughter to volleyball practice and my son to piano lessons. I have a headache.

It doesn't matter – God is love and God loves me! "Let them praise the name of the Lord, for his name alone is exalted; his splendor is above the earth and the heavens. And he has raised up for his people a horn, the praise of all his faithful servants, of Israel, the people close to his heart. Praise the Lord" (Psalm 148:13-14).

Do your circumstances make you joyful, or does being loved make you joyful?

Where in your daily challenges do you find joy?

Dear Jesus: I know that life is challenging, even at the best of times. Let me never forget that I am your creation and I can live in joy because of your love for me, because I am close to your heart. Thank you for that assurance. Amen.

53. IT DOESN'T HAVE TO BE PRETTY!

Bible Reference: "They crucified two rebels with him, one on his right and one on his left" (Mark 15:27).

Meditation: I always wanted my victories to be pretty. Preferably tied up in self-congratulation. You may have similar thoughts. The win would be hard fought but ultimately decisive. The student would pull through and fulfill her ambition. The alumnus would eventually come back to the school and admit that we had been right all along. Everything would be very clean and tidy. Being a victorious Christian would be so romantic. What could be better than Charlton Heston vs. Yul Brynner in *The Ten Commandments*? All so clean-cut and shiny. Followed by the Oscars.

Jesus isn't so easy to get along with. He died a Roman death along with two rebels. What I didn't realize until recently (courtesy of N.T. Wright), is that these two rebels show up earlier in Mark in a prophecy of Jesus: "Then James and John, the sons of Zebedee, came to him. 'Teacher,' they said, 'we want you to do for us whatever we ask.' 'What do you want me to do for you?' he asked. They replied, 'Let one of us sit at your right and the other at your left in your glory.' 'You don't know what you are asking,' Jesus said ... 'to sit at my right or left is not for me to grant. These places belong to those for whom they have been prepared' (Mark 10:35-40, edited). And at least one of those crucified rebels ended up in Paradise with Jesus!

It's a reminder to me as a Christian leader that life with Jesus isn't pretty. It's messy and dirty and inglorious, from a humanly proud point of view. It's a stable, and sleeping in a boat, and being hungry on a hillside, and going to Jerusalem where they killed the prophets. My job is to lead in those decidedly not pretty places.

Do I pray for my leadership to be more glorious?

What "thrones" am I looking to sit on? What might I look for instead?

Dear Jesus: I know I shouldn't expect it to be straightforward and easy. You said it was a narrow road I had to follow. But does it have to be so narrow? James and John expected you to be a victorious king on a Jerusalem throne. They were wrong, and so am I when I want the same thing. Help me to know that the true glory is in following you where you went. Thank you for your courage and example for me to emulate. Amen.

54. THE CHALLENGE OF FAMILY

Bible Reference: "Hearing that Jesus had silenced the Sadducees, the Pharisees got together. One of them, an expert in the law, tested him with this question: 'Teacher, which is the greatest commandment in the Law?' Jesus replied: *Love the Lord your God with all your heart and with all your soul and with all your mind*'" (Matthew 22:34-37).

Meditation: As the father of two daughters, I can say without doubt that the world's culture influences and seduces our children with its emphasis on popularity, materialism, and self-fulfillment. And therein lies the tension. The call of the world collides with the call of Jesus to focus on God and worship and glorify him alone.

Sadly, we increasingly live in a time where there appears to be a worldwide, all-out assault upon the home and family. All parents, but particularly Christian parents, are facing unbelievable and often overwhelming challenges today. We are not insulated from the stresses that pull apart families.

Children are a gift of the Lord and, by God's design, parents are the primary educators of their children. Parents have one of the most influential roles, if not the most influential role, in a child's life.

Raising children is challenging, but parents have been given the opportunity and privilege to raise their children in the fear and admonition of God. In this regard, the role of the Christian school is supplemental. To put it another way, children are God's homework assignments to parents. How then do Christian parents prepare their children to become godly men and women with a heart and desire to love and serve God? By acknowledging and understanding that the education of children is a 24-hours-a-day, 7-days-a-week process and making sure that the training of our children is a consistent effort.

In a proactive partnership, home and school can strive together to instill in our children a passion for love, humility, truth, and forgiveness that run counter to the world's call to self-fulfillment.

How do your families need you to partner with them in an age of new challenges?

What is your school's witness to the world about the strength and importance of family?

Lord, we give you our school. Give us the courage and the wisdom to set about the task of teaching that has your truth as its bedrock. Help us to strengthen and grow the partnership between home and school so that together, in partnership, we can raise a generation that loves and serves you with their whole heart. Amen.

55. TIME TO DO A HOUSE CLEANING

Bible Reference: "I am the true vine, and my Father is the gardener. He cuts off every branch in me that bears no fruit, while every branch that does bear fruit he prunes so that it will be even more fruitful" (John 15:1-2).

Meditation: Every year, in late November, I prune my crepe myrtle trees. When I'm finished, they look pretty sad. But, as spring approaches, those sad-looking, truncated stubs burst forth with glorious new growth and color that illuminates the whole yard. In the above scripture, Jesus talks about pruning of another kind – spiritual pruning.

Now, I'm the first to admit that spiritual pruning doesn't feel good because it often involves times of pain and uncovering our wounds. Sometimes we are called to step out of our comfort zones. So, why does God prune us? God wants us to be stronger, more productive, more fruitful, and he wants us to grow and blossom so that we can be more effective for his kingdom.

The fruit to which Jesus is referring is the fruit of the Spirit; which is love, joy, peace, patience, gentleness, goodness, faith, meekness, and self-control (Galatians 5:22-23). I don't know about you, but I could probably use a little growth in all of these areas. That's why I need to be regularly pruned. Pruning, or removing all that is an impediment to my spiritual growth, will hopefully let people more clearly see Christ living in me.

Pruning is not a one-off event. Pruning needs to happen every year if the tree is to remain healthy and productive. God's primary concern is not your comfort or even your happiness, but that you bear spiritual fruit. God will use circumstances to prune you. If you are facing tests, trials, or opposition, take heart. Rejoice! The Lord is likely pruning you to bear that precious fruit of the Spirit, and in doing so bring him honor and glory. As Jesus says later, in John 15:8, "This is to my Father's glory, that you bear much fruit, showing yourselves to be my disciples."

What circumstances is God using to prune you?

What kind of fruit might you bear after pruning?

Lord, the desire of my heart is to bring you honor and glory. So, Lord, I ask that you continue to cut away all that impedes my spiritual growth. Shape me and make me stronger and more productive, so I can bear fruit and share your goodness. Amen.

Christian School Leader's Devotional

56. STAND FIRM!

Bible Reference: Jesus answered: "Watch out that no one deceives you" (Matthew 24:4).

Meditation: In other Bible translations, "deceive" is expressed as "leads you astray." Whatever version of the Bible you read, the words of Jesus to "take heed" present a stark warning. It is both foolish and dangerous to think we can't be led astray or deceived.

You are responsible for the curriculum at your school. A curriculum is considered the "heart" of any learning institution, and deceit can be clearly illustrated in textbooks. As a student and teacher of history, I am constantly amazed at the attempts to revise historical events and movements. Here is just one example from an American history book:

"We whose names are under-written ... do by these present solemnly and mutually in the presence of God, and one of another, covenant and combine our selves together into a civil body politick." (Mayflower Compact, 1620)

What was edited from this important historical quote?

"We whose names are under-written having *undertaken for the glory of God, and advancement of the Christian faith and honor of our king and country, a voyage to plant the first colonie in the Northern parts of Virginia* do by these present solemnly and mutually in the presence of God, and one of another, covenant and combine ourselves together into a civil body politick."

The omitted segment clearly indicates the strongly religious nature of early American government documents and leaders, and its exclusion robs students of the opportunity to see the guiding hand of God at work in the foundation of this great nation. This is not an isolated occurrence.

It is essential that Christian schools stand firm in the Lord (cf. Matthew 24:13), our rock and foundation, and not be deceived by hollow philosophies as they design curriculum.

Where do we need to stand against deceit?

What does it mean to have a curriculum that's "true"?

Lord, your Word says to "stand firm," and that's what we will do, in the power of your Name. The enemy has no control over us, and we bring your Word of Truth as weapon against his schemes. We know that we do not fight alone, for you are constantly at work on our behalf, bringing to light what needs to be known. Help me as a leader to identify deceit and cling always to the Way the Truth, and the Life. Amen.

57. MY SCHOOL IS FOR CHILDREN

Bible Reference: When Jesus saw this, he was indignant. He said to them, "Let the little children come to me, and do not hinder them, for the kingdom of God belongs to such as these. Truly I tell you, anyone who will not receive the kingdom of God like a little child will never enter it." And he took the children in his arms, placed his hands on them and blessed them (Mark 10:14-16).

Meditation: Jesus loved children! During his earthly ministry, he often demonstrated this overwhelming love and concern for children as the above verse from Mark's Gospel shows us. He spoke to children, healed children, and blessed children. Jesus knew that a child's faith is pure and sincere and without reservations.

Daily, as you observe your faculty interact with your students, how often do you remind them that they are the hands and feet of Jesus that your students see every day? Everything about them, their demeanor, their dress, and their actions exemplify their Christian walk and witness. The Bible makes it clear that a child will be like his teachers when he is fully trained. To steal an old coaching phrase, your faculty really need to "walk their talk."

Every day, your students get to interact with their teachers. Do they see teachers whose faith is essential to who they are? Do they see teachers who model a Christ-like life in their living teaching and leading? Do they see humble teachers who have trust and dependence in Christ alone?

An unknown author once wrote, "Genius is undiscovered gold. Talented is the teacher who struggles, finds and helps students develop it." Every day, every student at your school should come to understand and be shown that he or she is unique, fearfully and wonderfully made in the very image of God. Students need to learn and celebrate that their Heavenly Father has given each and every one of them gifts, talents, and abilities just waiting to be discovered. What an honor and privilege that God has called and equipped you and your staff for this awesome responsibility.

What does it look like to model a Christ-like life in teaching and leading?

Ask the question: Is my school a welcoming place for children?

Lord, thank you that you always remind us about the importance of each child. Let me lead with that in mind. Let me also constantly remind those around me and those I lead that same lesson. Amen.

58. MANAGING TIME IS WISDOM

Bible Reference: "Teach us to number our days, that we may gain a heart of wisdom" (Psalm 90:12).

Meditation: Every day consists of 24 hours – 1,440 minutes – 86,400 seconds. That's a lot of time! Why then do most of us feel like there is never enough time to accomplish our never-ending to-do lists?

We are only given limited time here on this earth. That's why the Psalmist asks the Lord to number our days. This is a call to action – to really think about how we use the days we are given. It's a cry from the heart for the Lord to make all our days worthwhile.

Christian education is a sacred calling from God. Our charge is clear: to assist parents in their God-given mandate to "raise their children up in the nurture and admonition of the Lord" (Ephesians 6:4), teaching them to "Love the Lord your God with all your heart and with all your soul and with all your mind" (Matthew 22:37-38).

Implicit in Jesus' words is the mandate to instill in our students a Christian or biblical worldview, a framework of ideas and beliefs through which they will interpret the world and interact with it. According to research by George Barna, worldview is developed between the ages of 18 months and 13 years. By the time a teenager is 13 or 14, it's done. He says it may be refined a little through the teen years, but by your 20s, a worldview is solid.

In light of these findings, the time we have with our students is a scarce resource indeed. Ephesians 5:15-17 tells us, "Be very careful, then, how you live – not as unwise but as wise, making the most of every opportunity, because the days are evil. Therefore, do not be foolish, but understand what the Lord's will is." God is calling you to "make the most of every opportunity." This is a call to intentionality and purpose in all that you do. As a Christian leader, you must steward all of your resources with precision and diligence. Your school depends on it.

The use of time then becomes a moral decision. It's not just a matter of thinking "well now I'll do this or now I'll do that." Time use is a matter of wisdom – intentionally moving in a particular direction in order to benefit the students the most.

What is the one thing you are committed to completing today? Is this important or just urgent?

How do you lead the use of time in your school?

Lord, you want our limited time here on earth to have lasting significance in others' lives. Please use me this day to share your eternal truths with others. Amen.

59. THE LORD HAS DONE GREAT THINGS FOR THEM

Bible Reference: "Our mouths were filled with laughter, our tongues with songs of joy. Then it was said among the nations, The Lord has done great things for them" (Psalm 126:2).

Meditation: You came into work today and all the little details were waiting for you on your desk. It sometimes feels as if all the great things you were supposed to be doing have been reduced to answering emails and handling crises. How did it get this way?

Think what Saul and David had to do in order for Solomon to reap the benefits. They had to unite the 12 tribes of Israel, fight many battles, organize the nation's finances, set up the courts. They also had to face their own sinfulness, sometimes in the most dramatic ways. Saul tried to kill David. David did kill Abner. They had to move on.

You have "ancestors" on your journey too. They have done great things for you. Your school is where it is because of them. They were amazing people and they were also real people. Well, that's where you are too. You are an amazing person, filled by God's breath, made in his image. You dare not deny what God has given you. You are also a sinful person, making mistakes, acting badly, or sometimes not acting when you should. You have to move on as well.

Your measure of success is not whether you are perfect. Your measure of success is your ability to move beyond the details and get to the "great things" that fill you and those around you with joy and laughter. Solomon's Temple was the place where God dwelt – an incredible light shone from the Temple (1 Kings 8:1-11). Your measure of success is that the neighborhoods around you see that the Lord has done great things for you, see that the school is a place of light, and that you are filled with laughter and joy.

Who are the giants on your journey who have made you possible today? What mighty acts did they perform so that you could tread your path?

What mighty acts are you planning for your school? Who needs to be part of that, and what resources do you need?

Dear Jesus: I don't associate myself with mighty acts. I don't think of the school as my school. Still, you have given the school into my care and you have given the school me as a leader. We are both supposed to do "great things." Help me to move on from my own sinfulness and from the details that stop me achieving and being full of laughter and joy. I thank you for all the gifts you have given me personally – and all the people who brought me and this school to this moment. Help me to go to the next level and take the school to the next level as well. Amen.

60. UNEXPECTED HEROES

Bible Reference: When Jesus heard this, he was amazed at him, and turning to the crowd following him, he said, "I tell you, I have not found such great faith even in Israel" (Luke 7:9).

Meditation: Is it possible for you to be amazed? It seems to me that we tend to prize predictability in our lives, which is probably a good thing. However, that can become a hindrance to God's possibilities. I still remember as if it were yesterday becoming the Head of a Lutheran school in Ontario, Canada. I had written the first parent letter and I know that I'm a good writer (!). An unexpected source of wisdom happened by. Desi, a parent at the school, happened by and read it. She gently told me that it was terrible and needed significant work in order for the parents to be able to understand what I was saying. Happily, I understood that this was a moment of grace for me, and Desi became the proofreader for all my parent letters. She was indeed amazing, I was amazed, and the school benefited from her wisdom.

Here in Luke, Jesus is amazed at the depth of faith found in a Roman centurion. The hero of the story is a Roman, member of the occupying army, nice to the Jews but nonetheless an oppressor. Amazing! (In Mark, 6 Jesus is amazed at the lack of faith where we might expect it to be – his home town of Nazareth.)

Look around you in your school. You can see the expected heroes – the 4.0-GPA student headed to Princeton; the quarterback with the scholarship to the state university; the 40-year veteran teacher beloved by all. Can you see the unexpected amazing heroes – the friendless student's kindness, the contribution to school morale by the janitor, the 3.0-GPA student from a fragmented family, the faculty member counseling a child whom everyone else has given up on?

I can guarantee, if my own experience means anything, that just as Jesus was surprised to find such depth of faith in a foreigner that he could not find among his own people, you also will be surprised by the leadership coming from unheralded places.

Do you always look in the same places for your student and adult leaders?

Who are you not seeing? Are you open to amazement?

Dear Jesus: The centurion isn't the only unexpected hero in the Gospels. You constantly pointed out people who were great but didn't look like it, beginning with those you chose as your disciples. Thank you for your example. Help me to really see the people around me, both child and adult. Help me not to underestimate the grace you have given each one. Help me to appreciate and call upon wisdom, irrespective of title or worldly prestige. Amen.

61. THANK GOD FOR HARVEST

Bible Reference: "I tell you, open your eyes and look at the fields! They are ripe for harvest" (John 4:35).

Meditation: The harvest is hard to see sometimes. A physical harvest is obvious. It's not so easy to see the children for your school in the streets of your town or city. Nevertheless, the fields are ripe for harvest.

I am reminded of the story of Adoniram Judson. He was a Baptist missionary to Burma in the 19th century. He went at a time when Burma, largely Buddhist, was considered impermeable to Christianity. During his time there he lost 2 wives and several children; was tortured and imprisoned for a period of almost 2 years, including being suspended upside down for 7 days; and it took 7 years to gain his first convert. But the fields were ripe for harvest.

He died there aged 61. He had spent most of his adult life there, from 1813 to 1850. It might have seemed like a tortured and purposeless vocation. But it was not. He and his first wife learned to speak and write Burmese fluently. He translated the entire Bible into Burmese, and it was printed in 1835. By the time of his death, he had also begun work on a Burmese-English dictionary, had established 100 churches, and there were 8,000 believers. His translation is revered to this day – around 5% of Burmese are now Christian. The fields are ripe for harvest.

Do you face enrollment challenges as difficult as Adoniram Judson's? The fields are ripe for harvest!

How do I need to talk about enrollment with my team, my faculty, my parents?

What plan will I make and what actions will I take to reflect the ripe harvest?

Dear Jesus: I constantly talk about the challenges. Remind me that they are nothing new. Remind me of the saints who have gone before who inspire us with their stories of perseverance and hope. Let me pray Psalm 13 continuously, understanding how whiny the beginning sounds and how I must trust in your bounty: "How long, Lord? Will you forget me forever? How long will you hide your face from me? How long must I wrestle with my thoughts and day after day have sorrow in my heart? How long will my enemy triumph over me? Look on me and answer, Lord my God. Give light to my eyes, or I will sleep in death, and my enemy will say, 'I have overcome him,' and my foes will rejoice when I fall. But I trust in your unfailing love; my heart rejoices in your salvation. I will sing the Lord's praise, for he has been good to me." Thank you, Jesus. Amen.

62. JESUS, SON OF GOD

Bible Reference: "In those days, Caesar Augustus issued a decree" (Luke 2:1).

Meditation: Lots of people aren't mentioned in Luke – why Caesar Augustus? Well, it's delicious. The background is important and interesting. Augustus called himself the son of god, having called his adoptive father Julius a god. When he died, he was named a god. Luke was aware of that when he was writing since Augustus had died in 14 A.D. We have an Egyptian inscription that describes Augustus as a marvelous star "shining with the brilliance of the great heavenly Savior." There is a coin from Gaul describing him as the son of god. People took this seriously. In Asia Minor, the worship of the emperor was so serious that Christians were most fiercely persecuted in that region for refusing to worship him. This is the person we still remember in the month of August.

Now the command of Augustus fulfills the prophecy about Jesus' birth (Micah 5:2)! The true Son of God is to be born, Luke says, by command of the false deity, in Bethlehem. Ponder this verse at length. Luke is saying that all the principalities of this world cannot thwart the will of God in bringing about the kingdom of God. Luke mentions the phrase kingdom of God 43 times. The very last mention of this phrase is when Luke tells us that Nicodemus was waiting for the kingdom of God and then asks for the body of Jesus (Luke 23:50-53). The irony at the beginning of Luke and the innocent proclamation at the end of Luke!

You are a Christian school leader. You live in this irony and innocence every day. The rulers of this world try to set themselves up as "Augustus," but you know that God has you in the palm of his hand. You seek the kingdom of God, and the body of Jesus is delivered to you in the Last Supper – do this in remembrance of me (Luke 22:19). You are a resurrection leader – lead in and to the kingdom of God.

Do I really understand that I am a willing and often unknowing part of God's covenant plan?

What leadership attributes do I use to demonstrate that the kingdom of God is present for us?

Dear Jesus: Thank you for Luke and his amazing ability in a few words to lay out an entire story line that recognizes and reveres you as Lord of all. Help me to accept and trust that in my leadership. Give me the innocence of Nicodemus to just ask for the kingdom of God. Let me see your face, as the Psalmist says. Help me see you in every child and every adult in the school. Thank you for the confidence that Christmas brings that you are with me, your rod and your staff they comfort me. Amen.

ACT 2: TOILING AND TILLING (WINTER)

THE CHRISTIAN JOURNEY: EPIPHANY, LENT, AND EASTER

How is my mission statement affirmed or changing?
_____
_____
_____

My top 5 understandings as I enter Act 2

1. _____
2. _____
3. _____
4. _____
5. _____

What has surprised and/or touched me so far?
_____
_____
_____
_____
_____
_____

What is my journey buddy urging me to do?
_____
_____
_____
_____

63. EPIPHANY AND ALL THE NATIONS

Bible Reference: "Magi from the east came to Jerusalem" (Matthew 2:1).

Meditation: In Eastern Christianity, Epiphany is the birthday of Jesus – his manifestation. In Western Christianity, Epiphany is the Feast of the Magi, inaugurating a season that finishes with Candlemas, the presentation of Jesus in the Temple.

In Matthew's story, the magi come willingly to pay homage to the "king of the Jews." The king in this story, Herod, is not impressed, unlike Nebuchadnezzar and Pharaoh, and plots to kill Jesus. The magi do not play along. They go back home by a different road. Herod is a symbol of the people of Israel who do not recognize the Messiah, while the foreigners, people who practiced astrology, both recognize and worship the baby.

There are amazing leadership insights here. Where does wisdom come from? Is it always from the experts? Who are the special chosen people who are gifted by God? Are they always tall and handsome and wealthy? Who does God want to be a part of his kingdom? The ones who have the right accent and the right theology? The magi tell us that God is bigger than any stereotype. Jesus himself said that the outside was not a good sign of what was on the inside (Matthew 23:27 and others).

This is so important for you as a Christian school leader. Don't be swayed by the outside, adult or child. Don't be swayed by the title, the learning, the clothing. Don't be swayed by the power or the wealth. Don't be swayed by the good looks or the academic prowess. Don't be swayed by the gift or the swagger. Remember that God came to the foreign magi as Jesus comes to rich Nicodemus and lowly fishermen and the Samaritan woman and the dishonest tax collector. He is no respecter of persons (cf. Mark 12:38). Do likewise. Be a leader for every person.

Are there groups that I favor over others?

What are Jesus' criteria for praising and raising up a person?

Dear Jesus: You looked into the heart of those around you. That's hard for me to do. And so it's easy to be tricked by piety or influence or cleverness. Help me to have a discerning mind and heart. Let me acknowledge the magi in my school. Thank you for giving us so many examples of people who were on the outside. Thank you for calling me to lead every person in my school, both child and adult. Amen.

64. WHAT'S YOUR PURPOSE?

Bible Reference: "But the plans of the Lord stand firm forever, the purposes of his heart through all generations" (Psalm 33:11).

Meditation: Christmas is over. The goose has been roasted. The presents have been opened. But did I really get the point? God, from thousands of years ago, promised that Jesus would come. According to his mercy, Christmas happened and the angels sang. God, from thousands of years ago, promised that he would come again, and we look forward to that great day when "on earth as it is in heaven." God always works with purpose.

Are you leading a school with purpose? The reason I ask is that school after school that CSM visits does not know its own mission with accuracy and is not focused with laser sharpness on its "why", its purpose. That's odd. In the *Harvard Business Review* for August 2018, the authors of the article "Creating a Purpose-Driven Organization" write this: "In our consulting work with hundreds of organizations and in our research – which includes extensive interviews with dozens of leaders and the development of a theoretical model – we have come to see that when an authentic purpose permeates business strategy and decision making, the personal good and the collective good become one. Positive peer pressure kicks in, and employees are reenergized. Collaboration increases, learning accelerates, and performance climbs."

Amazing! A completely secular magazine that determines whether something is good by looking at whether the company has excellence shareholder return understands the power of mission! Wall Street meets Rick Warren!

So why is it so hard for you? Put your focused 25 word mission statement on every agenda (including every Board agenda), recite it together at faculty meetings, put it in front of you on your computer. Know it and make sure everyone else knows it. God works with purpose. Get rid of the January blues by reminding yourself and those who work with you that you have a purpose, too, that is connected to God's purpose. You are a purpose-driven organization.

How can you ensure that everyone knows the school's mission?

What obstacles do you have to being a purpose-driven school?

Dear Jesus: Even as a child, you were focused on your Father's business. You knew your purpose and even swatted Peter aside when he tried to move you from it. Help me be purpose-driven with the same energy and focus. Help me understand what the school's mission is and bend every sinew to making it happen in the lives of children. Thank you for the covenants you have fulfilled over thousands of years. Thank you for being with me to sustain me and the school I serve. Amen.

65. THE SIZE OF THE TASK

Bible Reference: "When he looked up and saw a large crowd coming toward him, Jesus said to Philip, 'Where are we to buy bread for these people to eat?' He said this to test because he himself knew what he was going to do" (John 6:5-6).

Meditation: It can be like that, can't it? You arrive at work and as you pull into the parking lot, the magnitude of the task just grabs you and you sit for a moment, wondering if you are capable of being the leader God has called you to be. You know you are called. You feel God's presence.

But you still can't help wondering, "Is it really me? Am I really the one to lead this school? Just look at the size of the task! The children pouring onto the playground; teachers and staff pulling into their spaces; the facilities looming; the gardens of flowers and the fields of grass; the parent waiting by my office; the upcoming Board meeting; that utility bill that seems too large to pay; the child yesterday in tears. Am I really the one?"

How amazing that Jesus is there before you to ask the question. Where are we to buy bread for these people to eat? Where are we to find the will to continue on? Where do I reach for the determination to succeed? Where do I find the joy in the midst of the challenges? Where do I cultivate the leadership skills I know I don't yet have? Jesus is already there asking the questions for us. He knows, and just the fact that he knows is sufficient for you. He knows that you are a single human being with a supernatural task, a single mind and heart to feed the crowd coming into that building.

There is a plan, and Jesus will hold your hand patiently while you figure out that you have what you need, that you have the wisdom to ask the right questions, to hire the right people, to get the needed professional development. He will stand next to you, so closely that you can feel the swish of his robes, smiling at your confusion as he did at Philip's. How can you feed so great a multitude? Bring your "bread" and he will bless it.

What are key strengths God has gifted me with?

Who are key people God has gifted me with?

Dear Jesus: It is easy for me to feel as if I am not adequate to the task. On my own, that's true. Please help me to bring everything you have given me back to you so that you can bless it. Help me to do that daily, even moment by moment. I am so thankful for your blessing and promise not to let it go to waste. Amen.

66. WHERE IS GOD'S HOME?

Bible Reference: "Jesus replied, 'Anyone who loves me will obey my teaching. My Father will love them, and we will come to them and make our home with them'" (John 14:23).

Meditation: Wow! You are not "going" to heaven! You are not "finding" salvation! You are not "searching" for God! When you obey Jesus' teaching, God the Father and God the Son will come to you and make you their home! Isn't that astonishing? Jesus did and does the Father's will (cf. John 15:10) and lives with the Father. Jesus has already sent us God the Holy Spirit, the Comforter, who is the source of our creativity and insight (cf. Matthew 1:20). God, the Holy Trinity, is also God with us, God with me, in totality. You can expect great things from our God to happen in your leadership. "In the morning, Lord, you hear my voice; in the morning I lay my requests before you and wait expectantly" (Psalm 5:3). That is literally awe-inspiring.

With that in mind, it must be true that God expects great things from you. You can even imagine that you will be enabled by grace to exceed all human expectations (cf. 2 Corinthians 8:5). You are to be a leader of transformations. With God, you are to have power as a Christian school leader. Grab onto Jesus. Lift your face to the Father. Hear the call of the Holy Spirit. Lead your school for this generation and for generations to come. There is nothing left to do but pray with Paul as he wrote in his letter to the Ephesians:

"For this reason I kneel before the Father, from whom every family in heaven and on earth derives its name. I pray that out of his glorious riches he may strengthen you with power through his Spirit in your inner being, so that Christ may dwell in your hearts through faith. And I pray that you, being rooted and established in love, may have power, together with all the Lord's holy people, to grasp how wide and long and high and deep is the love of Christ, and to know this love that surpasses knowledge – that you may be filled to the measure of all the fullness of God."

Now to him who is able to do immeasurably more than all we ask or imagine, according to his power that is at work within us, to him be glory in the church and in Christ Jesus throughout all generations, for ever and ever! Amen. (Ephesians 3:14-21)

67. LOVE! THAT'S ALL IT TAKES!

Bible Reference: "If you keep my commands, you will remain in my love" (John 15:10).

Meditation: That's all – and that's everything! This is part of the vine-and-branches metaphor. You are the branches, and Jesus is the vine, and the Father is the gardener. If you do not live in Jesus, the gardener will cut you off from the tree.

What do branches do? Their purpose is to be sun and water catchers. In more formal language, the leaves on branches are the "primary location for photosynthesis and production of hormones and other chemicals." I was intrigued by learning about trees producing hormones and other chemicals, so I investigated further. Here are 5 hormones in plants:

- Auxin is the reason plants bend towards the sun; it's also the reason that the tip of a branch does not splinter into 20 different stems – that's call apical dominance.
- Gibberellin makes plants grow longer. Dwarf plants don't have this hormone.
- Cytokinin is a hitchhiker travelling with water through the plant. It promotes growth and repair.
- Ethylene is a gas that affects how plants / fruits ripen and rot. It exists in the plant but also travels outside to other plants. Don't put ripe fruit with green fruit unless you want the green fruit to ripen much faster!
- Abscisic acids are the messengers to close the stomata when the plant is water-stressed (thirsty) so the plant doesn't lose more water.
- (from http://www.untamedscience.com/biology/plants/plant-growth-hormones/)

Creation is complex and wonderful, reflecting the creative impulse of the Creator! Let's take an imaginative leap. If you are a branch, you are a Christian leader who helps and supports the growth of your community, ensures it is always looking toward Jesus, heals the wounds of the community, and ensures the community is protected in times of crisis. That's not a bad definition of school leadership!

How do you think about yourself as a branch of the vine?

What is the evidence that your leadership team remains in Jesus' love?

Dear Jesus: Your love is earth shattering – its effect was earthquakes, the tearing of the Temple veil, the opening of graves. Let it be so in my life. Shake me, open me up, help me to heal division. Let me be a true branch in this school. Thank you for your love. Amen.

68. IT'S TIME TO REST ON THE SABBATH

Bible Reference: "Then, because so many people were coming and going that they did not even have a chance to eat, he said to them, 'Come with me by yourselves to a quiet place and get some rest'" (Mark 6:31).

Meditation: I am a doer. Most leaders I meet are doers. It's not surprising. Our schools tend to have few resources and enormous needs. There is only one learning-support person and 175 students. There is only one free period a day for reviewing student assignments and planning, and that time is often taken away by meetings. There is only $300 in the art budget and so I am going to spend Saturday going to garage sales in the hope of finding some cheap materials. There is only one of me and everybody wants a piece, preferably before noon. The to-do list is long and rarely gets completed.

Many leaders I talk to neither sleep enough nor do they eat regularly.

Jesus constantly tries to find opportunities to pray, to be by himself, to rest, and to sleep, even in the middle of a storm. Given that his to-do list was just as extensive as yours, it would seem wise to think about rest. The most profound form of rest is sleep. The following quotations come from by Alex Soojung-Kim Pang, published in 2016. I recommend it.

"Sleep gives the brain a chance to repair itself; it also takes the time to process the day's events and solidify its memory of new skills ... we engage in task consolidation and performance review while sleeping ... the growth of new brain cells ... the interpretation of experiences ... restore the body, repair damaged cells ... heightens our ability to learn and perform ... deepens our ability to remember and create as individuals and as a species" (pp. 152-156). "Deliberate rest helps you cultivate calm. It deepens your capacity to focus, which helps you complete urgent tasks while driving off anxiety. It encourages you to work steadily rather than wait for a burst of inspiration ... it deepens your emotional reserves and resilience" (p. 243).

Do you get 8 to 9 hours of sleep a night?

How do you ensure your entire community thinks about God's sleep?

Dear Jesus: You made us with circadian rhythms. Help me pay attention to the way in which I am created and be respectful of the rest part of that rhythm. Let me be convinced by your own example of seeking rest. Let me plan better today and going forward. Bless my sleep and bless what happens during it to give me greater health. Thank you for rest. Amen.

69. WHOM SHOULD WE INVITE TO THE FEAST?

Bible Reference: "I say to you that many will come from the east and the west, and will take their places at the feast with Abraham, Isaac and Jacob in the kingdom of heaven" (Matthew 8:11).

Meditation: Enrollment is an ever-present concern. Few schools can assume that their classrooms will be full in August or September. Some have told me that they are having to re-assess their admission criteria in order to cut a wider swathe. I am told, we must adapt.

Are we maybe reaping the whirlwind of policies that were problematic to begin with? Why did we think that Christian schools should be full of Christians? Where did we get the idea that Christian schools were only useful to Christian families? Who said that the Christian school is only Christian in "my" denomination? Are those concepts of Christian school scriptural? Let's make sure our enrollment discussions are driven by scripture and not by economics.

On this day, as you act as a Christian leader, Jesus challenges you to look for faith in the most unexpected places. He has just met the Roman centurion, a man of blood and obedience. He has just declared (hyperbolically or factually) that this Roman oppressor has more faith than anyone he has met in Israel – and those are God's chosen people. He's looking at a crowd of fellow Jews; he's looking at his disciples; probably there are at least one or two members of his own family in the crowd. That's a wow! In Jesus, redemption comes to the whole world, and some at least respond to the invitation.

If we could go back 30 or 50 or 70 years to the beginnings of our schools, when the churches were full, would we be willing to consider the implications of Jesus' mission to the nations? How should the Christian school be part of that mission in a special way? If all have sinned and fall short of the glory of God (Romans 3:23), whom should we invite to the feast?

When was the last time we looked at our enrollment criteria in the light of scripture?

Whom do we want to serve?

Dear Jesus: I thank you that you took me, unworthy as I am, and made me a child of God and inheritor of your kingdom. I thank you that you welcomed the little children. Help me lead thoughtfully and prayerfully as we look at our neighborhood and town and city. Inspire me to know what your will is as to whom we should serve. Thank you for being the suffering servant for me. Amen.

70. JANUARY IS A TOUGH MONTH

Bible Reference: "When Jesus spoke again to the people, he said, 'I am the light of the world. Whoever follows me will never walk in darkness, but will have the light of life'" (John 8:12).

Meditation: Dr. Cliff Arnell at the University of Cardiff makes the following calculation to discover what the worst day of the year is:

$$\frac{[W + (D-d)] \times TQ}{M \times NA}$$

The equation is broken down into 7 variables: (W) weather, (D) debt, (d) monthly salary, (T) time since Christmas, (Q) how long it took to give up on New Year's resolutions, (M) low motivational levels and (NA) the need to take action (https://tinyurl.com/yce4yrls). Wow! This results in January 24 being considered the most miserable day of the year. At least in the UK!

Is January hard for you?

Truth is that Christmas is a high stress season and not much of a break. We call it a holiday, but it really isn't. There's lots of company; presents are bought, given, and received; food must be prepared; there are Christmas services to participate in and go to. Christmas is amazing – who doesn't love singing Christmas carols? – but exhausting.

Another truth is that we've also been without light for quite a while at this point. If you spend most of your daylight hours inside the school during the winter, you are likely light deprived. Seasonal Affective Disorder increases the further north you go – it affects almost 10% in Alaska!

Focus in January on light in two ways: No. 1, go to the source of light, Jesus. Stay "in touch" at a time when lethargy might take you away. Maintain your discipline of prayer and Bible reading. Don't stop going to church. Meet with a friend once a week and intentionally include a spiritual moment. No. 2, get outside for at least 30 minutes of walking in sunshine during the day and again at the end of the day. Enjoy the idea of pick-up and drop-off line duty. Meditate or chat with a colleague. Remember to take care of your spiritual and physical light needs!

What kinds of mood do you have in January?
How can you connect to spiritual and physical light at all times of the year?

Dear Jesus: You are the light of the world. You made us both spiritual and physical – in fact, you intertwined the two of them. Help me to take care of the body you have given me during this winter season. Help me to be disciplined in paying attention to the importance of spiritual and physical light. You placed the sun in the heavens at the beginning of creation. You came as the light of the world within creation. Thank you for being and giving me the light of life. Amen.

71. KNOWING MY JOB AS A LEADER

Bible Reference: "But they did not understand what he meant and were afraid to ask him about it" (Mark 9:32).

Meditation: This isn't the only time that we are told that the disciples didn't understand what Jesus was talking to them about. But they were afraid to ask him about it and I don't know why. Jesus was certainly an amazing person to be with, but he was also kind and generous and constantly willing to share. Why were they afraid to ask him? I don't know.

What's your background as a Christian school leader? It's interesting that the disciples had terrible backgrounds for being disciples. They were fishermen and tradesmen. It's not surprising that Jesus' ministry lasted for 3 years – he needed that time to teach his disciples how to do their jobs, including internships where they went out and practiced; opportunities to fail where he could correct them; and the chance to learn how to teach as they listened to him.

But what about you? What training have you had as a Christian school leader? If you are like most of the leaders CSM meets, you have had little to no training at all. You were probably a teacher for several or many years and then were asked to or desired to take on leadership responsibilities. There is lots to know. Academic leadership is difficult enough given the changing social and economic context of teaching and the sometimes radically different characteristics of children compared with your own generation. But then there's leadership for enrollment, and leadership of the Board, and money leadership, and the list goes on.

The sting in the tail of this Bible passage is that the disciples were afraid to ask. That's often true of Christian school leaders. It's way too vulnerable to be at a conference with peers and say that you don't know! It's so much easier to pretend expertise while listening for grains of wisdom. It's easy to be intimidated by those who appear to know so much. Don't be afraid. Ask! Be vulnerable. And teach the leaders at your school to do the same.

What are areas of leadership where I need to grow?

How and where will I get the knowledge and skills I need?

Dear Jesus: You are often described as Teacher. You are certainly my Teacher as I study your Word and listen for you in the depths of my heart. Give me the courage to ask for help in order to grow as a leader. Don't let me be afraid of what people might think. Just like the children at my school, I am on a learning journey too. Help me find the teachers I need to be excellent. Help me also to share what I learn with those around me. Thank you for being the great Teacher. Amen.

72. KNOWING AND LOVING GOD

Bible Reference: "Love the Lord your God with all your heart and with all your soul and with all your strength and with all your mind" (Luke 10:27).

Meditation: One of my new favorite questions to ask of candidates during job interviews is when they were the most satisfied in their life and why. A look of pleasant surprise races across their faces as they quickly shift gears away from their previous preparation for anticipated questions. Their body language shifts. They become vulnerable and authentic. Their humanity emerges.

Examples include a very impressive young man early in his career proudly, yet humbly, describing how he broke free of his family's challenges to arrive at this opportunity. A woman in her mid-30s nearly cried tears of happiness recalling the first few weeks of her daughter's life. Another spoke of the incredible blessing he received from God by having space and time to spend with his dying father before he went to his eternal rest. Others have pointed to a particular project or assignment that provided meaning and significance, both personally and professionally.

We can all recall times when we focused on something or someone because that thing or person mattered to us. When we care about something or someone, we usually concentrate our whole mind and soul on that thing or person. The result is a stronger bond with the subject, and distractions are easily limited or disregarded altogether.

This is exactly what we need to do with our spiritual life and our relationship with God. In order for our hearts to be fully "glad and sincere" as we seek satisfaction – true peace and happiness – we should devote energy in knowing and loving God. Not surprisingly, most of the examples above have an implicit, if not explicit, reference to the hand of God in life's most satisfying moments.

What has been feeding my sense of satisfaction lately?

Am I currently reflecting the values, motivations, and priorities that I would want to communicate if I were making a first impression?

Jesus, the center of my life, in the midst of all the good deeds you did for God's people, you never failed to point them to the importance of taking care of their souls and spiritual life. Today I will focus on things that bring me true peace, happiness, and satisfaction, as I know they are personal, hand-delivered gifts from you. Amen.

73. CAN YOU ENDURE THE CROSS?

Bible Reference: "Then Jesus said to his disciples, "Whoever wants to be my disciple must deny themselves and take up their cross and follow me" (Matthew 16:24).

Meditation: For a long-distance runner, being able to endure is very important for success. Running over the course of miles takes patience, discipline, and thoughtfulness, all of which are marks of maturity. I'm reminded of the character played by Tom Hanks, Jimmy Dugan, and his classic line in *A League of Their Own*: "It's supposed to be hard. If it wasn't hard, everyone would do it. The hard is what makes it great." So too is fully living a Christian lifestyle.

Our faith walk amid the daily challenges and hardships of life is often methodical and inconsistent. And yet it is precisely our openness and willingness to be led where we would rather not go that is commendable to God. Immediately after Peter has been commissioned to be a leader of his sheep, Jesus confronts him with the hard truth that the servant leader is the leader being led to unknown, undesirable, and painful places – the place of the cross. Did any of us truly understand what we signed up for serving in Christian school leadership?

Any faithful Christian who wants to make it to the end and receive the crown of eternal life at the gate of heaven must endure all the hardships of the journey of faith. We must be so deeply in love with Jesus that we are ready to follow him wherever he guides us, trusting we will find life in him – and find it abundantly.

The way of the Christian school leader is not the way of upward mobility in which our world has invested so much, but the way of the servant ending on the cross. This way of Jesus is the hard, commendable path to the joy and peace of God, a joy and peace that is not of this world.

How much thought and prayer do I put into matters of upward mobility compared to the way of the servant?

Do I rejoice in or lament the suffering I endure in my Christian lifestyle?

Jesus, you endured so much for our salvation. You also called us to pick up our crosses daily and follow you. At times I may want to run away from the crosses and suspend my journey with you. But with your grace and encouragement, I will endure all the hardships and keep on carrying your cross to the end. Today, I will try to endure some of the difficulties of my day and some of the pains of being a Christian with a joyful spirit. Help me through the changes and chances of each day. Thank you for your example of the suffering servant. Amen.

74. WHOSE LIST DO I HAVE TIME FOR?

Bible Reference: "Teach us to number our days, that we may gain a heart of wisdom" (Psalm 90:12).

Meditation: There is never enough time to perform all of our roles as well as we would like. How do we number our days and decide what gets done and what does not?

I can recall the year where I lost my ability to manage the competing demands of my time. It was rough. A capital campaign, an intrusive construction project, and a new baby at home (our 3rd) were the added challenges to what felt like an already exhaustive life. I limped out of that school year feeling like a failure in every title I had: husband, father, school leader, Christian. I was isolated and cynical. I put an out-of-office reply on my email, stating I was "reconnecting to all that is important to me personally." I received a message from a Board member, Susan, whose response continues to support me in all the roles I hold. I will share in here in full, hoping it speaks directly to you as well:

"... Here is a little unsolicited advice from an old friend: Fr. Tang taught me that there is always time to do what God has planned for you. In other words, God's 24-hour plan for us is neither hurried nor stressed, so if we are feeling that way it must be because we are doing something outside of or in addition to his plan. Fr. Tang also said that the most important thing we might do in a day will come as an interruption to our day's plans. Such hard lessons to live by! Especially when I have a very long list of projects and things I want to accomplish. What I have learned over the years is that Fr. Tang is absolutely right. When I keep my project list in perspective and allow God to work through me in whatever way HE chooses, I find great peace. (On top of this, I am often MORE, not less, productive – Crazy!) The hardest part for me is that when I follow God's lead, some of my projects don't get done or aren't as perfect as I'd like. I need to remind myself that if God wants me to spend my time and energy on other things, I need to humbly accept this, surrendering my project list for his ..."

What areas of my life are taking my time contributing to a sense of stress or hurriedness?

How can I best sacrifice my list for his?

Loving and gracious God, teach me to number my days and gain wisdom in using them well in the most important ways. Grace me with your calming presence and remind me that I must do your to-do list. Give me a sense of liberation that the kingdom is not only beyond my effort, it is beyond my vision and capability. I ask that you walk with me, slowing me down as needed, to make sure my work is yours. Thank you for your Son's example of keeping his eyes fixed on Jerusalem, knowing what your will was, and listening to the prompting of the Holy Spirit in his life. Amen.

75. DO NOT ENVY

Bible Reference: "Do not fret because of the wicked; do not be envious of wrongdoers, for they will soon fade like the grass, and wither like the green herb" (Palm 37:1-2).

Meditation: It's time to attend that Finance Committee meeting. Yes, the one where you talk about the budget for next year. Once again, you will go through the process of seeing how little money you have. While your enrollment looks as if it will be the same next year as this, it's amazing how a small change can seem to totally upset the calculation. Last year, it was the family that left because the father's job suddenly moved out of state. The year before, it was the sudden 15% increase in health premiums. If it's not one thing, it's another. That school down the road, it's not even Christian and it's adding another set of classrooms. Or that Christian school up the road, they get lots of money from their church. They just don't have to do what we have to do!

The secular school down the road and your Christian competitor up the road are probably not "the wicked" in the sense the Psalmist, David, is saying. But your feelings are perfectly normal. It is easy to compare our school to other schools. It is easy to "fret" and even become "envious." After all, shouldn't we be blessed as they are?

Go to your finance session with a good heart. The Psalmist continues: "Trust in the Lord and do good; so you will live in the land and enjoy security" (vse. 3). God is blessing and will continue to bless you. Trust and do. Arrive at the meeting with confidence and share that confidence with the other members of the committee. They are waiting anxiously to see whether you are still leading. Trust and do. Go through the meeting dealing thoroughly with each issue; don't duck challenges – identify ways through. Trust and do. Bring snacks along so the lack of blood sugar does not become an enemy of good decision-making. Ensure there is a time for celebration. Rejoice. Trust and do. God promises you security in your land. Trust and do.

What words of encouragement will I bring to this meeting?

How is my budget a statement of God's love for me?

Dear Jesus: You were not born into luxury and you did not lead the grand life. You must have known how easy it is to envy. But you trusted in your Father in heaven and you did his will here on earth. Help me to lead in the Finance Committee in such a way that its members also trust in you and make the decisions that will help the school enjoy "security." You do not want us to lack anything we need to serve the children in our care. Help us be courageous in tuition setting and expenses stewardship so that we can carry out that service with excellence. Amen.

REFLECTION

It is time to take a break and think about the journey you are on. Use this page to reflect on how you can accelerate your impact as a Christian school leader.

_____
_____
_____
_____
_____
_____
_____
_____
_____
_____
_____
_____
_____
_____
_____
_____
_____
_____
_____
_____
_____
_____
_____
_____
_____
_____
_____
_____
_____

76. WHERE IS MY COURAGE?

Bible Reference: "They mounted up to the heavens and went down to the depths; in their peril their courage melted away" (Psalm 107:26).

Meditation: Christian institutions at every level, including schools, face two serious problems: insufficient courage to stand up for what is right and a lack of humility to beg the Lord for help. Our secular society tries to persuade us that there is no relevance for believing in God, that personal responsibility and a sense of accountability are flawed notions, and that right and wrong are individualistic.

These attitudes weigh heavy in the metaphoric backpacks of school leaders. Our cadence is slowed or broken unless we take heart in the knowledge we do not march alone. We just need to have the courage to do what is right despite our personal cost and ask God for help on our journey. "Be courageous and steadfast; have no fear for it is the Lord, your God, who marches with you; he will never fail you or forsake you" (Deuteronomy 31:6).

There is another tension in our daily roles. We constantly find ourselves living in the tension between justice and mercy, accountability and compassion, shepherding the flock and trying to save the outcast sheep. How do we respond to these tensions? Do we allow them to accumulate and tear away our judgment? Can we – and should we – disassociate one scenario from the next? Or should we reflect on our work more comprehensively? However we manage these challenges, we should rejoice in the knowledge that God will not forsake us. We must recognize and embrace this responsibility as God's work, always acting out of love and remaining steadfast in our purpose.

What is it that prevents me from acting with courage?

In what ways does God march with me in my professional role?

Lord, today help me to speak up for what is right and come out to defend the weak no matter the price. Thank you for giving me a conscience to know right from wrong. Give me courage to seek knowledge according to your will. Most importantly, give me the humility to ask for help in times of need rather than relying on myself or other worldly influences. Amen.

77. CONFLICT AND RELATIONSHIP

Bible Reference: "Jesus looked at him and loved him" (Mark 10:21).

Meditation: In many ways, the faculty and staff of our schools are like family. After all, we probably spend more time with our co-workers than our actual families. We lean on each other, support each other, push each other, and become intertwined in so many ways. And when we invest so much collectively, there's bound to be tension that occasionally spills over into conflict. Just like our families at home! Jesus' relationships involved many conflicts, including in this story of the rich man in Mark. It's amazing how full of patience Jesus was, even in the midst of disappointment.

What is the school leader's role in resolving conflict? "Bearing with one another and forgiving one another, if one has a grievance against another; as the Lord has forgiven you, so must you also do" (Colossians 3:13). As the scripture tells us, we must "bear" with one another first before we can get on the road to forgiveness and resolve the issue. There are plenty of professional resources that deal with conflict management, but the first word in today's scripture often gets overlooked. "Bearing" is a particular choice, suggesting a complex combination of patience, humility, discipline, restraint, dignity, and, in this context, a desire to preserve or restore the relationship.

Saying "I'm sorry" isn't the easiest thing to do. Yet school leaders are well positioned to enter into a conciliatory state since we spend much of our work exercising the above-listed virtues on behalf of others. We cannot be effective if we act impatiently, arrogantly, or without discipline. Being so, we must be the first brave individuals to admit our wrongdoings and ask for forgiveness, modeling to the rest of the school the kind of Christian behavior we expect.

Where in my school can I invest energy to prevent tensions from becoming conflicts?

What steps can I take to proactively address this situation?

Merciful Jesus, you never condemned or humiliated a repentant sinner in your years of ministry. Help me trust in your compassion and humbly apologize to whomever I need to as I find my way back to you. Give me strength to admit my faults and search for ways to improve myself each day. Amen.

78. LIFE IS NOT FAIR

Bible Reference: "A man was going down from Jerusalem to Jericho and fell into the hands of robbers who stripped him, beat him, and went away, leaving him half dead" (Luke 10:30).

Meditation: Imagine. Worshipping at the Temple in Jerusalem! The historian Josephus commented: "The natural magnificence, and excellent polish, and the harmony of the joints in these cloisters, afforded a prospect that was very remarkable …" The man was coming home from worshipping at THAT Temple. He headed for Jericho, his family, his business, the day-to-day. It was a letdown for sure. But worse followed. He was robbed, beaten, and left half dead. He didn't do anything to deserve it. He was just in the wrong place at the wrong time. Robbers were not uncommon, and this story told by Jesus would have resonated. Life is not fair.

Did you have a great Christmas? And were you inspired spiritually? Was it an amazing time with your family and friends? Then did you head for "Jericho" and fall into "the hands of robbers"? I don't know what it means for you to be stripped, beaten, and left for dead. It could be a combination of health and scandal. Maybe it's a spouse who leaves you. A child on drugs. Maybe the discovery of a deep financial problem, personal or professional. Maybe you have become depressed. Or the unending stress of days that are too long, jobs that never seem to be finished, and nights that are too short.

There are no holy answers that satisfy in times like this. This story was told by Jesus to a lawyer who had the holy answers down pat. Yes, I love God and I love my neighbor. But who is my neighbor? Jesus goes deeper than the holy language and makes it totally practical. Okay, he says, here's a story about neighbors.

I won't trouble you with holy language. I just want you to know that God surrounds you with neighbors who will bandage your wounds and take care of you. You are not alone. Don't withdraw into yourself. Reach out to your spouse, your best friend, to God himself, sometimes even an unexpected stranger – a Samaritan. You have neighbors. You are not alone.

Can you remember an unexpected time of grace from an unexpected source?

Are you willing to see, let alone accept, the Samaritan's outstretched hand?

Dear Jesus: Your story touches the deep places of my heart. You know that the road from Jerusalem to Jericho is unsafe. You know that I am hurt and wounded and sometimes feel left for dead. Let me see and accept the hand of the neighbor who stops to help me. I thank you for your encouragement and for your love. Thank you for Incarnation, and then thank you for Resurrection. I love and bless you. Amen.

79. DO SOMETHING! IT'S BETTER THAN NOTHING

Bible Reference: "Well then, you should have put my money on deposit with the bankers, so that, when I returned, I would have received it back with interest" (Matthew 25:27).

Meditation: It's easy to be immobilized as a leader by the enormity of the task. There is so much to do, so many items on today's list – and tomorrow's list is even longer. God gives us impossible tasks to do from a human point of view. The very enormity of those tasks fills us with weariness and dismay. How will I find 35 students? Where will that $135,000 come from? Whom can I ask to fill 5 positions on the Board?

Now this story told by Jesus is about the kingdom of heaven. Remember? It's a hard story to understand. I'm just struck that Jesus casts out the scared servant "into the darkness" because he hadn't, at the very least, taken his gold and put it on deposit for interest. The amount of money that Jesus talks about here is gigantic. A talent is equivalent to 6,000 denarii, and 1 denarius was the pay for a day's work. A bag of gold was an unimaginable amount of money! Jesus tells his audience that the servant would not enter the kingdom of heaven because he did nothing with what he was given. It reminds me of the story told by Jesus where "the master commended the dishonest manager" (Luke 16:8). God says he will spit us out of his mouth if we are lukewarm (Revelation 3:16).

Don't be paralyzed. Don't be scared of failing. You are only human. Do something! It's way better than doing nothing, even if it results in a judgment of shrewdness! Find one student; locate $1,000; talk to one person. It all begins with 1 or 2. Jesus doesn't call all 12 disciples at once. He finds a couple (Mark 1:17) and then another (Luke 5:27) and then another. He also failed. Not everyone followed him. One betrayed him. Most fled at the time of trial. But Jesus acted. And his Father raised him from the dead.

Act. And be resurrected in his kingdom.

What are you too scared to try?

Do you understand that success is the next step after failure?

Dear Jesus: You acted in real time when everyone around you didn't have faith. Your brothers didn't believe in you at the beginning. Certainly, the church leaders didn't believe you. You still acted. You talked to those who were prepared to listen. Help me to act even when the obstacles seem insurmountable. You promised me the kingdom. Help me to look to you for courage and strength and faith so that the kingdom will come near me and my school. Amen.

80. THE BEAUTY OF 'US'

Bible Reference: "How good and pleasant it is when God's people live together in unity! (Psalm 133:1).

Meditation: In an interview recorded in Convivium (vol. 5, page 28), Lech Walesa tells of his meetings with Pope John Paul II. He says: "We had very good relations. He was very well informed, so there was no need for me to tell him anything. Our meetings could be amusing. One time, the Holy Father greeted me and then began to talk for some time. He noticed that I was shifting in my chair and so he stopped talking. Then I began to talk and talk, and after a while, he began to shift in his chair uncomfortably, so I stopped talking! So in this way, we were together and it was very beautiful."

Becoming a leader is not necessarily a choice. You may not have wanted the position you are in. Or maybe you saw it as a fulfillment of the skills and talents that God has given you. Either way, leading can sometimes lead to disunity – the inability of leader and follower to hear each other or even see each other. Lech Walesa was very clear that John Paul was his leader. And yet, there was humility and love in each of them such that they didn't want to hog the limelight but were content to give each other time and respect. This was possible because they were deeply interested in what each had to say, recognizing that each could contribute.

Living together in unity in a Christian school is a vocation in addition to the vocation of leading. Leading requires being in unity with each other. Jean Vanier writes in his masterpiece *Community and Growth*: "Communities which start by serving the poor must gradually discover the gifts brought by those they serve. The communities start in generosity; they must grow in the ability to listen" (p. 142). Community / us means leading more and more by listening – to teachers, staff, parents, Board members, and most importantly, to the children we serve. They too have a voice: It's why they move uncomfortably in their chairs!

When do I lead by doing and when should I lead by listening?

What is the power of listening – what does it achieve?

Dear Jesus: You listened to the people around you all the time. There is no evidence of you ever interrupting anyone. And you always responded with words and actions of love and service. Let me be a leader who follows you. Help me to truly be interested in the people I serve, listen to them with my whole body, and then have the grace and wisdom to respond as you did. Thank you for listening to my prayer. Amen.

81. SEPARATE THE PEOPLE FROM THE PROBLEM!

Bible Reference: "Lord, don't you care that my sister has left me to do the work by myself? Tell her to help me!" (Luke 10:38).

Meditation: I have occasionally worked with schools and churches who want to separate their operations. The church doesn't want the hassle of the school; the school wants more independence; the church wants more space; the school can't get donations to build the buildings it needs. Lots of different reasons. The negotiations can be very difficult as the people involved struggle with issues of power, finances, relationships, control. Roger Fisher and William Ury speak realistically of the issues: "People get angry, depressed, fearful, hostile, frustrated, and offended. They have egos that are easily threatened. They see the world from their own personal vantage point, and they frequently confuse their perceptions with reality. Routinely, they fail to interpret what you say in the way you intend and do not mean what you understand them to say" (*Getting to Yes*, p. 19).

This is true of every kind of conversation or negotiation. For example, think of the last time an angry parent cornered you in your office and told you how badly her child had been treated. Or the Board member who takes you aside and dresses you down for sending out an email with a spelling error. Or the faculty member whose assignment you switched who sullenly resents your action. Or your spouse who thinks that your lack of attention is due to a lack of love. The problem is that the issue gets mixed up in the relationship.

Fisher and Ury ask us to listen to the "other" first and try to understand from his or her point of view. As they put it: "The ability to see the situation as the other side sees it, as difficult as it may be, is one of the most important skills a negotiator can possess" (p. 23). Think how Jesus listened first to Martha, waited for her to state the problem, and then separated the person from the problem. Martha's sister was not the problem. Martha's attitude to her sister was the problem. And sometimes I as the leader am the problem. Fisher and Ury again: "The basic approach is to deal with the people as human beings and with the problem on its merits" (p. 39).

In what direction do my conflicts usually go?

Where do I need to grow as a person in order to help others with problems?

Dear Jesus: I always think I am in the right. Help me to understand that it doesn't matter. Help me to treat others in love as I wish to be treated. Help me to listen and understand their point of view. Help me to really develop my skills in this area. Thank you that you loved every person you met, even Judas, even me, and died and rose to solve my problem of sin. Thank you. Amen.

82. SHOULD YOU NOT EXPECT WORKS OF POWER AND AUTHORITY?

Bible Reference: "At once Jesus realized that power had gone out from him. He turned around in the crowd and asked, 'Who touched my clothes?'" (Mark 5:30).

Meditation: I routinely ask groups of faculty and administrators to share with each other a story about a student of theirs who surprised them in amazing ways. The stories they tell are deeply moving and bring to the fore emotions that we don't usually show in public. I have my own stories as well. I remember well that 9th grader who had very poor literacy skills. By 12th grade, he had become an accomplished writer, but his professor father was quite unaware of his progress. On a visit to the school, I handed him a typed essay – anonymous! – and asked him to give me feedback. Where would this writer stand, I asked, among his 4th-year and graduate students at the University of Alberta? He read it carefully. "This is amazing," he said. "It would fit right in with my graduate students – I wish my son was this capable." "It is your son," I responded!

Why do we have such low expectations as leaders of what might happen, whether it is in the individual lives of students or teachers, or whether it is in the administration of our school in enrollment, retention, finances, fundraising, Board leadership? We are too often overwhelmed by the challenges in one or more of those areas and often focused on the deficiencies.

Christian school leadership begins with belief in the One who has such power that you only have to touch his clothing with faith to have his power flow to you! Of course, we have to know our jobs. Once we have an idea as to what to do though, it is time to expect what the Gospels call dunameis – works of power and authority – and paradoxa – unexpected events! Often, we talk about miracles which Scripture actually never mentions. And the word miracle is problematic, seeming to imagine an event that has little to do with reality. But Jesus had power and authority because he was doing his Father's work (John 10:25). And we are given that same power and authority and should expect the unexpected (Luke 10:17).

Can you be bold enough to say what you believe the Lord has in mind for your school?

Will you work, pray, and ask for that to happen?

Dear Jesus: You don't seem surprised by what you were able to do. You do seem to be exasperated by your disciples, who continually doubted. Please give me the faith to ask for the unexpected. Please help me to have the energy to do the unthinkable. Please give me the authority and power to lead my school as a child of God. I ask for these things on behalf of the children whom you welcomed into your arms. Amen.

83. SHOUT, AND THEN SHOUT LOUDER!

Bible Reference: "… but he shouted even more loudly, 'Son of David, have mercy on me!'" (Luke 18:39).

Meditation: Sitting at your office desk can sometimes feel so ordinary. You imagine your peers at the private schools around you doing exactly the same thing. You drive past their campuses, and it all looks the same. There are buildings, there are children, there are adults, there are signs, there are fences and trees and grass. It's easy to be intimidated into following the crowd. It's easy to be fearful of the consequences if you stick out like a sore thumb. What's a Christian leader to do?

Do you know that you are blind? Oh, I don't mean literally blind like the beggar in Luke. I mean intellectually blind, spiritually blind, emotionally blind, physically blind. The verse before this story is fascinating: They (the 12) understood nothing about all these things (vse. 34). The 12 who had followed Jesus around understood nothing. How long have you been a Christian? How long have you been a Christian leader? How long have you been a Christian leader in a Christian school? What do you understand?

Do you know that you are blind? If you don't, you won't reach out. You won't shout. You won't ignore the people trying to shush you. You won't break out of doing what everybody else is doing. You won't get Jesus' attention.

Find your blindness. Identify it. Then shout "Son of David, have mercy on me." Preferably do it in a crowd. Or just in your office. And if you shout loudly enough, Jesus will come to you and help you see. And you will be a better leader.

Why are you a Christian leading a Christian school?

When was the last time you shouted loudly enough for Jesus to hear you?

Dear Jesus: I am deathly afraid of admitting that I am blind in my leadership. I don't mind admitting I am a sinner. But I want so hard to believe that I "see" as a Christian leader. Help me shout each day to you. Then help me listen to the people you send me so that I can continually regain my sight and forward your kingdom through this school and in the lives of the children you have given me to shepherd. Amen.

84. WHICH STUDENTS SHOULD COME TO OUR SCHOOL? – PART 1

Bible Reference: "Which of these three, do you think, was a neighbor to the man who fell into the hands of robbers?" (Luke 10:36).

Meditation: It is admission season again. You are getting calls. You are praying for your school to be full next fall. The Admission Director is carrying out tours, talking with families, sharing the story of the school. Ponder this story of the Good Samaritan as a good admission story. The lawyer was asking about the boundary of the Jewish people. Who was a good Jew? Who was acceptable within the covenant? It's a good question in admission season. Who "belongs"? Who does not "belong"? Whom would we think of as normally within the school constituency who actually is a really poor fit? Who, on the other hand, look as if they are beyond the school's walls but actually will be really well served by the school? Who is an outsider? Who is an insider?

Each day you pass the mission at the entrance to the school. Each student you interview has to be mission appropriate. That's an important barrier. There are often other barriers to entrance to Christian schools – statements of faith cast in a particular doctrinal fashion, parental commitments, intelligence testing, observations of social behavior, ability to pay. You know how important the mission barrier is. You also know that there are practical barriers like class size and gender balance. What do you know about the other barriers?

Your answers to these questions will determine the character and purpose of your school. It's not easy to distinguish between wisdom and folly. It's not at all obvious what the answers are to admission dilemmas. It's easy when the school is full of the "right kind" of people. All those difficult questions are kept at bay by worldly success. It's harder when the seats are empty and philosophy becomes practical budgeting. Base your answers on the character of Jesus. "He said, the one who showed mercy. Jesus said to him, 'Go and do likewise'" (vse. 37).

In what ways am I using wisdom to lead the school in admission matters?

Which barriers to admission are mission-based, which are practical, and which are "additional"?

Dear Jesus: There are no easy answers. If there were, I wouldn't be struggling with this. It's not about the right number of students – it's about the mission of the school and its purpose in our community. Help me lead with wisdom and not with folly. Help me to follow you, however difficult that path is going to be. I want to understand your character and lead with mercy. Please help me listen and be convicted in how to do that. Amen.

85. WHICH STUDENTS SHOULD COME TO OUR SCHOOL? – PART 2

Bible Reference: "When the teachers of the law who were Pharisees saw him eating with the sinners and tax collectors, they asked his disciples: 'Why does he eat with tax collectors and sinners?'" (Mark 2:16).

Meditation: Diversity is a big deal nowadays. It is connected to justice and equity. To our shame, while Christ was all about every person whom God has created, Christianity has often taken the part of the rich and powerful against the poor and destitute. Even today, there are tinges of Christian teaching that somehow to be poor is shameful and a sign of God's disfavor and to be rich is a sign of God's favor. Dangerous territory!

But diversity isn't a new concept. Jesus reminded us of diversity when he treated all alike. It didn't matter whom he met, the foreigner, the Roman oppressor, the dishonest disciple, the rich and famous, the woman, the unclean, the diseased – there is no change of language, no change of attitude. He meets them all and asks them what they are looking for. He offers forgiveness of sins, healing for bodily and spiritual ailments, comfort to those who mourn the dead, a new beginning for the corrupt, always an opportunity to come closer to the God who already indwells. His Father's covenant was to all nations. And the Spirit spoke in many tongues to Jew and Gentile, black and white, male and female at the first Pentecost and thereafter.

Consider which Christianity your school should be a part of. Should it be about every person God has created, or should it be about those with influence / power / the majority? Too often, it seems to me, admission policy degrades into questions of classroom management, or having a homogeneous academic grouping where "I" can teach "the class." Where do our conversations begin? Do they begin by asking how do we meet the needs of the school or do they begin by asking how do we extend God's kingdom?

How homogeneous is my school? How representative of God's world?

Why might I want to invite the leper, the sinner, and the outcast?

Dear Jesus: You don't make it easy on me. My school can do really well with the students it has. I don't need any more hassle than I already have. Why do you constantly challenge me with your example and your Word? Leave me alone! Help me look to extend your kingdom first. Help me open my heart to the lost sheep. Help me to embrace your loving purposes. Thank you for not taking the easy road and reminding us that following you is a narrow path. Thank you for giving me wisdom to lead. Thank you for giving me great people around me to help me in these difficult conversations. Amen.

86. WHICH STUDENTS SHOULD COME TO OUR SCHOOL? – PART 3

Bible Reference: "Let the redeemed of the Lord tell their story – those he redeemed from the hand of the foe, those he gathered from the lands, from east and west, from north and south" (Psalm 107:2-3).

Meditation: Jesus talks in Luke 13 of the great eschatological banquet that will not have some folks that one might expect, but on the other hand, will include unexpected people from all over the world, echoing the Psalmist hymn of praise (cf. vse. 29). No one is a stranger or alien, but all covenant people are citizens of the kingdom.

It's always struck me as a bit odd, actually. Surely a club is much more comfortable, cozier. It's why we sit at meetings with people we "like," go to dinner with friends, enjoy the company of those who share our interests. Our friends often look very much like us. What's wrong with that picture?

Reality check. God doesn't care much for my thinking. His embrace is far greater than mine, and he challenges me to extend the hand of friendship way beyond those in my comfort zone. That's true of your school as well. Most often, those to whom we extend the hand of admission are those who are very like us. God asks us to think about the east and west, north and south.

Not so oddly, things work better with God's vision. Of the growth in GDP since 1960, 25% can be attributed to including more white women and black men and women. It's simple – it's actually using more of the talent that God has given. Diversity produces financial gains. The success rate of brand-new companies is 11.5% lower when investments are by partners who come from the same university. Wow! This thing about east and west and north and south actually works in practical, worldly terms as well! God is asking us to access ALL the talent he has put on earth because it produces better success. Your school will benefit.

What might it mean in my school to take students from east, west, north, and south?

What in my own attitude might have to change for that to be possible?

Dear Jesus: We constantly find that the advice and modeling that you give is meant for this earth. You actually are very practical when you offer us a new way to live. Forgive my surprise. Forgive my doubting heart. Forgive my lack of vision for my admission. Help me to lead a school that welcomes beyond the boundaries that make me content. Help me to be challenged to really think about the extension of your kingdom from east, west, north, and south. Thank you for reminding me that your banquet is for all. Amen.

87. TODAY I PLANTED A FLOWER

Bible Reference: "See how the flowers of the field grow. They do not labor or spin. Yet I tell you that not even Solomon in all his splendor was dressed like one of these" (Matthew 6:28-29).

Meditation: I watch people going into their schools all the time. They drive into the parking lot, they park, they get out of their cars, they walk across the asphalt and through the door into the building. I listen to Boards planning for change and for the buildings or renovations that they are excited about. Now don't get me wrong. God is not opposed to buildings or asphalt or cars. It is the "Holy City" that is coming in Revelation 21:2!

I invite you to try something different. Designate a day when everyone gets out of their car and goes and plants a flower, or a plant, or a bush, or a bulb. You plant many. You get your hands dirty. Soil gets under your fingernails. You have to bend over and crouch down. You have to actually look at your campus as the interaction of inside and outside. You have to think about where the birds build their nests, the worm throws its casts, the ant travels to find food, the spider creates its web.

On that day, have everyone learn the Scripture – not even Solomon in all his glory was dressed like one of these. Isn't that an amazing statement for Jesus to make? Why would he say that? Don't we human beings create much more beautiful things than a daisy or a flame azalea or a crape myrtle or the mountain yarrow or Christmas berry or the Jack o' the Rocks or the honey-suckle? Do your children even know that flowers exist?

You begin it. Plant a flower. Do it in private. Don't let anyone know. Reflect on the experience. Reflect on doing something better than the glory of Solomon. Then lead your community to do the same. In public. Speaking his words. Reflecting his glory.

What would happen if you planted a flower on your campus? What difference would it make?

God's gift is your whole campus. How are you leading your community in stewarding it?

Dear Jesus: I apologize. I haven't noticed the flowers, the weeds, the grasses, the shrubs, the animals and birds and insects that makes these places their homes, I haven't noticed them for quite a while. Thank you for reminding me that they are there, that your Father loves them, that they are reflections of his glory. Open my eyes. Get my hands into the soil. Remind me that I started as the gardener in Eden. Thank you. Amen.

88. REPENT, FOR THE KINGDOM OF HEAVEN IS AT HAND!

Bible Reference: "Produce fruit in keeping with repentance" (Luke 3:8).

Meditation: Repentance has always been attached to being good, and there's nothing wrong with that. Who will argue that we should not be good? But turning from your wickedness and living is a whole lot bigger than just being kind and truthful, important though they are. For your school, being a Christian community that repents is being a Christian community that seeks the kingdom. Think of the prodigal son (Luke 15:11-32). When the son comes to his senses and repents, it wasn't just that he now became a moral person. It was that he returned to the Father, having gone away from him. The outcome of going away was a life of despair. The outcome of coming back was a life of hope.

Leading your faculty and staff can sometimes descend into mere morality. While following the rules is not to be despised, you are not calling them to morality. Let's face it. We can never be good enough. Leading your faculty and staff into repentance as a Christian school leader should mean something much more important than that. Surely, being a Christian school does not just mean being good in the community? Having more volunteer hours than the secular school down the road?

Be more ambitious! Your message for your faculty and staff is far more dramatic: We live in a different kingdom and we follow a different King! We are living with Immanuel, God with us. We are salt to give things that are tasteless, like the prodigal son's pig swill, real meaning and life. We bring transformation to a broken world. We have a Person to share with our children and our neighbors who wants to live in and through us.

Being good is good. But easing the lonely heart is better. Healing the broken relationship is better. Serving without thought of return to change the possibilities of those we serve is better. Helping each other to replace hate with love is better. We are leaders of transformation, and repentance calls us to transformation, not just to good deeds. We must produce *that* kind of fruit!

Do I lead those around me to repentance?

What should a Christian school that repents be in its community?

Dear Jesus: John the Baptist called people to repentance and washed them in the river Jordan. You call us to repentance and wash us with your blood. You didn't do that just so that we could be good. You did it so we could be a resurrection people. Help me be a resurrection leader, not just a good leader. Amen.

89. LET'S COME FULL CIRCLE!

Bible Reference: "Then the eleven disciples went to Galilee, to the mountain where Jesus had told them to go. When they saw him, they worshiped him; but some doubted. Then Jesus came to them and said, 'All authority in heaven and on earth has been given to me. Therefore go and make disciples of all nations, baptizing them in the name of the Father and of the Son and of the Holy Spirit, and teaching them to obey everything I have commanded you. And surely I am with you always, to the very end of the age'" (Matthew 28:16-20).

Meditation: It is difficult to describe all of the various feelings as the school year comes full circle. After hundreds of hours of planning, praying, communicating, problem solving, administering, and ministering, we'd like to believe we have made a significant impact.

This scripture reminds us that Jesus had to come full circle with his disciples too, proclaiming the Gospel to them and to the world over a period of time. We should recall and appreciate that the first day Jesus met with his disciples, they were fearful and ignorant. After a process of learning from Jesus' leadership, they were transformed into the fearless, patient, and wise individuals who spread the Gospel to all nations. Jesus watched them take his lessons and apply them directly to their lives, even when they were doubtful. How proud and affirmed he must have been.

Create opportunities to come full circle with your students and staff as the year comes to a close. How gratifying is it to consider soon-to-be graduates at the honors program and recall their growth over the years? Our Registrar, describing the ways in which students grow, once quipped that our school turned a student from "Whoa!" as a freshman to "Wow!" as a senior. Of course, our work with students is never complete, but they will eventually leave us and use the lessons we've taught them to achieve success in the world. We pray the seeds we plant within them take root and continue to grow stronger over time. While we may never see it in this world, our work will eventually come full circle when we meet again in heaven.

Do I notice how my students' hearts and minds are being transformed?

Do we take time to be proud and affirmed in our mission through what is happening in the lives of our students?

Heavenly Father, help me to commit to the process of bringing myself in closer relationship with you as I minister to the students and staff in my school community. Challenge my hurriedness and support my diligence as I attempt to model a greater level of fearlessness, patience, and wisdom in my discipleship. Inspire me in my vocation, knowing my soul ultimately returns full circle to your loving embrace. Amen.

90. INTERRUPTION

Bible Reference: "While he was speaking, there came from the ruler's house some who said, 'Your daughter is dead. Why trouble the Teacher any further?' But ignoring what they said, Jesus said to the ruler of the synagogue, 'Do not fear, only believe'" (Mark 5:35-36).

Meditation: This reading starts with an interruption. While Jesus was speaking, several individuals came to announce "Your daughter has died." Throughout Scripture, Jesus was regularly interrupted both in his ministry and the more mundane tasks of his life. His speaking was interrupted. His travels were interrupted. Even his sleep was interrupted by his worried disciples. Others regularly brought their personal storms to lay before Jesus, believing he was capable and willing to calm them.

I must confess I occasionally treated my office as a sanctuary from the interruptions that would surely fall at my feet if I stepped outside it. It didn't take long before I encountered a parent, staff member, or student who would ask or say: "Do you have a minute?" "Quick question for you …" "There's something I need to get you up to speed on." "When do you have time to …" As a result of these simple interruptions, either my personal agenda for the day fell apart or my "to-do" list grew.

Jesus' life was filled with interruptions that he gladly welcomed. Being an all-knowing and powerful God who chose to live as a human, we can imagine that these "interruptions" weren't interruptions at all. Rather, they were moments where God intended his Son to be for the sake of his will. They were tasks given to Jesus to complete that weren't necessarily planned, but nonetheless welcomed.

As school leaders, we should always be ready for the unexpected. Some have heard the expression, "If you want to hear God laugh, tell him your plans." We can all appreciate the humor in the statement because we know things do not usually go according to plan. When that time comes, it is our job to recognize that those are unique opportunities to be more Christ-like to others.

Do I welcome interruptions as moments God personally invited me to?

Can I abandon my agenda to serve his?

Patient and loving God, help me to welcome interruptions with grace and warmth, as Jesus did. Strengthen my efforts to focus efforts on your love, so that I reframe my plans to become yours. For it is truly you who moves me to the places I need to be, the conversations I need to be a part of, and the positions I fill to carry out your will. Amen.

REFLECTION

It is time to take a break and think about the journey you are on. Use this page to reflect on how you can accelerate your impact as a Christian school leader.

_____
_____
_____
_____
_____
_____
_____
_____
_____
_____
_____
_____
_____
_____
_____
_____
_____
_____
_____
_____
_____
_____
_____
_____
_____
_____
_____

91. EACH PARENT IS PRECIOUS TO ME.

Bible Reference: "Who are my mother and my brothers?" (Mark 3:33).

Meditation: It might be hard to accept on some days, but each parent in your school is called by God to be ministered to by you, your team, your faculty. Jesus is so radical in this passage. He doesn't deny his own family standing at the door. He just includes all who hear his Word and follow him. That crossed all boundaries for his time – the Roman centurion, the renegade tax collector, the woman caught in adultery, his betrayer and rock of the church, the outsider and heretical woman. What about you and your school?

Of course, there are parents you adore. They behave appropriately. They give at the right times. They hold you accountable but in a kind and loving way. They volunteer their time. They bring others to the school. Sounds like Jesus' family too, who followed him through his ministry and then right to the foot of the cross and finally to the empty tomb.

There are parents who are not like that. How should you respond to them? I'm not talking here about those who are not called to the mission of the school and work actively against it. They need to be released from the school. I'm just talking about all those 'amazing' parents who just drive their children to school every day, just pay the monthly tuition on time, just volunteer occasionally, and every now and again advocate for their child with great energy. Do you pray for them? Do you love them?

What? For them as well? Yes. Hold yourself accountable for your partnership with all your families. Hold each parent up in prayer on a regular basis. You are not parenting their children. You are educating them. They, as parents, want and need your spiritual blessing on their work as you nurture their children daily. They came to the mission. They are your "mother" and your "brothers."

Who in your community creates your monthly cycle of prayer, including all children and all parents?

What is your attitude to your parents, not just the lovable ones?

Dear Jesus: It can be hard to think about each one of my parents positively. I know I shouldn't, but it's so easy to judge them – this one's too protective, that one's too permissive, that one shows movies I wouldn't. On and on it goes. Help me to love them because they came to the mission and allowed me the grace of their children. Lord, you were able to welcome all who did the will of God. Let me be a leader of a school that is welcoming to all of its parents. Amen.

92. HOW CAN I REACH THIS STUDENT?

Bible Reference: "And if he finds it, truly I tell you, he is happier about that one sheep than about the ninety-nine that did not wander off" (Luke 18:13).

Meditation: You lay awake last night thinking about a student. You just couldn't get her out of your mind. She could be doing so much better. She has plenty of brain power. She is talented in other areas as well. The music teacher says she has a beautiful voice.

But!

Yes, but! She makes no real attempt to get along with others; she refuses, almost angrily, to sing praise to God as part of the worship team. She has no interest in leadership. She seems entirely selfish. She flares up if a teacher corrects her. Her behavior is day to day. Should she be at the school? A couple of parents have mentioned that she has been rude to them.

"Answer me when I call to you, my righteous God. Give me relief from my distress; have mercy on me and hear my prayer" (Psalm 4:1). Yes, I call on you, God, for wisdom for this child. She does her work. She just wants to be left alone. She just seems so alone! Lord, how can I reach her, see her filled with joy?

"Tremble and do not sin; when you are on your beds, search your hearts and be silent," (Psalm 4:4). Maybe I am trying too hard. Being silent and listening is so hard when I want to help by doing. I stand in awe of your goodness and love. It is not me but you that changes the heart.

"In peace I will lie down and sleep, for you alone, Lord, make me dwell in safety" (Psalm 4:8). Lord, I bring you my broken heart. You will not despise it. I bring you this child of yours. I know that you will not turn away from her. Let the light of your face shine on her and fill her heart with joy and peace. Give me that same joy and peace so that I can rest tonight. I trust you, Lord.

How many of your students are in need of the peace and contentment of God?

In what ways can trust in God become a practical action in the life of a child?

Dear Jesus: There are times when I feel so inadequate. It doesn't matter how hard I try, it doesn't work. Help me understand that I can still have peace and rest by trusting in you. You are the Savior of the world. I am an instrument of your hands. I don't have to do it all. I can't do it all. Still, I pray for grace and wisdom to help the children given into my care. Maybe it's me, or maybe it's someone else who can touch this child's heart. Help me be or find that person. I am so anxious for her. Helping this one sheep is so important. Amen.

93. I AM CALLED

Bible Reference: "But the Advocate, the Holy Spirit, whom the Father will send in my name, will teach you all things and will remind you of everything I have said to you" (John 14:26).

Meditation: The Christian school is both an educational institution and a spiritual ministry. The ministry of Christian education is therefore not simply something individuals **can** do, but what they **must** do. It is a personal calling, the voice of God in an educator's life.

George Knight, in his book *Philosophy & Education: An Introduction in Christian Perspective*, says that Christian education is about restoring "the balanced image of God in students," and thus "education must be seen as a redemptive act." He goes on to explain how this has far-reaching implications for the Christian teacher: "The role of the teacher is ministerial and pastoral in the sense that the teacher is leading young people into a saving relationship with Jesus Christ."

For this to take place, the desire of every Christian school and every Christian school teacher is transformation in their students such as the Apostle Paul wrote about: "And we all, who with unveiled faces contemplate the Lord's glory, are being transformed into his image with ever-increasing glory, which comes from the Lord, who is the Spirit" (2 Corinthians 3:18).

Knight further suggests that the role of a Christian school educator is also pastoral in the sense that young people, once saved, need to be taught what it means to be obedient and transformed into Christlikeness. He describes Christian educators as simply being "in charge of different divisions of the Lord's vineyard." This is why it is critical that Christian school teachers and administrators have discerned a clear calling from God to the ministry of Christian education.

Only when Christian educators are functioning within the area of their calling is the Holy Spirit able to truly anoint their efforts. The Holy Spirit is a Helper, Teacher, and Friend who equips, guides, empowers, and sustains us so that we can accomplish all that our God has called us to do.

Have you indeed been called? Can you point to a time when God appointed you for the ministry of Christian school educator?

What does leadership mean in the context of calling or vocation?

Lord, you have a plan for me to give me hope and a future, a plan that will help me grace the world in the unique way that only I can. I pray now that your Holy Spirit will enlighten me with your wisdom so that I may come to know today, beyond any doubt, that you are calling me in my life and in my vocation. Amen.

94. I AM DIFFERENT – THAT'S GOD'S DESIRE AND HIS GIFT!

Bible Reference: "I praise you because I am fearfully and wonderfully made; your works are wonderful, I know that full well. My frame was not hidden from you when I was made in the secret place, when I was woven together in the depths of the earth" (Psalm 139:14-15).

Meditation: In Psalm 139, David expresses truths in a poetic style. As a leader at your school, perhaps the most profound truth is captured in the verses above: Each one of your students, faculty, and staff is a unique individual who is, like you yourself, wonderfully made. You are all a part of ongoing creation carried out by the Creator.

Your students, faculty, and staff are also multi-generational. Sociologists have defined these different generation based on when they were born: the Greatest Generation, the Baby Boomers, Generation X, Millennials, and iGen.

The challenge for leaders is that these distinct groups of children and employees differ in their concerns and needs in how they learn, how they communicate, and how they perceive workplace relationships to be. Understanding this, how then do you achieve mission and directional unity, a key component of highly effective teams?

In a multi-generational workforce, there is negative stereotyping or putting down that needs to be guarded against. Older faculty and staff perceive millennials as entitled, shallow, and preoccupied with technology. Conversely, younger faculty and staff perceive the older generations as entrenched in their ways and not open to new ideas.

Be aware of and understand generational differences. Celebrate and embrace the uniqueness and strengths of each child and employee. In this way you will be able to better leverage the distinct gifts of each person to create a synergy of purpose and direction where the rich intent of God is realized. Rajeev Behera, a performance management expert, offered this perspective: "Ultimately employees want the same thing – to be engaged at work and to have a good manager who acts as a coach and helps them achieve their specific career goals."

Do you and those in the leadership of the school realize and understand all the wonderful ways in which each person has been made?

What kind of listening is necessary for unity to occur?

Lord, as we work together to build your kingdom, help us to celebrate that each one of us is unique, "fearfully and wonderfully made." Help us to listen intently. Grant us the patience to move forward together. Teach us to work together with understanding and compassion in our hearts. Let us be the light that leads others to you. Amen.

95. MY CALL TO HUMILITY

Bible Reference: "For all those who exalt themselves will be humbled, and those who humble themselves will be exalted" (Luke 14:11).

Meditation: Effective, godly leadership is built on character, not style. Jesus pulls no punches. The clothes, the houses, the titles, none matter when God judges. He didn't just say it, he practiced it again and again in his earthly ministry. Paul talked about Christ's humility in Philippians 2:6-8 when he said, "Who, being in very nature God, did not consider equality with God something to be used to his own advantage; rather, he made himself nothing by taking the very nature of a servant, being made in human likeness. And being found in appearance as a man, he humbled himself by becoming obedient to death – even death on a cross."

Some of the most inspiring and the most influential leaders I know share the same often-overlooked quality of humility. In Psalm 51, the Psalmist writes: "My sacrifice, O God, is a broken spirit; a broken and contrite heart you, God, will not despise" (vse. 17).

Your calling to be a Christian school leader is also a call to humility. Jesus modeled this humility for us "just as the Son of Man did not come to be served, but to serve, and to give his life as a ransom for man" (Matthew 20:28).

In today's society, pride and assertiveness are the virtues often held up as worthy of imitation. The humble tend to be seen as feeble and weak. But is genuine humility really a weakness? Humility is a great value and a tremendous strength in leaders. A humble leader is authentic and genuine, and people sense very quickly who is authentic and who is not.

Humility is God's key to leadership.

Are you humbled to partner with parents who see Christian education as an investment rather than a sacrifice?

Are you humbled to work alongside faculty and staff who are willing to do whatever it takes to ground their students in the truth so that they are prepared for eternity?

How do you exhibit humility in your daily life?

What impedes humility from working and being exhibited in you?

Lord, your Word says that pride goes before destruction, and a haughty spirit before a fall. I begin to see the destructive nature of pride and the true blessing that comes from a heart that is humble. Teach me your ways and show me how I may clothe myself in godly humility toward those I serve and work alongside. Amen.

96. MISSION AND MISSION DRIFT

Bible Reference: "When the foundations are being destroyed, what can the righteous do?" (Psalm 11:3).

Meditation: There is a condition adversely affecting the health of many Christian schools. Well-intentioned schools that once had lofty, aspirational goals and great beginnings are discovering that something subtle has happened or is happening that is debilitating and impeding their witness and effectiveness.

What is it that has such an adverse effect on a school, and possibly is affecting your own school? **The problem is mission drift!** Peter Greer and Christ Horst, in their book *Mission Drift: The Unspoken Crisis Facing Leaders, Charities, and Churches*, say this, "Without careful attention, faith-based organizations will inevitably drift from their founding mission. It's that simple. It will happen."

Any builder knows that a solid foundation is essential to any building. Only once the foundation is firmly laid can the frame be put up and the structure built. Similarly, the mission statement is the foundation upon which effective schools are built.

The foundation of your school is represented by your mission statement. It is one of the most important tools in not only assessing where your school presently is but also where you need to go. It can provide everyone with guidance concerning day-to-day and strategic decisions that affect your school. If assimilated into the day-to-day fabric of the school, it gives all stakeholders a common set of beliefs and points toward a desired future. It can be described as the glue that holds your school together.

Sadly, many school mission statements, although often displayed on classroom walls and posted in the handbook, are rarely used to challenge, inspire, or guide a school.

A word of warning! Mission drift can be very subtle. Ask the question and see if you can answer it: What are you here to do? If you have difficulty answering that question in a clear, concise, and compelling way, your school may be experiencing mission drift.

Is your school's mission statement clear, concise, and compelling?

Do your faculty and staff know it? Can they state and implement it?

Lord, I thank you for the incredible mission you have given our school. Lord, may it burn in our hearts. Help us to keep our eyes on this purpose that you have given us. Take the words off the pages of the handbook and weave the mission powerfully into my own life and the life of this school. Amen.

97. GET OFF THE BEACH AND ONTO THE WATER!

Bible Reference: "And when they climbed into the boat, the wind died down" (Matthew 14:32).

Meditation: God has called you to be a leader. Leading is a privilege, but also a risk.

If you want to fulfill that calling, there is no place for timidity. Once you discern what God wants you to do, you must have the courage to step out and do it. You must be willing to take some risks and make some mistakes. You must be able to take criticism, be misunderstood, and even be slandered without giving up.

If you think about it, risk is intricately woven into every aspect of our daily experiences. You simply cannot live without taking risks. The greatest hazard in life, however, is to risk nothing, because the person who risks nothing accomplishes nothing.

A life committed to following and serving God is a life of risk taking. Christ is calling each of us to take risks for the sake of the kingdom. The Lord often calls us, as followers, to tasks that sometimes seem incomprehensible and, if we are brutally honest, even a little reckless at times. But isn't faith all about taking up your cross and following Jesus, whatever the cost?

As a school leader, what is important is that you do not become afraid to take calculated risks. This is an essential ingredient for growth in every area of your school. As you prayerfully take these calculated risks, remember that Jesus didn't calm the storm to allow Peter to walk on the water. No, the wind only calmed after Peter got into the boat!

As you step onto the water like Peter, you will experience times of struggle and doubt but also times of incredible accomplishment and blessing. As the leader of your school, you have choices and decisions to make every day. Note that Jesus holds Peter's hand on the water – he will hold yours as well.

How can you trust Jesus to hold your hand as you step into the boat?

What is the water you have to walk on in order to move your school forward?

Lord, you are worthy of my life. I trust the truth of your Word as my guide. I pray that you would empower me to take risks for you and to live and lead with courage and conviction in a school that sometimes needs risky action. Hold my hand, please, and bring me safe to land. Amen.

98. WHEN WAS THE LAST TIME YOU WORKED OUT SPIRITUALLY?

Bible Reference: "Trust in the Lord and do good; dwell in the land and enjoy safe pasture. Take delight in the Lord, and he will give you the desires of your heart" (Psalm 37:3-4).

Meditation: The elliptical machine in the corner was hidden with hanging clothes. So, a few summers ago I joined a military-style "boot camp" workout program. Three times a week for an hour at a time, outside in the "cool" of a Houston summer! My goal was to get back in shape. Despite repeatedly telling myself pain is simply weakness leaving the body, the excitement soon faded. In reality, the fitness project wasn't turning out like I expected. It was much harder than I had anticipated, and the transformation was also taking much longer to complete than I had anticipated. The initial enthusiasm definitely faded. There were days when it would have been very easy to quit.

Although we as Christian school leaders won't admit it, many of us treat our faith like beginning a new exercise program. We work out hard for a while. However, when the excitement dissipates and the muscles start to hurt, we hide our faith and enthusiasm away in some dark corner (perhaps even hanging things on it) or in a forgotten closet. Every now and then, when we hear an especially uplifting sermon or a song on Christian radio, we flex our spiritual muscles again.

Here is my confession. More times than I'd like to remember, I have found myself becoming spiritually complacent, misguidedly thinking that at least some of the time, mediocrity in my walk with the Lord was okay. Through my example, I gave others around me permission to do the same. I rationalized these times by assuring myself that I can't be expected to be excited about the Lord all the time, can I? Well, according to Paul writing in Romans, the answer is yes! "Never be lacking in zeal, but keep your spiritual fervor, serving the Lord" (Romans 12:11).

If you're lacking in zeal, take it to the Lord. Ask him to fire up the Holy Spirit that abides in all of Christ's followers so that it burns fervently in us and shines brightly through us. Ask him to speak to you through his Word and get those spiritual muscles working out again.

On a scale of 1 to 10, where are you in your spiritual exercises?

Who can be a spiritual warrior to encourage you in your 'gym'?

Lord, people today are concerned with their physical fitness and good health, but you are concerned more about our spiritual fitness. I know you made us and you want us to take care of our bodies, but our spiritual health is even more important. Fire us up, Lord! Make us zealous for what you have called us to do. Get our spiritual muscles working again. Amen.

99. HAVE PLAN: SUCCEED; HAVE NO PLAN: FAIL

Bible Reference: "Suppose one of you wants to build a tower. Won't you first sit down and estimate the cost to see if you have enough money to complete it? For if you lay the foundation and are not able to finish it, everyone who sees it will ridicule you, saying, 'This person began to build and wasn't able to finish'" (Luke 14:28-30).

Meditation: I have heard it said that Christian schools are not businesses. People argue that spreadsheets and things like bottom lines can never accurately measure the purpose or success of a school's mission. While there is some validity to this perspective, to then conjecture that business principles and models are "secular" and therefore have no place in how our schools operate is not a natural corollary. Good principles are good principles. Period. This means that the works of Patrick Lencioni, Jim Collins, Peter Drucker, and their ilk can and do apply to Christian schools.

The successful leader of any organization, let alone a successful school, knows that strategic planning is the key. Your school's mission addresses **why** you're doing what you do, but strategic planning addresses **what** you want to see happen in the future and **what** you're going to do about it. Strategic planning is the practical working out of God's will within the context of your school's mission.

As a leader, you do not have the option to simply let things happen. Strategic planning is a skill that, when exercised, allows you to spend your time and energy proactively building and developing your culture, people and programs, rather than reactively putting out constant fires and spending your days dealing with unforeseen problems that happen in the absence of foresight and planning.

Moses, Joshua, and Nehemiah thought and led strategically to accomplish the plans of God. Jesus Christ is part of his Father's strategic plan to provide salvation for a fallen world. Don't be content to simply let things happen. Be intentional in seeking God's heart and planning how you will accomplish his mission and purpose in your school.

What will happen if your school does tomorrow what it is doing today?

What will it take for your school be here for the next generation of children?

Lord, forgive me for sometimes getting ahead of your plans. Forgive me for sometimes having no plan at all. Help me to stop and listen for your direction. Your Word tells us that you know the plans you have for us, good plans to prosper us, to give us a hope and a future. Open my heart and my mind to those plans for this your school so that we can in all things bring honor and glory to your holy name. Amen.

100. TEACHERS HAVE ENORMOUS INFLUENCE IN A CHILD'S LIFE

Bible Reference: "The student is not above the teacher, but everyone who is fully trained will be like their teacher" (Luke 6:40).

Meditation: Think for a few moments about the teachers you have had throughout your life. What do you remember most about them? Is it what they taught? Or do you, like many of us, remember how they lived and acted the most?

A teacher's personal conduct has a powerful influence on children. If the teacher's words and actions are not in harmony, it sends contradictory and potentially harmful messages to the students. Evidence suggests that up to 90% of what students ultimately retain from their education is what they learn from watching their teachers. That's what Jesus is intimating here.

I am certain that every one of us can recall a situation or conversation where a person's actions spoke so loudly that they completely drowned out his or her words! That's why, as Christian teachers and administrators, you must endeavor to ensure that the lives you lead are in harmony with the lessons you teach. D.L. Moody once said, "It is a great deal better to live a holy life than to talk about it. Lighthouses do not ring bells and fire cannons to call attention to their shining – they just shine." C.S. Lewis said it this way, "What we practice, not (save at rare intervals) what we preach, is usually our greatest contribution to the conversion of others." A teacher's influence cannot be overestimated.

As a Christian school leader, you are instrumental in the selection of teachers. It is imperative then that you hire teachers not only for their professional competence, but also for their heartfelt and evident Christian commitment and lifestyle. By doing so, students will see Jesus in them and be more ready and willing to follow their leading.

Encourage your faculty and staff, as they stand before their students every day, to pause and remember the influence they exert. They are teaching not only what they know but also who they are. And make no mistake – their students will see them for who they really are and what they really believe. In Titus 2:7 we are given a pattern worthy of imitation: "In your teaching show integrity, seriousness and soundness of speech that cannot be condemned, so that those who oppose you may be ashamed because they have nothing bad to say about us."

Where is the pattern worthy of imitation at your school?

In what ways do you nurture and appreciate it?

Lord, I give you thanks for all our faculty and staff. Thank you for the way in which they give so freely of themselves each day in the classroom, serving and teaching the next generation. May all of us be found worthy of our calling to Christian education and live accordingly. Amen.

101. LEADERSHIP IS AN EXERCISE IN TEAM

Bible Reference: "How good and pleasant it is when God's people live together in unity! (Psalm 133:1).

Meditation: You were created in Imago Dei, the very image of God. You are not designed to live or work alone. God designed you, like the Trinity, to be in relationship. We are called to be people in unity.

In practice, getting a team together and on the same page takes much time and energy. So rather than engaging in these time-consuming efforts, some leaders prefer to work alone, misguidedly believing that going it alone is quicker. Many school leaders have even collapsed physically and mentally under such a heavy load. There is certainly enormous arrogance in the idea that "only I" can do it! Here are three clear and tangible benefits to assembling a unified leadership team:

First, a team is capable of accomplishing things that no individual could do alone. One example of this is found in Ecclesiastics 4:9-10 (and following), where we're told that "Two are better than one, because they have a good return for their labor: If either of them falls down, one can help the other up. But pity anyone who falls and has no one to help them up."

Second, teams consisting of people fully utilizing their various gifts, talents, and strengths toward a common goal can accomplish much more than an individual acting alone: "As iron sharpens iron, so one person sharpens another" (Proverbs 27:17).

Third, teamwork helps people to feel productive, appreciated, needed, and unique, while at the same time broadening the leadership base: "The Lord God said, "It is not good for the man to be alone. I will make a helper suitable for him" (Genesis 2:18).

I've personally witnessed the incredible power of a unified team to create energy and growth. Part of the success of your ministry hinges on your ability to develop a strong team with a deep sense of team spirit.

A team spirit is never accidental; it is always intentional. How are you equipping and empowering others to cooperate, collaborate, and to work in unity?

What skills do you still need to develop for team building?

Lord, I thank you that you created me in your image. I am not designed to work alone. Give me the wisdom I need to equip and empower my team to join together in unity. Thank you for your example of the disciples. Let me be inspired by their accomplishments. Amen.

102. A YOUNG PERSON'S LODESTAR

Bible Reference: "How can a young person stay on the path of purity? By living according to your word" (Psalm 119:9).

Meditation: To a casual observer, modern day America seem to have become so engrossed in having more and bigger and better that aspects of Christianity such as honesty, integrity, and character are often scoffed at and dismissed as an impediment to success.

In Romans 12:2 Paul tells us, "Do not conform to the pattern of this world but be transformed by the renewing of your mind. Then you will be able to test and approve what God's will is—his good, pleasing and perfect will."

Not conforming does not simply mean the avoidance of worldly behaviors. Paul also exhorts us to "renew our minds" or, put another way, to think and act biblically in accordance with God's Word. In 2 Timothy 3:16-17 we are told that "All Scripture is God-breathed and is useful for teaching, rebuking, correcting and training in righteousness, so that the servant of God may be thoroughly equipped for every good work." We have a lodestar.

Douglas Wilson emphasizes the importance of developing a Christian worldview that is converted into action: "A Christian worldview is not the same thing as Christian worldview jargon. ... Having a Christian worldview means living like an obedient Christian in all of life."

This deeper understanding will give students a new way of looking at their life. Minds that are renewed and transformed in this way give students new perspectives as they make decisions. For example, they no longer don't do something because it isn't *safe*, they don't do it because it's *wrong*.

The need is great for Christ-centered schools that know who Jesus is, bear his witness, model him daily, and diligently teach spiritual truth to their students.

If not us, then who? If not now, then when?

Do I have the resources I need to take on this task and execute it brilliantly?

Lord, the education of children is a tremendous responsibility. Our desire is transformation in every one of our students. I pray for every one of our teachers today. Give them insights on how to lead those they teach in connecting the Scripture to the subjects they teach and move in the hearts and lives of the students they teach so they would come to know you more. Amen.

103. YOU ARE A TRANSLATOR LEADER

Bible Reference: "Calling his disciples to him, Jesus said" (Mark 12:43).

Meditation: Looking back on my leadership, I made a lot of assumptions. I assumed that the team would be able to fill in the gaps in what I said; that they would know the background to statements I made, having done rich research; that they would be able to see with my experienced eyes. What I found was that they pretended a lot. They pretended to understand and carried out what they thought I said in ways that irritated me and even made me angry. They pretended to understand and didn't do anything for fear of getting it wrong. They pretended to understand to make me happy.

Jesus has a different approach to leadership. The disciples are at the Temple and watching the normal events of the day. Rich and poor people are freely giving to the Temple's upkeep. Jesus calls his disciples to him. Look, he says, rich and poor people are giving. Do you see the significance of this poor widow's offering? I appreciate all the gifts being made, but I have a special thanks in my heart for this poor woman. Do you see her? This is what her gift means to me. Mark doesn't record the disciples' reaction, but we can only imagine them saying something like: "Wow, we didn't really think about it that way."

Think about your own leadership. Does everyone on your team really understand and agree as to what the school mission means? When was the last time you reviewed the Board's strategic plan together and renewed your understanding of the school's direction? How did you interpret that event last week that made everyone uncomfortable? What steps have you taken to regularly take your team aside and talk together about what all this *doing* really means?

Maybe paradoxically, taking this kind of time will actually free up a lot of time – the time that used to be spent redoing or covering up or pretending or even firing. Be a translator leader.

In what ways are you already a "translator" kind of leader?

How do you want to improve this skill? Plan one action to take today!

What other examples can you find of Jesus as translator?

Dear Jesus: I can be so impatient with people who don't get it. I rarely stop to ask what have I done to explain the whys and whats and hows and wheres. Help me see your modeling of leadership, and let it be an inspiration to me. I commit to being a leader who is constantly improving my skills. I am awed by your example and vow to follow it daily. Amen.

104. I AM REALLY ANGRY!

Bible Reference: "Let them be put to shame and dishonor who seek after my life. Let them be turned back and confounded who devise evil against me" (Psalm 35:4).

Meditation: I am really angry. I think bad words. I am tempted to have a large drink of something strong. I want to do evil myself. My emotions are almost out of control. I am saying things like "I hate" and "I wish" and "life is not worth it." I feel as if my enemies are really out to get me. "Let them be like chaff before the wind with the angel of the Lord driving them on" (vse. 5). Yes, I am even calling on God to bring down vengeance on them. That's how strongly I feel. "Let their way be slippery and dark with the angel of the Lord pursuing them" (vse. 6). I am almost happy thinking about how they will have a worse time than I am having.

And it's not as if I brought it on myself! "For without cause they hid their net for me; without cause they dug a pit for my life" (vse. 7). I did nothing wrong. They were the ones who conspired against me. I know what they're thinking. "But at my stumbling they gathered in glee" (vse. 15). I know how they talk behind my back. Oh! "Let ruin come on them unawares" (vse. 8). Being angry feels so good! "Then my soul shall rejoice in the Lord" (vse. 9). It will be so amazing when they are brought low and I am vindicated!! Poor me!! "You deliver the weak from those too strong for them" (vse. 10). I am full of self-pity.

Come on, God. Why aren't you on my side? "How long, O Lord will you look on? Rescue me from their ravages" (vse. 17). What is taking you so long? Haven't I been a faithful servant? How do I deserve this? "Wake up! Bestir yourself for my defense, for my cause, my God and my Lord!" (vse. 23). I want them on their knees, "put to shame and confusion," and "clothed with shame and dishonor" (vse. 26). If that happens, I'll be happy again. "Then my tongue shall tell of your righteousness and of your praise all day long" (vse. 28). But not until then.

Why is it so irritating when people say you shouldn't be angry?

How does this Psalm make you think about the way in which you and members of your team react to people and the things they do and say?

Dear Jesus: I am so angry. It's a real emotion. Please help me not to sin because of it. I can rage all I want but let me not sin because of it. And help me move beyond it before I go to sleep so that I do not give the enemy a foothold. I acknowledge that my anger is not a righteous anger. I think I am better than the person I am angry at. But only you are truly good. Let me look at your redeeming love and allow you to redeem my anger. Today. Thank you. Amen.

105. TODAY IS A HAPPY DAY!

Bible Reference: "I will give thanks to you, Lord, with all my heart" (Psalm 9:1).

Meditation: It doesn't happen every day! Today it is happening. Today is a happy day. The children are engaged and productive and joyful; chapel was amazing, with student leaders singing and dancing to the Lord; parents complimented me on the truly transformational impact the teacher was having on their child; I had time to walk around and see focused classes in action; and I'm home for supper with my family and only have three phone calls to make this evening. Yes, I'm happy.

"I will give thanks to you, Lord, with all my heart; I will tell of all your wonderful deeds.
I will be glad and rejoice in you; I will sing the praises of your name, O Most High" (Psalm 9:1).

Of course, I know I should praise God for his goodness when I am and when I am not happy. But today it's good to praise God in the midst of richness – children are being nurtured in the love of the Lord, we can pay our bills, and the community is unified in its purpose and about its future.

"I will praise the Lord, who counsels me; even at night my heart instructs me. I keep my eyes always on the Lord. With him at my right hand, I will not be shaken" (Psalm 16:7).

I danced out of my house this morning, eager to get to school. My children asked me what happened because I was smiling so much at dinner. My heart is light, and today I have no fear. I looked into the eyes of my spouse and saw the eyes of love. I am blessed beyond my deserving.

"Clap your hands, all you nations; shout to God with cries of joy.
Sing praises to God, sing praises; sing praises to our King, sing praises.
For God is the King of all the earth; sing to him a psalm of praise" (Psalm 47:1, 6-7).

Are you good at being happy? Do you "practice" it?

How does your life reflect the desire of God to bless you?

Dear Jesus: I praise you and bless you for your goodness. I know that every day won't feel this way. But today I am full of joy, and I thank you for that. It is such a gift, and I bless you for that. You have made me righteous, and I sing your praise. You have given me the gift of leadership, and I thank you for that. You have loved me and do love me and will love me until I am living in the house you have already prepared for me. You are my God. You are my Savior. I bless you and thank you and praise you. Amen.

106. I AM BLIND

Bible Reference: "Two blind men were sitting by the roadside and when they heard that Jesus was passing by, they cried out, 'Lord, Son of David, have pity on us!' Jesus stopped, called them and said, 'What do you want me to do for you?' They answered, 'Lord, I want to see'" (Matthew 20:30-33).

Meditation: Jesus did a lot of healing during his years of ministry on earth, and there are multiple instances in which he cured blindness. Not being able to see seems to be one of the most difficult things a person must endure. Our sense of sight provides so much of our understanding of the world and our relationship with it. Sight connects us with everything outside of ourselves, igniting a sense of wonder and possibility. And yet, how ironic it is that our world suffers from a terrible problem of spiritual blindness. This seems largely due to a tendency to resort inwardly, evaluating things with ourselves at the center. This has caused all sorts of problems and outbursts in our society and in the lives of young people.

As school leaders, we often hear of the importance of having a vision for our schools, helping them aspire to something greater. This scripture reminds me that fundamental to that vision is the simple, poignant request of the blind men in the scripture: Lord, my vision must start with you. You alone are the one who will lead my vision, who can remedy my blindness. As my eyes are fixed on you, help me to see my life's purpose so I can continue your healing work at this school in a world that desperately needs to see your truth and love.

Isn't it intriguing that Jesus, knowing all things, still asked what the blind men wanted? He does not force me to see. He invites me to see. Let me cry out to Jesus and, when he stops and asks me what I want, let me know what to ask for and have the courage and wisdom to make the ask!

Where in my day did I fail to see?

What contributes to my blindness?

Dear Jesus: Today, I call out to you to help me seek your presence in everything I see and do. You are my vision and guide for this life. Take pity on me because I thought I could see but now am blind. Help me see through your eyes and your heart. Help me see clearly so that I can lead with a vision that is filled with your loving purpose. Thank you for the gift of vision you gave so often while you were here on earth. Thank you for that continuing gift even now in my life and in my school. Amen.

REFLECTION

It is time to take a break and think about the journey you are on. Use this page to reflect on how you can accelerate your impact as a Christian school leader.

_____
_____
_____
_____
_____
_____
_____
_____
_____
_____
_____
_____
_____
_____
_____
_____
_____
_____
_____
_____
_____
_____
_____
_____
_____

107. I AM A SERVANT

Bible Reference: "Take my yoke upon you and learn from me, for I am gentle and humble in heart, and you will find rest for your souls" (Matthew 11:29).

Meditation: As the school's leader, you should consider yourself the head of the school's body. This is a statement of fact, not opinion. When was the last time you reflected on your title? Our titles matter to others more than we realize. Head, President, Principal, Superintendent, all communicate a certain power and level of importance to others. We have many people who report to us, we delegate work to others, we hold sensitive information, and we get to (or have to) make significant decisions. And, given this stature as Principal, how powerful is it when we perform a humbling act or go out of our way to do something kind for people within the organization?

I find myself amazed at the gifts and talents of the faculty and staff as we deliver our school's mission to students. And yet I don't speak that fact aloud to them nearly enough. I do not know how the honors chemistry curriculum has changed. I do not know how to reboot the server after a power outage. I do not know how to retrieve video from surveillance cameras from the event 4 days ago. I do not know when the last time the school's elevator was inspected. I do not know when it's time to renegotiate the utility rates. St. Paul reminds us: "There are many parts, yet one body. The eye cannot say to the hand, 'I do not need you,' nor again the head to the feet, 'I do not need you'" (1 Corinthians 12:20-21).

Lord Jesus, you once told your disciples if they want to be the greatest or the head of everyone else, they need to be the servant of all. Help me learn to be the servant of others and dignify the work of all parts of the school's body. Teach me to be humble in my thoughts and actions so that I will bring glory to you and not myself. Open my eyes to see that if I am only the head without other parts of the body, then I have failed. Only by working in concert with others will I bring about the fruitful result that you intended for your disciples.

Who needs to be affirmed for their contributions?

Where do I need to see with new eyes?

Lord, help me to remember that all employees contribute valuable service as we realize our mission together. Help me to reach out to all people around me with acts of appreciation, kindness, and care. Amen.

108. IT'S HOW YOU SAY IT

Bible Reference: "And passing along by the Sea of Galilee, he saw Simon and Andrew the brother of Simon casting a net in the sea; for they were fishermen. And Jesus said to them, 'Follow me and I will make you become fishers of men.' And immediately they left their nets and followed him" (Mark 1:16-18).

Meditation: How's that for persuasion? Can you recall a time when you had this effect on someone? Was Jesus' success in this moment due to divine intervention or a deft skill he developed over time?

We know Jesus was both fully human and fully divine, but I tend to believe it isn't what Jesus said that made them react that way, but rather how he said it. And I also believe this is a skill that we can develop within ourselves as a tool for evangelism. With such confidence and calmness, Jesus offers to them a way of life that involves not only purpose, but a greater vision. At some level, Simon and Andrew believed that this loner on the shore knew what he was talking about and they needed to follow him. They may have thought he was a little nuts, but they went with him nonetheless.

Our school community will recognize very quickly if we, like Jesus, have a vision for them. I would suggest they need this more than anything else. And isn't one of our main objectives as a school leader to clarify for our followers why it matters and therefore what to do? It is so valuable to begin the year with a developed vision, then speak and act with great confidence in our abilities to teach our community this vision. Like Jesus, we must radiate a peaceful confidence that touches the souls of our students, teachers, and school community to the point that they will know we are part of something special regardless of how mysterious or difficult the path ahead may be. When we implement our vision in the hearts of the school community and unify our efforts, we too will be "fishers of men," just like Jesus.

Why do people follow me?

How can I better develop confidence and calmness in my leadership?

Lord Jesus, lead me to a place of calmness and confidence so that others may come to know you and the work we do together. You didn't often speak in really complicated ways. You were direct and pretty clear. Let me have the desire to develop the skill of communicating with integrity, purpose, and love. Thank you for all you shared with us and did for us. Amen.

109. THE CHALLENGE OF BEING A HYPOCRITE

Bible Reference: "For you have taken away the key of knowledge; you did not enter yourselves, and you hindered those who were entering" (Luke 11:52).

Meditation: At what point do you become the obstacle to progress? When do you fear those around you who are more able than you are? What makes you hesitate before allowing your colleagues, your direct reports, and even your students to be truly great?

"Oh, I don't do any of that!" It's our immediate response. If so, read no further.

But maybe it's worth asking not how we have opened the gate to knowledge but how we have taken away the key. I have a book on my shelves called *Breakpoint and Beyond* by George Land and Beth Jarman. On p. 153 they write: "One of the authors gave eight tests of divergent creative thinking to 1600 children in the early days of the Head Start program. He gave the same tests to these children over several years. The first tests were given when the children were between three and five years of age. 98% scored in the genius category. Five years later only 32% scored that high. Five years later it was down to 10%. 200,000 adults over the age of 25 have taken those same tests. Only 2% scored at the genius level." School qua school is not an inevitable good. In fact, your school can pose significant obstacles to children's real growth.

Are you willing to acknowledge that it is at least possible that you are an obstacle to progress? Are you willing to acknowledge that it is at least possible that you yourself are blind and are passing on what happened to you to the next generation? Are you willing to acknowledge that it is at least possible that you are a "hypocrite" (Luke 12:1), that what you say you want for children is not what you are actually giving?

Land and Jarman offer the thought that kindergartners use the word yes a lot. Can you sing? Yes! Are you artists? Yes! Can you run? Yes! Are you special in God's eyes? Yes! Can you learn from kindergartners and say Yes! a lot more to the possibilities in your school?

In what ways are you the limitation on what's possible?

How can you give the key of knowledge away in more frequent and more profound ways?

Dear Jesus: You convict the lawyers and the Pharisees. You convict me at the same time. Lord, I want everyone to be the genius you created them to be. Help me believe that it is possible. Help me to lead in a way that makes it possible. Help me to say Yes! to those directions that open up opportunity to my students, my staff, my faculty, and myself. Thank you for being the Good Creator. I acknowledge you in my heart and in my words and actions. Thank you for acknowledging me before the angels. Amen and Amen.

110. THE CHALLENGE OF BEING NEW

Bible Reference: "No one sews a piece of unshrunk cloth on an old cloak; otherwise the patch pulls away from it, the new from the old, and a worse tear is made" (Mark 2:21).

Meditation: In the first decades of my professional life, I taught at schools in Alberta, Canada. Those were definitely not in the days of political correctness, which is to say that I began teaching in 1977, well before microaggressions! I am still in touch with many of my students – they have been kind to remember the good things we did together. What I remember vividly about those days, though, was the challenge we were often posed by students who came to the school and needed to change radically. It wasn't just chipping at the edges for these students; it was hard-core reformation of the interior heart and brain. As far as I know, we sometimes failed, and the boy or girl had to leave the school. But just as often we succeeded and a boy/girl who previously was failing academically and empty spiritually would leave at graduation with a new lease on life.

That's the challenge for us as Christian school leaders. We are not called to sustain an organization. We are called to constantly renew it and to bring the vibrancy of the Gospel into each child's life. We know that our children are facing significant challenges irrespective of the financial richness of their lives. Families are challenged to stay together; parents and their children desire intimacy but don't always know how to achieve it; children face stress and exhibit stress indicators that I never knew about in my early days of teaching; the siren of secular success often inhibits and compromises healthy living.

Our schools are new cloth. We are not called to patch but to renew. We are not called to go along with but to challenge. We are not called to be secular schools but Christian schools. We are called to serve in the real world. You lead a real community – you have to deal with real people and real budgets and real constraints. If you are just a Christian patch, you will actually end up being a worse school than your secular counterparts.

In what ways does our school truly challenge its own constituency with the witness of Jesus within the reality of living in the world?

What characteristics as a leader do I have that give me authority and credibility in that challenge?

Dear Jesus: I ask for your forgiveness for using my gifts to just be successful. Create in me a new heart to use my gifts to be transformative. I don't want my school just to be a patch but to be a means to new creation for every child in it. Bless me as I lead my school into new life. Amen.

111. IT'S TIME TO SAY GOODBYE

Bible Reference: "So Jesus told him, 'What you are about to do, do quickly'" (John 13:27).

Meditation: This is a pretty dramatic scene. It is the Last Supper, the Passover meal, a journey that Jesus is taking in order to be the Lamb of God that takes away the sin of the world. Even to the last, Judas can go with him on that journey. But at that very moment of communion in Jerusalem, Satan enters Judas and he falls. Jesus tells him to leave.

This is a pretty dramatic meditation. Maybe too dramatic. But the stakes are high for you as a Christian school leader. Who is on your team matters for the success of the children and therefore the generational success of the school. As you think about signing contracts for the coming year, are you willing to say "leave" to the teacher or staff member or administrator who cannot or will not carry out the mission?

My children went to a Catholic parochial school when we first moved to Delaware from Canada. They were there for 2 years and had a good education. It was an important school for an underserved and relatively poor part of town. It was a beacon of light for a neighborhood. The parents of the children there were enthusiastic and committed, understanding the importance of the nurturing being given their children.

It had a receptionist who was one of the most unpleasant people I have met. She was rude, uncooperative, and seemed to be permanently depressed. I am ashamed to say that I judged her rather than prayed for her. For the school, she was entirely the wrong person to have as the first point of contact for a new parent. Two years after we started there, the school closed. She was not the entire reason, but the Principal's refusal to fire her (because of her decades of service) was a symptom of the reason.

In a number of ways, this has been true at many schools. Is yours one of them? Do you keep a teacher the parents take their children out of school to avoid? Do you have a receptionist without the gift of hospitality? Do you have an administrator who can't connect with the children? You must say to them: "Leave!" Do it this year. Don't wait.

Do you know who it is who should leave your school?

How can you say "leave" with grace and humility?

Dear Jesus: It doesn't always work out. The point is not whom or how to blame. The point is to ensure that the team is united in its vision and actions. The point is to have a team that can serve the students under your sovereignty. Help me to continuously strive for that team. Help me to lead with courage. Thank you for showing me how to lead graciously and implacably. Amen.

112. THERE'S A RAINBOW IN THE SKY!

Bible Reference: "You know how to interpret the appearance of the sky, but you cannot interpret the signs of the times" (Matthew 16:3).

Meditation: Do you enjoy storms? Yes, they can be destructive and a little scary. They are also amazing displays of power; they bring us often much-needed rain; they are an impressive artistic display; they are always fascinating and never dull. I will sit or stand at a window looking out at the sky and feeling very small in this great creation. My children, both when younger and even as they moved into the teenage years, loved to run out into the stormy blast and yell and shout as if to join in the revelry.

Storms have also been incredibly influential in Christian symbolism, providing us with sermons, poetry, images, hymns. What fun it is to look out at the rain lashing down and sing as loudly as possible: "O God, our help in ages past / Our hope for years to come / Our shelter from the stormy blast / And our eternal home!" Or maybe your tradition is a little different and you sing: "From every stormy wind that blows / From every swelling tide of woes / There is a calm, a sure retreat / 'Tis found beneath the mercy seat."

And the ending of storms is comforting. Out comes the rainbow, that symbol of God's covenant with Noah (Genesis 9:13-14). You might like to join with our Jewish friends when you see a rainbow and say a blessing. The traditional text for such a blessing is as follows:

ברוך אתה הוהי אלהינו מלך העולם זוכר הברית ונאמן בבריתו וקיים במאמרו
Blessed are you, Lord, our God, King of the Universe, who remembers the covenant, and is faithful to God's covenant, and keeps God's promise.
Baruch ata Adonai, Eloheinu melech ha-olam, zocher habrit v'ne'eman biv'reetoh v'kayam b'ma'amarav.

*When was the last time I really **saw** a storm and thanked God for the rainbow?*

What does the rainbow mean for you in your vocation?

Dear Jesus: Thank you for your creation. Thank you for being the Word that brought everything into being. Thank you for the storms and rainbows of nature. Help me to appreciate them and recognize their symbolism for my life and vocation. Help me to understand the signs of the times for my students, my school, my staff, my Board members. May the rainbow be a blessing for me. Thank you. Amen.

113. THE TRUTH WILL SET YOU FREE

Bible Reference: "'What is truth?' retorted Pilate" (John 18:38).

Meditation: Drake Charles, former Head of Linfield Christian School in California, used this phrase that really struck me. He said: "Bend reality with the weight of truth." Maybe Pilate should have asked, "What is reality?" Leading in a Christian school can be a constant tension between truth and reality. I can't say exactly what Drake meant, but I think he was thinking that what seems to be the reality in which we live can be transformed by the truth that we proclaim as Christians. Having to replace the air conditioners does not go away, knowing that donations are needed to get that 3D printer is real, reaching full enrollment is important to both Christian and secular schools. But truth transforms these realities and places them in a different context.

Jesus says that "everyone on the side of truth listens to me" (John 18:37). It seems pretty clear that Pilate was not one of them! But what does being on the side of truth mean for us in leadership? How does that translate into fundraising, into inviting families into the school, into evaluating faculty? Here are 3 ways of thinking about this:

1. A simple call to integrity – truthfulness is basic to the invitation to join the school community, to contribute to the school, to participate in the school's governance, to lead in the lives of children. While this is the simplest part of truth, it is not always paid attention to. It involves honest and open communication and the ability to confront with love. Just at this level, it has transformational ability.

2. On a bigger canvas, the school teaches its children and influences its parents and mentors its employees as "truth" in a world that follows the "father of lies" (John 8:44). The school represents God's kingdom on earth where God's will is done.

3. Finally, it is a call to follow Jesus himself, who described himself earlier in John as "the truth" (John 14:6). Pilate fails to recognize that the answer to his question is standing in front of him. The school has an educational mission and yet it is inevitably part witnessing as well, to the children, and then to its community.

How is the school community truthful along these three dimensions?
In what ways do I lead in a truthful way?

Dear Jesus: I want so much not to miss the obvious answer to Pilate's question. It will take more insight than Pilate had to acknowledge you. It will take more courage than Pilate had to go against the stream. It will take more character than Pilate had to sometimes stand alone. Give me insight, courage, and character to stand with you. Amen.

114. I DON'T TAKE MY WELL-BEING FROM THE MEDIA!

Bible Reference: "The Word became flesh and made his dwelling among us. We have seen his glory, the glory of the one and only Son, who came from the Father, full of grace and truth" (John 1:14).

Meditation: I want you to think about what the Jewish people looked back to at the time Jesus came: The great Temple of Solomon had been destroyed, the Temple where God literally came and lived and erased the barrier between God and man. Ezekiel tells us that God abandoned it and Nebuzaradan destroyed it. The 2nd Temple had been built, but it was not the same – God never came down to dwell there with his creation. It was not the statement of God's return that the Jews had hoped for. At the time of Jesus, it was newly magnificent because of the renovations of Herod the Great – but there was no glory shining from it – only the gold leaf that made it visible from far off.

John offers us a completely different answer to the question as to where Israel's salvation was going to come from. He says that the Word dwelt among us and used the term "tabernacled" (ἐσκήνωσεν) – the Word was a human temple who came and lived with us. I want to apply that to how you feel about the world around you as you lead your school. As I write, the media headlines declare tragedy and chaos: various governments terrorize their own populations; buildings collapse because of poor construction; in North America itself, our water supply is under threat because of lead pipes and groundwater contamination. Create your own list! It's easy to be depressed. It would be human and we are all definitely human.

You are a Christian school leader, however. John says to you, the Word has already lived among us! There is still great pain and suffering around us and also in our schools. We are not naive. But this is not the result of God's vengeance on the earth. The Word has already come in great love, and God yearns to draw all people to himself. Every child in your school, every teacher, every administrator, every staff member, every parent, every Board member. "The light shines in the darkness and the darkness has not overcome it" (vse. 5). It's real to see the darkness. You lead a school that is light in the darkness, the Word made flesh, resurrection children.

What is my reading material and what do I watch?

In what ways can I understand reality and still be light in the darkness?

Dear Jesus: Thank you for being the Word made flesh. I praise you for being my strong deliverer. Remind me that you are not overcome but that you overcame. Help my mood be one of optimism and hope as I look forward to the new Jerusalem, the new heaven and earth. Help me lead my staff as a resurrection leader. Amen.

115. WHAT DO YOU MEAN? I HAVE A GREAT ATTITUDE!

Bible Reference: "The eye is the lamp of the body. If your eyes are healthy, your whole body will be full of light. But if your eyes are unhealthy, your whole body will be full of darkness. If then the light within you is darkness, how great is that darkness!" (Matthew 6:22-23).

Meditation: Your attitude is one of the most significant factors in your pursuit of your life's purpose. A report from the Stanford Research Institute found that only 12.5% of your success in life is determined by knowledge; the other 87.5% comes from attitude. More than ability, education, or aptitude, your attitude dictates your success in life. As the saying goes: If you think you can, you probably will. If you think you can't, you probably won't. Your attitude is the lens through which you view life. That's what Jesus was saying in the above scripture from Matthew's Gospel.

I get it. In the midst of the pressures you encounter every day, it is often hard to maintain a positive attitude all of the time. This is because we wrongly believe attitude is something that happens to us as a result of circumstances rather than a choice we make. Attitude is not something that goes on around you, but rather it resides within you.

One of my favorite images in the Bible is the image of a soaring eagle in Isaiah. How many of us long to live our lives like this every day; strong, graceful, and effortless.

"But those who hope in the Lord will renew their strength. They will soar on wings like eagles; they will run and not grow weary, they will walk and not be faint" (Isaiah 40:31).

Eagles are large birds that have to work hard to get up into the air, but once airborne they're masters of using rising air currents to stay aloft with minimal effort. The updrafts and thermals they need to soar and glide are only found at altitude. If you want to soar and glide like the majestic eagle, then remember that your attitude determines your altitude.

What can you let go of right now without losing anything?

What could you be positive about right now, if you really wanted to?

And this is my prayer: that your love may abound more and more in knowledge and depth of insight, so that you may be able to discern what is best and may be pure and blameless for the day of Christ, filled with the fruit of righteousness that comes through Jesus Christ – to the glory and praise of God. Amen. (Philippians 1:9)

116. SATAN IS THE ACCUSER

Bible Reference: "If a kingdom is divided against itself, that kingdom cannot stand" (Mark 3:24).

Meditation: Jesus carried out a number of exorcisms and seemed to consider it an important part of his ministry. It seems clear that this was part of the coming of the kingdom (Matthew 12:28) and that Jesus was far more preoccupied with the struggle with Satan than he was with any possible struggle with the Roman Empire. This person (only mentioned in 3 books of the Hebrew Scriptures – Chronicles, Job, and Zechariah) is both real as a person (Mark 1:13) and used metaphorically to illustrate the barrier between man and God (Mark 8:33).

It's good to remember this in the midst of the culture wars. Our struggle is not with "Rome" but with the one who has "authority to throw you into Gehenna" (Luke 12:5). It is highly intentional that Jesus' own prayer finishes: "Deliver us from the evil one" (Matthew 6:13).

And Jesus was confident that he had already defeated Satan, seen through his account of the temptations (Matthew 4:1-11). We can be equally confident that, while Satan certainly continues and will continue to roam until the 2nd Coming, throwing weeds among the wheat stalks, Jesus reigns triumphant now, in the present time, in your life and in your school. The sign of Satan's influence is the presence of a kingdom divided against itself.

Where Satan is the accuser, the answer to disunity is not a resort to power and a claim to positional authority. The answer, Jesus says, is in taking up the cross. The kingdom can only come through you walking the 2nd mile, giving up your cloak, and you turning the other cheek. Leaders don't create unity through dictate but through serving and inviting to service. Our leadership begins with washing feet. The kingdom comes through the gifts of bread and wine.

What is the character of my leadership?

Where do I face the accuser, Satan, and where does my school find him hidden within?

Dear Jesus: You had no doubt that our leadership would be tested, just as that of the disciples was tested. You also knew that we are ambiguous leaders full of courage and fear, resolution and timidity, pride and humility, love and indifference. Give me your strength of will to face my Jerusalem, wash my followers' feet, and offer myself in service. Thank you for your gift of your salvation so that we can truly step forward as children of the light. Amen.

117. MEASURING SUCCESS

Bible Reference: "And the child grew and became strong; he was filled with wisdom, and the grace of God was on him" (Luke 2:40).

Meditation: Do you sometimes struggle with how to describe the success of your school? In a technical sense it's probably not that hard. Did you do what the Board wanted you to do this year? Did you meet the key metrics of the financial plan? Did your students achieve the "right" results on their standardized testing? Did you get enough press attention in your town? I have seen Principals measure success in all these ways just over the last few months. And none of them are wrong or bad.

So why not stop there? Isn't that good enough? The school has students, can pay its bills, the parents are happy, I have a great relationship with the Board, my family life is going well – isn't that enough?

Well, yes. Yes, of course, feel great about your leadership.

And no. What makes your leadership Christian? All of these objectives, important as they are, can be replicated in any school around you. The local public school has a strategic plan, wants test scores to be good, wants to maintain enrollment numbers, tries to have a good relationship with its parents. What is your Christian success? Does the parenting of Joseph and Mary provide us with a clue? Their parenting resulted in the child (Jesus) becoming strong and wise, with the grace of God on him.

Ask your teachers what success looks like and listen acutely to their answers. Which ones will take you beyond what everyone else is doing? Are you committed to strength of body? Is your nurturing of the child going to result in wise thinking and action? What does the grace of God, the favor of God, look like in the lives of your children?

What assumptions do we make as an educational community about child-rearing?

What assumptions should we be making?

Dear Jesus: You have given me the great privilege of leading in a Christian school. You have given me the example of yourself becoming strong and wise, and experiencing the grace of God as you grew up. Give me the wisdom to lead in my community so that we can give our children that same experience. I know that we have to be successful in worldly ways – just help me to have the courage to give that success a foundation that is rooted in you. Amen.

118. I AM AN ESCHATOLOGICAL LEADER!

Bible Reference: "Ask the Lord of the harvest, therefore, to send out workers into his harvest field" (Luke 9:38).

Meditation: How many books on leadership have you read? Yes, I've read a lot too. Very occasionally it mattered. Not often. The reason it usually didn't matter, even if truly entertaining, is that most leadership books end up with platitudes, e.g., here are 10 things (not 5, 7, 150); never stop learning (as if you could); be creative (often not helpful); be a servant leader (whatever that means), etc.

As a Christian leader in a Christian school, you are a different kind of leader than most described by these books, even Christian books. You are a worker in the harvest. Okay, it's a nice metaphor, but doesn't it almost have a sense of platitude to it? Only if you leave it at the most surface level! If your school claims a Biblical worldview, it is entirely different.

Harvest is an eschatological image – it is the time when the people of Israel will be brought out of exile for the last time, when justice will come to the earth, when God's kingdom will come, when what happens on earth and what happens in heaven are congruent (cf. Isaiah 9:3, Hosea 6:11, Joel 3:18, Amos 9:13-15, etc.) You are a worker in the harvest!

The "Lord of the harvest" is an eschatological Lord who is both Alpha and Omega, beginning and end, Creator, Redeemer, and Sanctifier. When you walk your school corridors full of "harassed and helpless" (vse. 36) people, you are not just walking but you are "sent" as a shepherd to them. You are a worker in the harvest!

The coming of Jesus himself means that the final days are in progress, that God's blessings have been released in a new way through his Son. God's plan is coming to fruition and the prophets' voices through the ages are being fulfilled. Eschatological leadership means that you are part of that plan, part of the fulfilling of the kingdom of heaven. You are a worker in the harvest!

Does being sent out into the harvest result in arrogance or humility?

What meaning does planning take on when it is placed in the framework of eschatological leadership?

Dear Jesus: You came to earth as a light to the Gentiles. But you never left Israel. Instead you sent me out to bring in the harvest that you have watered and fed. Help me to be a leader that brings the kingdom of heaven to my students, my faculty and staff, my Board, my parents. Give me the strength and wisdom to be light to the Gentiles. Amen.

119. WHOM DO I LISTEN TO?

Bible Reference: "It was Mary Magdalene, Joanna, Mary the mother of James, and the others with them who told this to the apostles. But they did not believe the women, because their words seemed to them like nonsense" (Luke 24:10-11).

Meditation: When and from whom do you look for advice? Who gives you advice, sometimes when you aren't looking for it? I remember a turning point in my life when my wife became, for the shortest time, my career counselor (cf. Genesis 21:12). Listening to her, really listening to her, and following her advice led us as a family to a new country. God gave her an insight about me that I didn't have myself and that no one else had seen either. It was key to my own development as a person and as an educator.

When and from whom do you look for advice? Mary Magdalene and Joanna were Jesus' fundraising group. This group of women were also close enough to Jesus to have heard and remembered his teachings in a similar way to the disciples. Joanna was an important woman in her own right. But they were women. Women were not allowed to testify in court; they only went outside heavily veiled; their status had significantly diminished since the times of Miriam and Deborah and Sara. Their words about critically important things were considered nonsense.

When and from whom do you look for advice? Who in your school lacks status and therefore voice? I was at a very large Christian school where I interviewed the Director of Security – he outlined for me what should be in the strategic plan, and he was about 90% accurate. He was appreciated deeply at his school for his security role but was not considered to have insight outside that. I was at another Christian school and interviewed students who were proud of their school but did not enjoy it. The faculty were astounded. They had never listened to the students deeply.

When and from whom do you look for advice?

List the typical individuals and groups who provide advice to you.

Who else might provide key insights and divergent approaches?

Dear Jesus: Your example of interaction was revolutionary then, and it still is today. Your disciples constantly tried to keep people away from you who didn't fit the mold. You constantly talked to, ate with, healed, and listened to those very people. Help me to be a leader who is open to each person as an image of God. Help me to listen deeply, open to the possibility that good advice can come from any of my staff or students or volunteers. Thank you for the richness of talents you have given to each of us. Amen.

120. IT'S NOT YOUR MIRACLE!

Bible Reference: "Here is a boy with five small barley loaves and two small fish, but how far will they go among so many?" (John 6:9).

Meditation: Don't beat up on yourself so much! You are working 50- to 60-hour weeks; you are counseling families, both parents and their children; you are trying hard to lead the Board and think not only for today but for tomorrow as well; you are being a good steward of what you have. But it is still easy to go home and worry in the evenings (those that are not filled with meetings) that you are not enough, that you cannot lead the school.

Let's be honest. Sometimes that's true. Sometimes the mirror tells a story that you would do well to pay attention to. Leading a school or leading in a school may indeed not be your gift. But my experience is that, much more often, you are being unrealistic. Worse, you are trying to **be** God rather than **rely on** God.

It's hard to know what Andrew was thinking as he diffidently pointed out a totally inadequate few loaves and fish. Was he being ironic? Was he impudently asking for a sign? Was he exasperated by the situation? Was he being faithful? I like to think that the first part of the sentence was addressed to Jesus, while the second part was addressed to the other disciples to try to avert inevitable scorn and mockery. After all, that's what we do as humans, right?

But Jesus actually takes him seriously. He accepts what the boy has given and looks up to his Father (Luke 9:16) and says: "Blessed be you, O Lord our God, King of the world, who has caused bread to come forth out of the earth." And God feeds the 5,000. We are not so arrogant as to look up to heaven, but we too must bring our loaves and fish, say the blessing, and expect God to act. It's not your miracle. They are not even your loaves and fish. You only bring to God what is his and expect him to be God. Don't make it so hard. Just bring the loaves and fish.

What is the difference between arrogance and faithfulness?

In what ways do you need to become more like a child?

Dear Jesus: I need help being thankful and following your example. Thank you for being my Savior. Thank you for my school. Thank you for each blade of grass on the fields and flowers in the flower beds. Thank you for each precious child given to us for feeding. Thank you for each staff member *(name each one)*. Thank you for each teacher *(name each one)*. Thank you for each of my leadership team *(name each one)*. Thank you for each brick and stud in our building. Thank you for every dollar in the bank. You know our needs before we ask. Thank you for that too. Amen.

REFLECTION

It is time to take a break and think about the journey you are on. Use this page to reflect on how you can accelerate your impact as a Christian school leader.

ACT 3: CELEBRATION AND ANTICIPATION (SPRING)

THE CHRISTIAN JOURNEY: PENTECOST

In what ways is my thinking about mission deepening?
_____
_____
_____

My current top 5 leadership gifts

1. _____
2. _____
3. _____
4. _____
5. _____

How can I be more of a resurrection leader?
_____
_____
_____
_____
_____
_____

What emotions are being stirred in me, and how is my spirit strengthening?
_____
_____
_____

121. PRAISE GOD!

Bible Reference: "Praise him with tambourine and dance; praise him with strings and pipe; praise him with clanging cymbals; praise him with loud clashing cymbals!" (Psalm 150:4-5).

Meditation: Have you ever wondered why? You're human, so of course you have! I have wondered 'why' many times in my life, and some of those times has been around Psalm 150. I didn't get it. All the churches I have attended have been Bible-believing churches. None of them have seemed to believe these 2 verses of Psalm 150. I was constantly being told to "shush" in church. I have never seen a cymbal in church except at a concert. I have certainly never seen a loud clashing cymbal in a service.

What about in your school? Where does praising the Lord fit into your daily walk? What about noise? Do you have cymbals in your worship services? Apparently, cymbals were the rhythm section in Temple worship, so maybe the bass guitar or the drum set serves that function. Obviously, the ecstasy of Psalm 150 is the climax of the Psalms, as it can be the climax of worship. It is not for every moment of every day. But when it happens, when the Spirit of joy and thankfulness moves, do we expect it? Do we welcome it?

I've often wondered why kids are so noisy and adults treasure quiet. I am turning away from the explanation that, as we get older, we get wiser and recognize reflection and contemplation as somehow superior. I am wondering instead if the noise of children is not something to be continued into older age, whether I am too quiet and not noisy enough. Psalm 150 reminds me that the sounds of children are voices reaching to heaven; their instruments are a sweet sound to our God.

Where is the space for noisy praise in our school's life?

Do I as a leader rejoice as a child – or maybe recoil from children's exuberance?

Dear Jesus: Help me to treasure cymbals, even clashing cymbals. Help me to keep the child in me appreciating their noise and rejoicing. Help me to be a leader that loves the noise of children and urges my team to do the same. I want Psalm 150 to be a part of my life as much as being still. I love you, Lord. Let my heart rejoice in the fullness of sound. Amen.

122. ADMISSION SEASON FOR ALL THE NATIONS

Bible Reference: "Praise the Lord, all you nations! Extol him, all you peoples! For great is his steadfast love towards us, and the faithfulness of the Lord endures forever. Praise the Lord!" (Psalm 117 cf. Romans 15:11).

Meditation: Who is your school for? You're in admission season and it's a good question. You may think you have answered it, but I'm going to ask the question anyway – who is your school for? Few schools that I have gone to have really gone into this in any depth. They are still leaning on 20th-century hopes that good Christian families from good Christian churches will come to their school. The Psalmist challenges that. Of course, the realities of today's society challenge that. But, more importantly, the Psalmist challenges that.

Who's going to praise God? All you nations! That's a wow! In the Hebrew Scriptures we might have expected a call to the Jewish nation, specially chosen by God. But no, it's to all you nations. Paul makes it clear that means to the Gentiles as well as the Jews. What are the implications for us? Our schools are not just for the chosen people, but for all nations. Why? The Psalmist tells us: because God loves all of us – he died for all of us, Paul adds, and rose again – because God's faithfulness is forever!

This is a short Psalm but not in the least trivial. It is dead center in the Bible. Yup, that's right, 589 chapters before and after it. This message is central to our school's message. The reason for this message is central to the reason for our school. Are you ready to listen to it?

Have you written down the criteria for children to come to the school? Do they reflect Psalm 117?

How "all the nations" is your school? What would that look like in your setting and with your mission?

Dear Jesus: I'm not sure about this call to all the nations. Aren't I supposed to help the household of faith first? I'm puzzled. Help me follow your example in greeting all people in your ministry on this earth and in even applauding the faith of a Roman centurion above all others. Help me lead the school in an "all the nations" kind of way. Help me understand what that means. I am so grateful that I am included in all the nations and that you came and died and rose for me. Let me share that in my school. Amen.

123. SING PRAISES TO OUR GOD

Bible Reference: "Praise the Lord! How good it is to sing praises to our God; for he is gracious and a song of praise is fitting" (Psalm 147:1).

Meditation: What is it about song? About music? Martin Luther said that "Next to the Word of God, the noble art of music is the greatest treasure in the world." If it's been a while since you released your inhibitions and belted out a really good tune (even if you sing out of tune!), you really need to get to it. We **say** the Psalms, but the Jews and Jesus **sang** the Psalms. Who knows if they knew the technical reasons for doing so, but we know a lot about singing. It releases dopamine, a neurotransmitter that makes you feel happy. It improves immunity-boosting antibodies and cells that protect against bacteria and other invaders. Music is used to treat health conditions ranging from premature birth to depression to Parkinson's disease. It increases gray matter volume and improves brain functions like auditory processing, learning, and memory. I could go on and on.

So the Psalmist is on to something when he tells us that it is "good" to sing praises to our God. It's not just that it is a good thing to praise God – that's obvious. But to sing is itself a good thing. Music is a gift that has been given to us in order to connect heaven and earth. David C. Mitchell writes in *The Song of Ascents*: "Melody fills our minds and souls … Melody connects us with our ancestors when we sing their ancient songs. Melody connects us with the ancient church when we hymn their hymns. Melody touches our spirits" (p. 219). Rhythm connects us to the rhythm of our mother's heart, the rhythm of day and night, walking on 2 feet, sleep and wakefulness, hunger and being full, walking and running.

So sing. Singing is good for the soul. Sing praises to our God. What greater pleasure can there be than praising the God who made us, who saves us, who prepares a place for us to be with him? Praise the Lord!

In what ways do you make time for music in your life?

Does your school community take seriously the Psalmist's encouragement to "sing"?

Dear Jesus: I know that you sang psalms. Even after the last supper, you went to the Mount of Olives singing a psalm. Help me to sing your praises every day. Help me be open to children making a "joyful noise" to you. Give me courage to make the psalms an important part of my life and the life of my school. I thank you for them. Amen.

124. SPRING IS IN THE AIR

Bible Reference: "Sing to the Lord with thanksgiving; make melody to our God on the lyre. He covers the heavens with cloud, prepares rain for the earth, makes grass grow on the hills" (Psalm 147:7-8).

Meditation: I don't know where you live as you read this. My home is farther north than many people's, and I enjoy each season in its turn – winter, spring, summer, fall. The coming of spring is a great transformation of the earth from frozen, cold, and white to soft, warm, and brown/green. The winter has brought its own contribution to life – the daffodils won't bloom without 12 weeks of cold; dormancy is needed by many plants and animals; the cold kills off diseases. Spring is a wonderful opportunity to praise God for his care of us in bringing new life. It has always been a wonderful metaphor for transitions, for rebirth, for the creative life. They are not opposites; rather, each is a meaningful aspect of life.

Your life is going through a similar change as you lead from year to year. You are testing new skills as you discard methods and thinking that have not or are no longer serving you well. You are looking at new challenges and wondering how they can be met. You are going to be recruiting new teachers and thus leavening your culture. At the same time, you are dusting off ways of being and leading that seem as relevant today as when you first learned and practiced them. You are standing on the rock of Scripture that tells of Jesus, the same yesterday, today, and forever.

Spring asks you to make melody. The melody of spring is different from the melody of winter or fall. Whatever school you are in, whatever its size or wealth, the melody of spring needs to be sweet, persistent, and loud. Sweet because you want those hearing it to be drawn to its tone. Persistent because you can't bear the thought that anyone will miss its tune. Loud because you are full of thanksgiving and want it to cut through all the text messages and emails and phone calls. Sing to the Lord a new song!

What will your spring message be this year?

In what ways will it call your children and the adults in your school to thanksgiving and new life?

Dear Jesus: Thank you for the opportunity to sow new seed and prepare for a new harvest. Thank you for your call on my life to be a harvester in your Father's vineyard. Bless me as I sing a melody of spring for those I lead. Bless my melody and make it sweet, persistent, and loud. Inspire me with your Messenger, the Spirit, to be a humble singer. Inspire me to be a singer with authority. May this spring be a blessing to my school. Amen.

125. GOD'S REVELATION; MAN'S PLANNING

Bible Reference: "If it is not possible for this cup to be taken away unless I drink it, may your will be done" (Matthew 26:42).

Meditation: The whole universe is full of secrets. Much of our lives is spent searching for meaning and discovering things both visible and invisible. While God encourages our pursuit of this meaning, it can be frustrating for many people. We want answers. We want things to be revealed to us on our timeframe. Thank goodness God's wisdom supersedes our impatience. He has a plan for each of us whether we know it or not, whether we want to believe it or not. There is no figure in the Bible who received full instructions for his or her life, no one for whom the future wasn't a mystery. While it is God's prerogative to reveal a bit of his will for a person's life, no one gets the whole script.

And so it is for school leaders as you begin to approach the end of each academic year. "Beloved, we are God's children now; what we shall be has not yet been revealed. We do know that when it is revealed we shall be like him" (1 John 3:2). Even now you start to think about the coming school year. As the school community begins to get excited about summer break – and the rest and freedom that will surely ensue – you can be overwhelmed by trying to uncover what the next school year will look like. There are many questions that you are responsible for answering as the end of the year shakes out. How will we overcome next year's budget shortfall? What the heck happened to enrollment? How can we possibly replace that valuable employee who won't be returning? What's the domino effect of teaching assignments as a result of one departure? How significant is the change in Board leadership?

As you stare down these questions, sometimes desperately seeking to resolve them, so you too must trust in the wisdom of God's timeline. You must work faithfully while trusting he will reveal his plan soon. In the revelation, blessings will come from the disruption. And so, despite not knowing all you'd like to know, approach the challenges of planning next school year as an opportunity to be more like Jesus: may your will be done.

Why is it difficult for me to await God's revelation?

In what ways does God expect me to use the insights he has given me?

Heavenly Father, open my heart and mind to welcome your new revelations to me each day, and the conviction to see each day through without fear, anxiety, or complaints. Help me pause throughout this day to see what you are trying to reveal to me. Help me not to fear the future but to trust as Jesus did and know that you always desire the best for us. Thank you for showing that so dramatically through the death and resurrection of Jesus. Amen.

126. UNMERITED FAVOR

Bible Reference: "May God be gracious to us and bless us and make God's face shine upon us, that God's way may be known on earth, God's salvation among all nations" (Psalms 67:1-2).

Meditation: We often hear the term "gracious" used in various contexts. We are often given a "grace period" to pay a bill. Or someone has been a "gracious" host by preparing the guest's favorite meal and making other thoughtful selections with the guest in mind. A gracious person is kind, caring, giving, generous, thankful, and cheerful, almost always putting the needs of others ahead of his or her own. This type of person certainly sees God in other people.

One of the simplest, best working definitions I have ever heard for any word is for the word grace: *unmerited favor.* Many of our societal systems lean heavily on the notion of merit. Our students are admitted into college (or even some kindergartens!) on the basis of 'merit'. Degrees or certifications are essential to earn the job. A good credit score delivers a better interest rate. But merit and achievement are not synonymous, and our schools are more susceptible to merit than we may realize. Our schools are not immune from the pressures of standardized testing. Our schools may employ a merit-based compensation model. Accreditation and strategic planning processes require benchmarking and documentation that validate or seek to improve the notion of merit.

While these realities can help drive continuous improvement, they can also, sadly, lead us away from the school's true value to the community. However your school's specific mission statement reads, we're sure to agree that our schools must be filled with good people who bring the face of God to life through our words and actions. We must be the ones who make God known to others by the gracious behavior we exhibit, offering kindness, hope, and wonder to those we encounter. Through an unwavering relationship with Jesus and a desire to serve others, our schools will flourish not because of our merits, but because we are building God's kingdom though God's graciousness.

How can I seek to improve the level of grace in my school so that we better reflect a Christian community?

In what ways is grace evident in my own leadership?

Loving and gracious God, you were always concerned for the well-being of others and aware of their needs. Your heart was filled with care for all, especially the downtrodden. Help me have a gracious heart and be kind and gentle to others, especially when I have a bad day. Help me act toward others as you acted toward me. Thank you for giving me such unmerited grace. Amen.

127. THE PROBLEM OF EVIL – PART 1

Bible Reference: "All in vain I have kept my heart clean and washed my hands in innocence. For all day long I have been plagued and am punished every morning" (Psalm 73:13-14).

Meditation: What a cry from the heart this is! The rich in the world, the successful in the world, the popular in the world, even the seemingly happy in the world often seem to be those who have not kept their hearts and their hands clean. It's easy to look around at other schools and pour scorn on their ethics, on what they are "selling," on how they pander to the world around them. Sometimes that can even be true of our Christian schools. We might look at the success of a Christian school down the road and think envious and highly uncharitable thoughts about the motives of its donors or the worldliness of its Board or even the nature of its faith.

Lord, I have done no evil! I have gotten up every morning and worshipped you! I have as pure motives as it is possible for a human to have! I have sacrificed my life in service to you! For all this, where is my reward? Why do the evil prosper?

The Biblical reality of evil is that it is not logical, at least not in the sense that we can create a system out of it and wrap it up neatly in a bow. Stoics shrug and say, "Deal with it." The Epicureans say, "Find pleasure." The radical sinfulness that we all, Jew and Gentile, find ourselves in is far more fundamental than just the idea that bad things happen to good people. Evil is so intrinsic – it's why we feel despair and hopelessness.

Then St. Paul says, "Against all hope, Abraham in hope believed and so became the father of many nations, just as it had been said to him, 'So shall your offspring be'" (Romans 4:18 / Genesis 15:5). Knowing evil is there, knowing it is intrinsic, we nonetheless live in hope. Abraham hoped in something that came about over 2,000 years later. We are to be Abrahams in our generation, witnessing to the hope that has already justified us.

Is the evil others do a problem for me?

Where do I find hope on a daily, every moment basis?

Dear Jesus: I know evil is here, not just in "them" but in me. Thank you that, despite that, I can live my vocation in hope. I can work with my team in hope. I can look at each child with hope. I can look in the mirror with hope. Thank you for justifying me. I know it doesn't make evil go away. I know that evil is here until you come again. I thank you that you are a just God, that you came in love, and will come again to live with us in love. Amen.

128. THE PROBLEM OF EVIL – PART 2

Bible Reference: "Therefore pride is their necklace; violence covers them with a garment. Their eyes swell out with fatness; their hearts overflow with follies" (Psalm 73:6-7).

Meditation: Remember the child in your office this year who complained about the treatment you gave her? Remember what she said? "It's not fair!" she complained. "Why am I being punished?" You said it as a child; we hear our children say it to us. "It's not fair." The child is not wrong! The adolescent who knows that her peer cheated on the test and received a higher mark; the boyfriend who cheated on the girl and still ended up with the prom queen; the student who anonymously lied about another student on social media and was never found out; the possession, stolen during recess, that was never found. From a child's point of view, no, life is not fair.

As adults, we still echo our childish plea of "It's not fair!" It doesn't seem so childish to us when we say it with a more mature voice. It seems to be a legitimate cry against odds that can often feel stacked against us. As the leader of the school or of my area of the school, why do I not get more respect? As someone who is well educated, why am I not listened to more? As a person with experience, why am I not thought of as wise? Especially so because the ones who are respected, are listened to, are thought of as wise, they don't deserve it! Worse, they are full of pride, put down those who disagree with them, and often lead in a foolish direction. Surely God is good (vse. 1), but this makes the problem worse, not better. Why do they have "shalom" when shalom is a gift of God?

Take heart. Like Asaph, the writer of this psalm, it is not surprising that you / we are troubled. But your work as a Christian school leader has an eternal significance, and your leadership has impact far beyond your current observation. God is trustworthy and holds you by the hand (vse. 23), he guides you personally (vse. 24), and will justify you in his time (vse. 24). You may feel helpless, but God is your strength and your salvation (vse. 26).

When do you feel most vulnerable in your leadership?

How do your alumni often give you confidence that you will be justified in God's time?

Dear Jesus: You must have felt the same way when you were here on earth. I remember how you cried out on the cross, wondering why God had forsaken you. Yet God held you in the palm of his hand, and you are with me and call me Child of God. Give me your faith and understanding in your Father so that I can lead with confidence in you. Evil is nothing compared with love. Let me love with your love and make my leadership transformational. Thank you. Amen.

129.   THE PROBLEM OF EVIL – PART 3

Bible Reference: "But when I thought how to understand this, it seemed to me a wearisome task until I went into the sanctuary of God; then I perceived their end" (Psalm 73:16-17).

Meditation: How wearying it is to live with despair and envy and regret! How intolerable is life when we look at the work of the Accuser, the Satan! Seen through his eyes, the very reasons for hope are dashed to the ground; life itself becomes a burden; one's dearest friends seem far away. Is it surprising that we live in times when suicide is so common? For every two murders, four people kill themselves! How wearisome life can be!

When he goes to the Temple, however, Asaph writes, he looks elsewhere and sees with different eyes. Looking through the eyes of the Deceiver is to see pointlessness. To look through the eyes of God is to see purposeful love. A problem with thinking about evil is the perspective you take. God says to us: "Where were you when I laid the foundation of the earth? Have the gates of death been revealed to you or have you seen the gates of deep darkness?" (Job 38:4, 17). Job, like Asaph, sees with different eyes and responds: "I had heard of you by the hearing of the ear but now my eye sees you: therefore I despise myself and repent" (Job 42:5-6).

As a Christian school leader, leading both children and adults, the problem of evil is not that you don't understand it. The problem is that it takes your eye away from seeing life as it really is, not as the illusion it is. Enter the Temple of the Lord. Fix your eye on Jesus. Study his Word. Resist the devil and the devil will flee from you. Teach your children that they should "awake" (vse. 20) and see the "phantoms" for what they are. Teach your adults that "God is the strength of my heart" (vse. 26), and it is enough to be in his presence.

When I get up in the morning, where do I look?

Is my customary place to be the "Temple" or the places where the "arrogant" walk?

Dear Jesus: I don't pretend to understand. I acknowledge you as the Creator and the Savior. Help me to look at life through your eyes, understanding that you will bring justice in time, and occasionally even in my time. Let me understand that leadership has an eternal framework. Give me the power to lead from inside the Temple, praising you and glorifying you. Thank you. Amen.

130. A RESURRECTION LEADER

Bible Reference: "He breathed on them and said, 'Receive the Holy Spirit'" (John 20:22).

Meditation: Here you are heading into the end of the school year. What emotions must be going through your mind and body! So much to be thankful for – and also so much to try and comprehend. Why was there so much challenge? Why am I so tired? Why did that donor take back the gift? Why did that family leave? Why was that faculty member so obstinate? Why did the Board not carry through on what it promised? Thankful for so much blessing and questioning why so much sin!

And Jesus says to you, I breathe on you. You have the Holy Spirit, the Comforter (John 16:7). Think of how amazing this is. This is the day of resurrection. Jesus echoes the breath of creation – "And the Lord God formed man of the dust of the ground and breathed into his nostrils the breath of life; and man became a living soul" (Genesis 2:7). He echoes the breath of resurrection: "This is what the Sovereign Lord says: Come, breath, from the four winds and breathe into these slain, that they may live" (Ezekiel 37:9). Jesus says to you, I created you, I saved you, even now today, I breathe life into you.

Let's not deny the sin. But that's not what makes the world go 'round. It's life that energizes and fulfills, and it's that kind of life that Jesus wants you to have. Focus on the sin, and you focus on death. Focus on blessing, and you focus on life. The sin is there, but you are given the Holy Spirit to figure out how to deal with it. The Holy Spirit influences your intellect to reason solutions; influences your emotions to improve self-control; influences your love to look to your brothers and sisters to help with the answers. Jesus breathed on the disciples then. He breathes on you today.

In what ways do my human emotions get in the way of me being a resurrection leader?

How can I recognize the reality of sin without being overwhelmed by it?

Dear Jesus: Thank you for the blessing of the breath of life. Breathe on me, breath of life. Breathe on me, breath of God. Fill me with life anew that I may love what thou dost love and do what thou wouldst do. Don't let me duck the challenges of sin. Help me find ways through under your enduring grace. Amen.

131. TODAY IS A HAPPY DAY!

Bible Reference: "My soul glorifies the Lord and my spirit rejoices in God my Savior, for he has been mindful of the humble state of his servant. From now on all generations will call me blessed, for the Mighty One has done great things for me – holy is his name" (Luke 1:46-49).

Meditation: My grandmother, and yours too probably, used to say "Count your blessings!" It was sometimes irritating to count my blessings when I really wanted to wallow in sorrow, bemoan my fate, complain about those around me, and genuinely enjoy my self-pity. But today is a happy day!

Let's think about that for a moment from Mary's point of view. "I am an unwed young teenager with a baby that came out of nowhere. I have had visions that those around me frown upon. I am going to go and have that baby about the same time my fiancé and I have to travel to Bethlehem because of the Roman oppressors. So my family won't be around me, and I will be in unfamiliar surroundings. But my soul glorifies and my spirits rejoices. Today is a happy day!"

Wow!

Maybe it's Elizabeth who gives us a clue as to why it's possible to be happy when humanly we should be overwhelmed and fearful. "Blessed is she who has believed ..." (vse. 45). Today is a happy day because we have heard God's voice and we have believed. More than that, our belief has been followed by execution–by acting on that belief–and by thinking through what we should therefore do. Happiness is obviously not about comfort or being in control. It is about the relationship we have with the Mighty One who has already and will continue to do great things for us when we act in accordance with his will. It is about trusting in the Mighty One who is merciful and forgives us our imperfections. Holy is his name!

Count your blessings! Rejoice! Today is a happy day, not because we are successful or the sun is shining, but because God has been mindful of our humble state, has already carried out his promises to Abraham, and will continue to do so for us, his descendants.

Are you sometimes tempted to believe that happy days are only those days that are going well?

How can you rejoice on all kinds of days, sunny and gloomy?

Dear Jesus: Mary did not have a simple path to follow. She probably wondered how successful she was being many times. Thank you for her example of faithful obedience. Help me to sing the Magnificat, the "my soul glorifies," in thunder and in sun, in wealth and in want, in sickness and in health, in success and in failure. Help me to trust your promises and lead in active faith. Amen.

132. TEND MY SHEEP

Bible Reference: "Do you love me?" (John 21:16).

Mediation: The first two times Jesus asks this question, he uses αγαπαω / *agapao*, meaning a high and devoted love. Peter replies using a different and more humble word – πιλεω / *pileo*, meaning a friend's love. Jesus, the 3rd time, challenges Peter using his own word πιλεω, do you love me?

Jesus challenges you too. Do you love me? Whatever way you answer that, Jesus will come back to you and use your own words and say, okay, wherever you choose to place yourself, I'm still going to ask you the question. And whatever response you give, Jesus has the same two commands: Follow me (vse. 19) and Feed my lambs / sheep (vse. 15-17).

As you look back on your year, you can see the successes. I'm sure Peter looked back on his three years with Jesus and thought about being sent out and all the amazing things he was able to do in Jesus' name. But for him, as for you, I'm sure he discounted those experiences because he knew he had failed Jesus when it counted most, denying him in the garden. There are things this past year that you are not proud of. There are words you said that you wish you could take back. There are relationships that still have to be mended. For all the excitement about graduation and awards and the stories you can tell about individual students and families, there's a nagging doubt in your mind as to whether you were the leader you wanted to be.

Jesus says: Follow me and tend my lambs / sheep. He says to you as to Peter, yes, stuff happens. Look forward. There is so much to do. All will be well. Just follow and tend. There are years of leading I am still calling you to, and generations of children and teachers and staff to shepherd. Follow me and I will be with you in the planning of next year, the hiring of new teachers, the admitting of students over the summer. Jesus says: I know that you love me. I love you too. Follow and tend.

Is there guilt that you find it hard to let go of?

Who is your confessor who will advise you through your spiritual trials?

Dear Jesus: Thank you for loving me so much that you can forgive my betrayals, overlook my failures, and see only a redeemed Child of God. Thank you for telling me that I can look forward and be forgiven for my past. Help me to follow you more clearly and be a better and better shepherd of the school you have given into my care. Amen.

133. IDENTITY AND PURPOSE

Bible Reference: "Then he opened their minds to understand the Scriptures, and he said to them, 'Thus it is written, that the Messiah is to suffer and to rise from the dead on the third day, and that repentance and forgiveness of sins is to be proclaimed in his name to all nations beginning from Jerusalem'" (Luke 24:45-47).

Meditation: It's like a mission statement, isn't it? Thus it is written ... It was obviously the mission statement for the disciples at that point. They proclaimed repentance and forgiveness in the name of Jesus from Jerusalem throughout the whole world. It was pretty focused even though there were hiccups along the way. But they never had any doubt they were headed out to do something very specific.

How about you? As you look forward to next year, what is your focus? Are you clear as to who you are and what your purpose and your mission are? I'm talking about you personally – not the school. I want to quote Viktor Frankl from *Man's Search for Meaning*. You will remember that he survived the German concentration camps and wrote about the difference between those who stayed human and those who descended into the depths of degradation. He said this, and I quote at length: "Don't aim at success. The more you aim at it and make it a target, the more you are going to miss it. For success, like happiness, cannot be pursued; it must ensue, and it only does so as the unintended side effect of one's personal dedication to a cause greater than oneself or as the by-product of one's surrender to a person other than oneself. Happiness must happen, and the same holds for success: you have to let it happen by not caring about it. I want you to listen to what your conscience commands you to do and go on to carry it out to the best of your knowledge. Then you will live to see that in the long-run – in the long-run, say! – success will follow you precisely because you had forgotten to think about it."

Substitute mission for conscience, or maybe add mission to conscience, and it challenges you to answer those 2 questions: Who are you, and what is your purpose? Is your purpose a dedication to a cause greater than yourself and a surrender to Jesus? Or has it decayed into the desire for a secure job and a safe place? Take this time to re-evaluate and answer the 2 questions: Who are you, and what is your purpose?

Who can you talk to who will challenge who you are?

What Bible passages might you collect that assure you that God calls you to a vocation?

Dear Jesus: It's easy to get lost in the "doing" of a job. Help me to grow as a leader by knowing better and better who you called me to be and what you called me to do. Give me people to challenge and comfort me. Give me your Holy Spirit to set me on fire to do your will. Amen.

134. THIS IS A DAY WHEN I WANT TO GIVE UP!

Bible Reference: "If I make my bed in the depths (Sheol), you are there" (Psalm 139:8).

Meditation: I still remember the day. I was deeply distressed and probably depressed. I had been under stress for months, leading change in a school in very difficult circumstances – poor accounting, no paperwork, isolated campuses, no resources, poor compensation, and more. The Board was supportive but not very helpful. I didn't know what I know now, so I was flying by the seat of my pants. I reached out my hand and picked up the phone to call a counselor and ask for help. I remember it being physically difficult to reach out, as if there were a force holding me back. I remember thinking, "Now I understand why it's so difficult to ask for help!"

Are you there? It's not a sin. We come to moments in our lives when we are overwhelmed at the thought of what there is to do, let alone actually doing it. We try to survive on less and less sleep. We put on a brave face so no one, sometimes not even our spouse, is truly aware of the turmoil inside. We feel as if we are dying at the same time as we smile and laugh. In the silence of our thoughts, the pain of being so inadequate, of bearing so many burdens, of feeling so much anger brings us to a blackness that no night can replicate.

O Lord, you have searched me and known me. You discern my thoughts from far away. You hem me in behind and before and lay your hand upon me. Where can I go from your spirit?

Yes, even the thought of God's love and mercy is too much. The accuser, Satan, afflicts my mind and heart to such an extent that to come into contact with the living God feels like torment. I don't know where to turn. Guilt stops me from returning to the loving arms of Jesus. I am not good enough. Who can save me?

And God says, "I am there with you. You don't have to find me. I am with you, even in Sheol."

What help do you need?

What phone do you need to pick up?

Dear Jesus: Your sweat was like drops of blood. You also experienced anguish. And God delivered you from the depths and raised you from the dead. Help me believe. Help me know your presence and trust your grace. Help me find answers. Help me. There is nothing left. You are left. You are still with me. You walk with me in the valley of the shadow of death. With you, I fear no evil. Thank you. Amen.

135. MAKE THE WORLD A BETTER PLACE

Bible Reference: "Children are a heritage from the Lord, offspring a reward from him. Like arrows in the hands of a warrior are children born in one's youth. Blessed is the man whose quiver is full of them" (Psalm 127:3-5).

Five-dollar-plus coffee is a very foreign concept to me! Consequently, it's been quite a while since I visited a Starbucks, but I remember a few years ago when quotations from a variety of people began appearing on the coffee cups. Under the title "The way I see it #209," I remember reading: "Growing up my parents always said, you will leave this world the same way you came into it – with nothing. It made me realize that the only things we do in this world that count are those things that make the world a better place for those who will come behind us." The author is Tyrone B. Hayes, biologist and herpetologist. (Bonus points if you know what herpetology is – a branch of zoology concerned with the study of amphibians!)

Today, Christ-centered, Christ-honoring schools are uniquely positioned to challenge their students to do just that – make the world a better place – by being Jesus' ambassadors of light, love, and hope in a world consumed with darkness, animosity, and despair. Christian schools have been given a tremendous opportunity and charge to shape lives that shape the future.

Sadly, I am sure you have heard Christian parents reject the option of a Christian education, saying that they want their children to be "salt and light" in public schools. This is a worthy sentiment; it's a noble one too. Every one of us should strive to be salt and light wherever we find ourselves. But we have to be pedagogically mindful that our children are generally not equipped to defend their faith and influence others.

Let me encourage you today to say "thank you" to your school families for their partnership with you in bringing up their children to make the world a better place. They are being trained in the Word of God and in a deep understanding of what salt and light means for the world.

When did you last call school families to simply say, "Thank you for trusting us with your most precious possession every day?" Do it today.

In what ways are your students demonstrating their faith in ways that others are not?

Lord, I praise you for your love and faithfulness. Thank you for each child. Children are a gift – an amazing blessing from you. We know that there's a battle over our families today, and the enemy would love nothing more than to destroy all that we hold dear in this life. Lord, I pray for your protection and care over our families. Continue to equip us and lead us as we seek to train up a generation that will be your hope and light in this world that so desperately needs it. Amen.

For Jesus; Through Mission; With Students

REFLECTION

It is time to take a break and think about the journey you are on. Use this page to reflect on how you can accelerate your impact as a Christian school leader.

136. PREPARING FOR THE CHALLENGE!

Bible Reference: "O Lord, you protect me and save me; your care has made me great, and your power has kept me safe. You have kept me from being captured, and I have never fallen. I pursue my enemies and catch them; I do not stop until I destroy them. I strike them down, and they cannot rise; they lie defeated before me. You give me strength for the battle and victory over my enemies. You make my enemies run from me; I destroy those who hate me" (Psalm 18:35-40).

We have not always prepared our children for the challenges to their faith that they will face in the world. Why is this? The problem seems to be that we have retreated for so long that there is nowhere left to retreat. G. Tyler Fischer writes, "We built the walls around our *Christian* institutions higher and higher. We put more locks on the doors. We put up stronger gates at the entrance. We finally realized that we had not succeeded in locking the world out – but we had found a way to imprison ourselves."

We must lead our schools down a different road. Christian schools will and should absolutely continue to protect our children from evil and unbelief but not by teaching them to retreat or run away. We will give them the spiritual weapons to defend themselves, teaching them how to fight against the evil that is in our culture and advocate for love, life, sacrifice, and service.

The great British parliamentarian Edmund Burke once wrote, "The only thing necessary for the triumph of evil is for good men to do nothing." By choosing a Christian education for their children, our parents have refused to do nothing. They have said "enough is enough" and made a stand. They have refused to sacrifice their children to an educational system that does not ground them in the truth of God's Word.

We can no longer retreat behind the walls of our Christian schools. We must engage. Together, as partners in the education of our precious children, parents and Christian schools must continue to do battle for Jesus Christ by challenging and preparing our sons and daughters to be his ambassadors to a hurting, lost world that desperately needs love, hope, and resurrection. May the Lord continue to find us faithful.

Does your school build walls or embrace its neighbors?

How might your school charge forward with love, hope, and resurrection into a hurting world?

Lord, we confess that too often we play it safe and retreat when we need to charge. Help us to understand what we need to do and why. Equip us for your work. Give us your strength and courage to move beyond our walls and bring your love and hope to a world that so desperately needs it. Amen.

137. I HAVE TO FIGHT A LION TODAY

Bible Reference: "The Lord is my light and my salvation – so why should I be afraid? The Lord is my fortress, protecting me from danger, so why should I tremble?" (Psalm 27:1).

Meditation: I have a confession to make. I am attracted to catchy book titles! A few years ago, I read a book with a rather catchy title: *In a Pit with a Lion on a Snowy Day*. It is based on the story of Benaiah, found in 2 Samuel 23:20, who, as the title says, went down into a pit on a snowy day and killed a lion! Now, I can't speak for you, but my first reaction upon encountering a lion in a pit on a snowy day – or on any day, come to think of it – would not automatically be to jump in there and take it on in hand-to-hand combat. In fact, my reaction, and I'm sure yours as well, would be to turn tail and run away as fast as I could.

But what if we didn't run away? What if God actually wants us to jump into the pit and face the lion? When we don't have the guts to step out in faith and chase lions, then God is often robbed of the glory that rightly belongs to him.

As a follower of Jesus Christ, I believe that our calling is to do so much more than play it safe and run away from what's wrong. I believe that it is exactly when we boldly face new frontiers and new challenges in our lives that we better understand what our Creator's plans for us are, and what he has called and equipped us to do.

My point is this: Benaiah didn't see a problem, run away, and go on with his life as usual. He saw an opportunity, and he was willing to take a risk and strive, for God's best. And if you read the rest of the story, God rewarded him as David made him the head of his bodyguard, one of his "mighty men."

I've read that there are 2 types of regrets; regret of action (wishing you hadn't done something) and regret of inaction (wishing you had done something). I am convinced that your greatest regret at the end of your life will be the lions you didn't chase. You will look back longingly on risks not taken and opportunities not seized. With Christ leading us, we are called to be lion chasers like Benaiah – to look for God-given opportunities in the midst of these obstacles and challenges.

What lions have you been running away from?

Who is with you as you 'jump into the pit'?

Lord, there are things happening that I do not understand. Some of these things make me feel weak, helpless, and afraid. Even in the midst of this, I know that you are the Lord. I know that the situation is in your hand, and I trust you. Give me strength and wisdom to fight lions and bring glory to your name. Amen.

138. LOOKING BACK; UNDERSTANDING THE PRESENT; FORESEEING THE FUTURE

Bible Reference: "I will remember the deeds of the Lord; yes, I will remember your miracles of long ago" (Psalm 77:11).

Meditation: The close of a school year can be hectic! It's filled with finals, last-minute projects, concerts, budget deadlines, hiring needs, and much more. There is always a perceptible tension between things that are urgent and things that are important, and, far too often, the urgent wins. Slowing down is simply not something we are good at. As a leader, our focus always seems to be on moving the organization forward faster.

Taking time to reflect – to look back – on the school year can be extremely effective in helping your school to progress. I like to think of it as looking back to move forward. The Psalmist looks back to understand today and to be able to think about tomorrow. The people of Israel were always looking back to the Exodus event as a way to see how God worked in their lives and to renew their trust in the covenant. What is the value of reflection for you today?

- Where are you compared with where you intended to be? Did you meet your goals and objectives and advance your vision? If you did, how will you sustain that success? If you did not, although painful to do, ask yourself why. There are valuable lessons to be learned from both successes and failures.
- What did we do right this year? Where could we have done better? These questions help you take a step back from the day-to-day operations and examine the very nature of the school. Areas that need attention and unproductive habits become clearer.
- On a personal note, just as we need annual check-ups for our physical health, reflection helps us to "check in" on the state of our spiritual health – our strengths and weaknesses. It allows us to retool our relationship with our Lord and Savior and in doing so become a more effective servant leader.

Looking back to evaluate your past and understand how God has been at work is the key to moving forward with vision, direction, and hope for our future. Be still, reflect, and know that he is God!

Do you schedule regular times to get away, be still, and reflect on all that God has done?

What might reflection look like with the leadership team?

Lord, forgive me for the many times that I only focus on what's to come, and I neglect what has been. In so doing, I fail to see your faithful hand at work every day protecting, leading, and blessing your school. Help me to take time to reflect on all that you have done as we look forward expectantly to all you are yet to do in us and through us. Amen.

139. DO YOU NEED SUCCESS TO BE ON FIRE?

Bible Reference: "But the Advocate, the Holy Spirit, whom the Father will send in my name, will teach you all things and will remind you of everything I have said to you" (John 14:26).

Meditation: Late March usually marks Opening Day, the beginning of the baseball season, a game once famously described by baseball legend Yogi Berra as "90% mental, and the other half physical." Ernie Banks, the Chicago Cubs Hall of Famer, is acknowledged as one of the greatest players of his time. Surprisingly, he never played in a World Series or a play-off game, and the Cubs were perennial cellar dwellers of the National League. In a radio interview he was asked how he could continue to play with such passion when there was little to play for and little or no hope of ever playing in a World Series. His response was, "You have to love the game itself and not love yourself in the game."

It's easy to love school leadership when the school is doing well and being recognized, when enrollment is flourishing and the phone is ringing off the wall with inquiries, and there is an absence of red ink on our budgets. Oh, how we wish it could always be so! Sadly, school doesn't always operate this way. What about those times or seasons of the school's life when there are no awards, no accolades, and little tangible success? During those times it is tempting, and some might say understandable, to allow our spiritual passion and drive to drop precipitously.

As a leader, God calls you to be steadfast in your spiritual passion every day, even when you feel like you are losing. Just like Ernie Banks, you have to love this vocation of Christian education, not love yourself in the vocation. Today, particularly if your school is faltering, let me encourage you to examine your heart to see if your passion and fire for leadership at your school still burns strong. Is it ablaze, or is it flickering and in danger of being extinguished?

If your passion is growing colder, it may be time to rekindle your spiritual fire. Just as a fire needs fuel to keep it burning, your spiritual passion for your ministry also needs fuel to keep it burning. That fuel is the Word of God. Feed your fire and let the fire of the Holy Spirit burn anew in your heart with a renewed strength and passion.

Is success the adrenaline I need to keep going?

Where is my coach who will remind me of the vocation I am called to?

Lord, let your Holy Spirit give me a fire and a passion for your kingdom every day, not just on the days things are going well or only when we are perceived as winners. Thank you for the Spirit who accompanies me on each day, good or bad. Amen.

140. ARE YOUR CHILDREN GOING TO BECOME A STATISTIC?

Bible Reference: "Then the Lord said to him, 'Now then, you Pharisees clean the outside of the cup and dish, but inside you are full of greed and wickedness. You foolish people! Did not the one who made the outside make the inside also?'" (Luke 11:39-40).

Meditation: At the risk of sounding overly alarmist, let me ask you a question. Could we be America's last Christian generation? In his book *Battle Cry for My Generation*, author Ron Luce estimates that only 4% of children born since 1985 will claim to be Bible-based believers. Comparing that to 35% of the Baby Boomers who are already struggling with the role of faith in their lives, he asks the question, "Are we living in what could become America's last Christian generation?"

It's true. Our children are becoming increasingly less Christian in how they think. As their view of life becomes increasingly secular, they see the need for salvation less and less. "The Spirit clearly says that in later times some will abandon the faith and follow deceiving spirits and things taught by demons" (1 Timothy 4:1).

Perhaps more than ever before, our children need a Christ-centered education to stand strong against a society that is increasingly hostile or, perhaps worse, disinterested in God.

The importance of Christ-centered education has long existed. Martin Luther, the great reformer, wrote, "I advise no one to place his child where the Scriptures do not reign paramount. Every institution in which men are not increasingly occupied with the word of God must become corrupt."

Paul, writing to Timothy, perfectly captures the importance of placing God's Word at the center of all we do, "All Scripture is God-breathed and is useful for teaching, rebuking, correcting and training in righteousness, so that the servant of God may be thoroughly equipped for every good work" (2 Timothy 3:16). Leading your school is a great responsibility, to ensure that your children do not become one of Ron Luce's statistics.

How can disinterest in things eternal be changed through the Christian school?

What is the evidence that you are being successful in fighting the good fight?

Lord, I acknowledge that we are in a mighty battle for the hearts and minds of our students. Help us to teach our children to follow you and so hear and act on your Word as truth and applicable to all areas of their lives. Help them to be no longer conformed to the pattern of this world but to your pattern, and to be transformed by the renewing of their minds. Thank you that you bring comfort and salvation to our aching hearts and minds. Amen.

141. WHEN IS A STORM NOT A STORM?

Bible Reference: "Then he got into the boat and his disciples followed him. Suddenly a furious storm came up on the lake, so that the waves swept over the boat. But Jesus was sleeping. The disciples went and woke him, saying, 'Lord, save us! We're going to drown!' He replied, 'You of little faith, why are you so afraid?' Then he got up and rebuked the winds and the waves, and it was completely calm. The men were amazed and asked, 'What kind of man is this? Even the winds and the waves obey him!'" (Matthew 8:23-26).

Meditation: Leadership can be tempestuous, tossing us around with waves of exhilaration and challenge, but also affecting us with anxiety and disappointment. The storm Matthew is referencing is no ordinary storm. In Greek the word used for storm is "seismos," from which we get the word seismic. This is the type of storm that threatens to destroy everything and turn your world upside down. Every one of us experiences storms like this in our own lives. They may come in different intensities and differing durations, but they come.

Sometimes these are relational storms when a spouse or trusted friend or colleague betrays you. Sometimes they are professional storms and you find yourself embroiled in struggles at school. Sometimes we see these storms coming from a long way off, and sometimes they just pop up with no warning. The reality is we all face these storms. Perhaps you are in the middle of such a storm right now.

Although Jesus is in the boat with them, the storm still scares the disciples to death! "Lord, save us" they cry out, "We are going to drown!" We feel that way at times–times when the winds are too strong, the waves are crashing over the boat, and we feel as if we are going to drown.

Don't miss what Jesus was doing as the storm raged. He was asleep at the back of the boat! Jesus experienced the storm just as much as the disciples did. But he saw past the storm to the salvation that he was in the process of bringing. God never promised us this life would be easy, but he is bigger than any storm we will ever face in this world. And he's always working for our good, even in the circumstances that we don't fully understand. He promises to never leave us or forsake us. Even when he's asleep!!

When storms come, do your fears stop you seeing Jesus?

How do you lead your team in the school's storms?

Lord, you don't promise that we won't go through storms in this life, but you do promise that you are with us. When the storms come, help me to know that you are near and to know that you are always working for our good. Amen.

142. PREPARING FOR GRADUATION

Bible Reference: "For where your treasure is, there will your heart be also" (Matthew 6:21).

Meditation: I was at my daughter's graduation from Ursuline Academy, a Catholic girls' school in Wilmington, Delaware. She was an excellent student who worked hard for her marks and achieved honors standing. She was a varsity athlete in volleyball who had played for several years and rarely missed a practice, even during those months when she just sat on the bench and watched. I was interested in how they would conduct graduation. Most schools would praise their students for their great worldly achievements, the colleges they would attend, the championships they had won. But my daughter's school took a different tack.

I was awestruck! As each of the girls approached the stage to receive her diploma, there was no declaration about how great that student was. Instead, a gowned administrator read aloud the causes the students had dedicated themselves to during their time in high school and the number of hours they had spent of themselves. For my daughter, it was the Delaware Children's Theater and 700+ hours. She wasn't even close to the highest in terms of the number of hours spent!

Why did the school do it in this way? Because it was centered on its mission – Serviam (I will serve). Graduation was therefore centered not on college entrance, not on scholarships and dollars won, not on prestige and vainglory, but on whether the students had imbibed the spirit of the school through serviam.

What is your mission? And will your graduation celebration be centered around it? I urge you to consider the intended outcomes of your mission and how your students exemplify that. It doesn't matter whether your graduation is for seniors, for 8th-graders, or even that cute ceremony you run for kindergarten. Whatever age the student is, mission outcomes should be exemplified in that child's life – <u>that</u> is the celebration.

In what ways is the mission specifically carried out in your school's life?

How can your graduation ceremony be made of eternal significance by celebrating your students' embodying of your mission?

Dear Jesus: It's so easy to get carried away by the fantasies of the world. I know that getting into college or into the next grade is important. Help me lead in my school so that we all understand that they are just a means to an end. Inspire me with the "treasure" that never rots or goes moldy. I thank you that you kept your eye on the main thing and never lost your way. I am moved by your focus and commit to the same in my school. Amen.

143. EXODUS AND BAPTISM

Bible Reference: "Prepare the way for the Lord, make straight paths for him" (Luke 3:4).

Meditation: You have students or their siblings who may be baptized at Easter. This is an ancient tradition connecting the new birth of baptism with the risen Christ. Of course, they may be baptized at any time of the year – it doesn't really matter. They will be baptized in a church. What part does the school play in this amazing step of faith?

The school prepares the way and continues the process of nurturing the faith of the child after. Your influence on the child is likely greater than that of the church, certainly of most churches. In your school, deep relationships form between child and teacher / model, strong peer influences lie beneath meaningful friendships, and committed parents bond within the school community. Preparing the way is an Exodus moment. Unlike the original 40 years of wandering in the desert, God's path to new life is straight (cf. Isaiah 40, Luke 3, Revelation 11:8).

The school's responsibility is also outlined in Psalm 27: "Teach me your way, Lord; lead me in a straight path because of my oppressors" (vse. 11). It's always a challenge to make that teaching experience personal and feeling fresh. Chapel services can become formulaic and routine. Bible classes can seem patronizing and unreal. Teachers can sound simplistic. How do I lead preparing the way for the Lord?

Let's not forget the power of Exodus? And the challenges for the people of Israel in staying the course despite the slavery from which they had been delivered. Our children can experience the power of Exodus (from slavery into freedom) but will likely also experience time in the wilderness, times of fear and betrayal, and times of exaltation. As an Exodus leader, you follow in the footsteps of the One who makes the path straight. Be an Exodus leader for your children.

What does Exodus mean for me and other leaders in the school?

How can Exodus help us as a leadership team understand our opportunities and challenges better?

Dear Jesus: My children are on a journey, and I don't always know how to lead a straight path. Lord, as they stumble and waver on their Exodus journey, help me to be an Exodus leader with focus, faith, and fortitude. Let me lead in a school that provides them with encouragement, your saving grace, and a fresh understanding of you in a fast-changing world. Amen.

144. PENTECOST – PART 1

Bible Reference: "'Come, follow me,' Jesus said, 'and I will send you out to fish for people'" (Mark 1:17).

Meditation: I worship at an evangelical church where the pastor forgot Pentecost. That's interesting, isn't it? How do you forget Pentecost, the birthday of the church, the celebration of the coming of the Holy Spirit in a special way to the early church, and the beginning of true evangelism? But it's easy for us to forget that Jesus didn't just say "follow me." He continued to say that following him meant that we were and are to act on his behalf – "I will send you out to fish for people."

Our Christian schools are not neutral places. We are places of academic learning but within a context that demands a response from our students. As Trinity Christian High School in Monterey, California, puts it: *Discover your purpose, your passion, and your potential in Christ*. The context is always "in Christ." We are not mindless atoms wandering hopelessly around a formless universe. I am created in the image of God, designed with clear purpose in mind, known down to each hair on my head, and my life is to give glory to God. That is the call of Pentecost, the call of Jesus, the call of the Holy Spirit.

As a Christian leader, am I led astray by other concerns? Does my worry about public relations get in the way of "in Christ"? Does my determination to beat last year's annual fund target get in the way of my call to "fish for people"? Is my popularity a stumbling block to my students following Jesus? It's funny. The success of the school requires attention to money, to graduates prepared for college and for life, to the strategic plan. But these are all under the Pentecost call: "You will receive power when the Holy Spirit comes on you and you will be my witnesses" (Acts 1:8).

Am I really clear about the meaning of Pentecost for my life?

In what ways can I lead in the power of the Spirit for my school to be a witness?

Dear Jesus: I follow you. Help me to be a fisher of people. I love you and worship you. Help me to be a fisher of people. I repent and have been baptized. Help me to energetically carry out my calling. The disciples were fishers in many different ways. Help me find my way anew. Thank you for their example and their faith in times of joy and of sorrow. Thank you for Pentecost and the gift of your Spirit in my heart. Amen.

145. PENTECOST – PART 2

Bible Reference: "If anyone would come after me, he must deny himself and take up his cross and follow me. For whoever wants to save his life will lose it but whoever loses his life for me and for the gospel will save it" (Mark 8:34-35).

Meditation: Peter declares that Jesus is the Christ. Jesus tells him that he doesn't understand the fullness of what he is confessing. Jesus **is** the Christ. But in a way that is totally opposed to the power structures of Caesar, Herod, Pilate, Caiaphas. In Acts though, Peter declares salvation in Jesus (4:12) and declares that Jesus is the Christ, this time with complete understanding. Pentecost is the transition from the upper room in fear, to the street and palace in service.

Pentecost calls on the Christian school to be countercultural. It is both political and apolitical. It is apolitical because it is neither liberal nor conservative, socialist nor libertarian. Political because it speaks to a new way of living that the Satan who still has dominion over the world strives to make contemptuous. "There were no needy persons among them. For from time to time those who owned lands or houses sold them, brought the money from the sales, and put it at the feet of the apostles and it was distributed to anyone as he had need" (4:34-35).

Imagine that as the economy of the school you serve! *There was no needy child in the community. For from time to time, those who had knowledge, skills, understanding, willingly served the needy child whenever the child had need. And this was done freely, without coercion, without obligation. And all of them were healed* (5:16). As a Christian leader, you are under the Pentecost call: You will receive power when the Holy Spirit comes on you and you will be my witnesses (1:8).

How much am I leading conformity to this world and how much am I leading by losing my life?

Where does my school need to go to heal each child authentically and with power?

Dear Jesus: You are amazing. You are the Christ, and yet you do not force but only invite! But you invite with the power of love. Help me to be like the 2nd Peter – a witness who truly understands your message that is opposed to the way of the world. Help me to witness to the power of your sacrifice. Thank you for Pentecost and the gift of your Spirit in my heart. Amen.

146. PENTECOST – PART 3

Bible Reference: "Do not stop him," Jesus said, "For no one who does a miracle in my name can in the next moment say anything bad about me" (Mark 9:39).

Meditation: It's not always easy to see who the "real" Christians are. Whether in the adults or the children at the school, who knows what is in the heart of each person except the Lord? It is apparent throughout Jesus' ministry that his followers were a strange mix of people. We know about the disciples, of course. There were the 12 apostles, and Luke's 72, and all the disciples who stopped following Jesus. There was the Roman centurion who had more faith than anybody in Israel. There were the 500+ Jesus appeared to after his resurrection. There were all the women who followed him and were the only ones at the cross (apart from John). There were 120 believers in Acts 1.

In this passage from Mark, the 12 imagine that being a disciple was like being in an exclusive club. Only people who look like this, or who dress like that, or who speak in this way, or who do these church actions, or who (fill in the blank) are part of the club. Our schools can seem to be rather like a club, with those who are in and those who are out. We think we don't make it obvious, but students are keenly aware of our prejudices and reflect them within their own groups.

Is our school truly a Pentecost school with Parthians, Medes, Elamites, Mesopotamians, Cappadocians, Asians, Phrygians, Egyptians, Libyans, Italians, Cretans, Arabs in it? That's a lot of colors, languages, customs! Would we be willing to sit down with each other and see how many different kinds of Christian we have? Would we be willing to see what obstacles we put up to students being Christian in our school? Obstacles that show students they are not valued equally? If we believe we have received power, how are we being witnesses? (Acts 1:8)

Can every student in my school be a Christian?

In what ways is my school full of "clubs," and what should I do about it?

Dear Jesus: Your example of openness to all people is humbling to me. You welcomed everyone who came your way and invited them all to be part of the kingdom. Help me to lead an open community and not a club. Help me to stay humble and be more worried about my own failings than the failings of others. Thank you for your promise in Joel to pour out your Spirit on all people. Thank you that you have been gracious and invited me to part of your kingdom as well. Amen.

147. WHOSE SIDE?

Bible Reference: "If the Lord had not been on our side …" (Psalm 124:1).

Meditation: It's interesting to ask the question, are you on the Lord's side or is the Lord on your side? What difference does it make? Who is the subject and who is the object? Grammar is so important in our faith!! Well, it may not be your cup of tea, but imagine how the Psalm would have read if we had reversed the subject and the object: if I had not been on the Lord's side. The focus is egocentric; it makes me the key actor in the action. Thanks be to God that he takes the initiative and saves us!

The end of this Psalm of Ascents, to be spoken going up to Jerusalem and / or going up the 15 steps into the Temple of the Lord, reads: "Our help is in the name of the Lord, the maker of heaven and earth." It emphasizes our dependence on God the Creator. It brings us back to the reality that we are the creation. And the author, David, now looking forward to the construction of the Temple by his son Solomon, seems to be reflecting on his reign and appreciating what it has taken to get this far.

So with you. You are not on the Lord's side. He is on your side. Think about your journey to this point. What have you "escaped" (vse. 7) from? What forces have "attacked" (vse. 2) you and your school on the journey? Your Christian school is an affront to the accuser, Satan, who would love to use dissent and conflict and mistakes and struggle against the kingdom. Yes, he would love to make you impotent, lacking in charity, powerless, watering down the Gospel resurrection message and teaching your children pablum. Thanks be to God that he is on your side, encouraging and inspiring you with his Spirit.

We don't have to feel burdened and bowed down by the fact of this struggle. This is a battle where the victory has already been won FOR US! Yet again, God goes before us in fire and cloud and rolled back stones. Jesus tells us that God's "burden is light" (Matthew 11:30). We do not fear the accuser. We have solutions to the challenges of running our school. David says, if the Lord had not been on our side. Thanks be to God that he has been, he is, and he will be. Amen.

What struggles have seemed overwhelming to you?

Do you know that the accuser has no power over you, that God is on your side?

Dear Jesus: I thank you for the cross, the rending of the Temple veil, and the open tomb. I thank you that you already went before us, throwing the Tempter into confusion and taking away his power. Lift me up and lift my school up so that we can proclaim your kingdom in word and deed in our neighborhood. Thank you for being on our side. Amen.

148. WINNING ISN'T ANYTHING!

Bible Reference: "But seek first his kingdom and his righteousness, and all these things will be given to you as well" (Matthew 6:33).

Meditation: It's hard to put first things first. It's hard to look at the needs of our school, the "money" we need, the "clothes" we have to wear, the "buildings" we have to live in, and not spend all our time in seeking them. Jesus tell us in a gentle fashion that we are mistaking the primary cause for the secondary cause. Jesus says if we seek the kingdom, the King will look after us.

Now this is not so complicated, I think. He's not saying if we have enough dogma and holy propositions and worship services and immovable principles, we will have enough students and money. He's also not saying just pray and everything will show up that you need. Not only is he not saying that, it is demonstrably untrue! In the previous verses he warns against "religiosity" – charity, prayer, and fasting! He's saying if we seek the kingdom. What does that mean in my school?

Remember, he was teaching the disciples, so it can't be that hard (!). "Therefore" (vse. 25, 31, 34)! What a great word! Seek first the kingdom, and we can stop worrying about the other stuff. Work hard. Think clearly. Plan well in advance. Imagine what could be. Collaborate. But don't worry about it. Have regular Board meetings. Strategize with the Finance Committee. Write an enrollment plan. Get in touch with social media. But don't worry about it. If we seek first the kingdom, the King will look after us. <u>Therefore</u>, we shouldn't worry.

Let's listen to the King again as he finishes his discourse in chapter 7: "Therefore everyone who hears these words of mine and puts them into practice is like a wise man who built his house on the rock. The rain came down, the streams rose, and the winds blew and beat against that house; yet it did not fall, because it had its foundation on the rock." **Amen.**

What are the reasons I am so worried about all the things I have to do to succeed?

What practices would help me put the kingdom first?

Dear Jesus: Worrying is as natural as breathing. It creeps up behind me, it knocks me sideways, it attacks me from the front. There are times when worry is so great, I have to talk to a counselor. Help me to put the kingdom first. Help me to trust your word and to trust you as The Word. Let your love drive out my fear. Thank you for always keeping your covenant with us. Thank you for always being with me even when I don't believe it. Thank you for promising that I will be in the kingdom, in a house you have prepared for me. Amen.

149. WHICH CHILDREN ARE HONORABLE?

Bible Reference: "When he noticed how the guests chose the place of honor he told them a parable" (Luke 15:9).

Meditation: Who is on the walls of our hallways and in the trophy cabinets in the front entranceway? Go and have a look. Make a list. And then pray over it, reading the school's mission between each heartfelt petition. Ask the question: Who are we missing? I've often wondered how Christian schools I visit determine whom to honor so publicly. One school I've gone to has the names of all the donors on the walls. Almost every school has a proud sports trophy cabinet next to the gym or in the entranceway. Schools that end with grade 8 or grade 12 will put up photos of their entire graduating classes, always looking splendid in beautiful suits and dresses or caps and gowns.

Is that the mission of the school? Does that represent your mission? Does it tell the visitor that you are a Christian school? But let's dig a little deeper still. Which children have we forgotten to honor because they just do the conventional actions or join the conventional clubs or sports? The lead in the musical, the quarterback, the valedictorian, those who stand out – these children are well honored. But do they obscure or hide from us those who are deserving of a high seat at the table? If your mission speaks of leadership, do you honor servant leaders (cf. Luke 1:38)? If your mission speaks of service to others, do you honor those who give willingly to the community, often behind closed doors (cf. Matthew 6:3)? If your mission speaks of glorifying God, do you honor those who lead God's worship (cf. Psalm 68:24-26)?

Think about the messages that your school walls tell. I often bring to mind that great scene in "Chariots of Fire" where Eric Liddell is lining up for his 440-yard run, having refused to run the 100-yard race on a Sunday. An American runs up to him and puts in his hand a piece of paper with a quotation from 1 Samuel 2:30, "Those who honor me I will honor." He ran, won, and broke the world record. Your leadership can be a reflection of that verse – honor those who are truly enacting the school's mission. Then your walls will be a witness to a powerful and inspiring story.

When you look at your mission statement, who is being missed who should be honored?

What does honor mean at my school? What makes it different from the schools around me?

Dear Jesus: It's pretty easy to be seduced by the world's version of honor. You have given us a different standard to live by. Help me to be inspired in my leadership to recognize children, certainly for the traditionally honorable achievements, but also for those achievements that are not so obvious. Help me to believe that those are really important too. Amen.

150. I AM A LIGHT

Bible Reference: "You are the light that gives light to the world. In the same way, you should be a light for other people. Live so that they will see the good things you do and praise your Father in heaven" (Matthew 5:14-16).

Meditation: As a Christian educator you have chosen a life of light-giving! Wow!

Jesus teaches us that the most esteemed men and women are not the movie stars, political leaders, or the CEOs of Fortune 500 companies. On the contrary, Jesus teaches that the greatest among us are those who choose to minister and serve, relieving the darkness and shining light on the shadow of death.

We lead by the words we speak and the lives we live, but not necessarily in that order. Dark and light cannot survive together. We must make certain that the lives we lead are in harmony with the lessons we preach. Leading with light includes leading with hope, with resurrection joy, and with enacted love in every situation.

So an important part of God's yoke for you as a leader is found in the example that you set for your school. Are you the kind of leader whose life serves as a memorable model of righteousness and godliness? Do you inspire for the future? Are you resolute in the storm and a healer of the wound? Remember that you are a powerful force for good in your school and in the world. The messages that you teach and the life that you lead can have a profound impact upon your school. All of us can fondly remember teachers who greatly influenced our own lives. Now it's your turn. Our schools need and deserve encouraging leaders and mentors and worthy role models. As you stand before your staff and students each day, remember you teach not only "what you know" but also "who you are."

As you start to think about next year, look to the example of our Savior Jesus Christ who humbled himself and became a servant. He is the Light of the World. He is your example.

Is your leadership full of light?

What does a leadership of light mean for you and your colleagues?

Lord, I want to be a light for you and your kingdom. Help me to keep my character and reputation above reproach. Give me wisdom as I seek to communicate clearly and competently. Help me to love people just as you love me. May all I do be for your glory alone. Amen.

REFLECTION

It is time to take a break and think about the journey you are on. Use this page to reflect on how you can accelerate your impact as a Christian school leader.

151. I CAN BE ANGRY AND HURT!

Bible Reference: "O Lord, do not delay!" (Psalm 70:5).

Meditation: A friend of mine lost his 8-year-old son to a boating accident. It wasn't just one of those things. It was and is a heart-wrenching tragedy that has no explanation. "Be pleased O God to deliver me, O Lord make haste to help me!" It wasn't my son, and yet I felt strangely moved because I knew of this friend's goodness and faith. Why does evil happen to good people?

It's at times like this that shouting can really help. I hate it when people say stupid things like, You'll get over it, or maybe worse, God will teach you through this. He very well might, but I can't believe he wanted it to happen. What sense would that make? "Let those be put to shame and confusion who seek my life. Let those be turned back and brought to dishonor who desire to hurt me. Let those who say Aha Aha turn back because of their shame" (2,3).

Events in your professional life can bring you to the same point of anger and hurt. It's not uncommon at Christian schools. A new pastor brings discord from the church. A married teacher you admired runs off with another person. There is a fire. A child dies. You are unjustly fired by your Board. Every year, there are myriads of stories. "Let all who seek you rejoice and be glad in you. Let those who love your salvation say evermore, God is great" (4). We need hope. We need a future. We need trust.

Don't repress that anger and hurt. With the Psalmist, be truly human. We were given emotions and they are useful to us. With the Psalmist, speak to God, rail at him! He sheds tears with us and will hold us in his arms as a parent holds a raging child. And in the depths of our hearts, he speaks love, compassion, and peace to us. "But I am poor and needy; hasten to me, O God! You are my help and my deliverer; O Lord do not delay!" (5).

Are there events and relationships that you have not expressed anger and hurt over yet?

Are you able to be real with your God who himself walked this earth?

Dear Jesus: You know what it is to get angry. You know what it is to be betrayed and hurt. You know what it is to love and for that love not to be returned. Help me to have the courage to be a real person, to be angry and hurt, to accept the feelings that I have. Then, let me also turn to you for solace and lean on you as you leaned on your Father in heaven. Amen.

152. IT DOESN'T HAVE TO MAKE SENSE

Bible Reference: "Near the cross of Jesus stood his mother, his mother's sister, Mary the wife of Clopas, and Mary Magdalene" (John 19:25).

Meditation: Obedience is a funny thing. We are brought up, and we bring up our children, to be rational, to ask for the reasons for things. We provide reasons to our children for what we want them to do. We believe it has to make sense.

But obedience isn't nice and neat and tidy like that. We know that with our children because there are not a few times when we get to the point of saying, "Because I said so!" The child just can't understand the long-term consequences of doing / not doing an action. Or the child doesn't understand the importance of habit-forming. "Because I said so" is short-hand for me saying that, as an adult, I know this is important for you even though you don't understand it today.

We are the children of God in exactly the same way. God asks for our obedience, not because He is an angry King who demands subservience, but because he is a tender, loving Father who wants the best for us and knows that understanding will come as we mature in the faith, gain experience, practice love of God and mankind, study his Word. How else can we think of the scene at the foot of the cross where Jesus' mother and closest friends all stood in sorrow too deep to even express? How could they understand that their obedience would make sense at the empty tomb?

Let us practice obedience ourselves. It is for our own good that God asks it of us. Some things he gives us to understand now. But other things are "through a glass darkly." When we travel through the veil of death, we will understand the why.

What am I impatient with, wanting to know the reason for?

Can I be obedient even as Mary, mother of Jesus, was obedient?

Dear Jesus: Obedience is hard. I am a stubborn and willful person. Help me trust your loving goodness. Help me be obedient and model that in my leadership. Thank you for the obedience you showed your Father as you went to the cross. Thank you for the obedience of your mother and friends. Let me "take captive every thought to make it obedient" to you. Amen.
(2 Corinthians 10:5)

153. HEALTHY OR SICK?

Bible Reference: "It is not the healthy who need the doctor but the sick. I have not come to call the righteous but sinners" (Mark 2:17).

Meditation: There's no simple answer to the question: Who is your school for? We all are concerned to ensure that our children are protected – we do not want to put them at risk either physically, emotionally, intellectually, or spiritually. We are also concerned to bring children into the loving embrace of a school that embodies Jesus. Which children does that include?

In academics, we make the decision about admission with attempted precision. We give tests; we observe in a school visit; we read references; we interview the student and the parents. We decide whether we can serve the child with the resources we have.

What about spiritually? Can we make that decision with precision? Some of us try to by standing on our denominational identity. It's the equivalent of an academic test. If you are in our church, you qualify; if you are not in our church, you don't qualify. Or we have a statement of faith, sometimes so long and complex, it's hard to imagine most people reading it let alone understanding it. Some of us almost ignore the "religious" side, deciding that we'll worry about that once the child is in the classroom. We even change our mind about the qualification depending on our enrollment numbers.

Is it simpler than that? Is the call of Jesus the simplest spiritual qualification? As we determine whether we can meet intellectual and physical needs through some objective assessment, I wonder if, from a spiritual perspective, we should just call out: "Follow me!"

I am a leader in a Christian school. Which children do I want to follow Jesus?

What is it that makes the invitation of a Christian school authentic?

Dear Jesus: In your ministry on earth, the requirements for being a member of your group were very simple. Is it really that simple for our school? Lord, give me a discerning heart to understand what to do with "follow me." Help me know where to lead my school – how to think about the children who come to our doors. Thank you for your Incarnation and presence here on earth. Thank you for your amazing open invitation to me. Amen.

154. A TRIPTYCH: PSALM 7

Bible Reference: "Lord my God, I take refuge in you; save and deliver me from all who pursue me" (Psalm 7:1).

Meditation: How many enemies do I have? Oh, I know I'm not supposed to think in that way, and maybe it's a bit extreme. But there are days when I feel surrounded by foes, when the Satan seems to be gnawing at my heels and frustrating my every move. I am pursued by frustration, it feels, at every turn.

- My Board shows up once a month and just tells me I'm doing a good job – they don't want to get their hands dirty, unless they have a complaint about their own child's experience.
- I slaved last year and we still lost students.
- Just last week, I had to clean up after one of my teachers who upset a parent completely needlessly.
- The budget is so lean I can't even bring doughnuts to the faculty meeting anymore.

How much can I take? Lord, don't let the naysayers triumph! Don't give the heathen the satisfaction of my failure! Don't let those who desire this school's downfall succeed!

Is it my fault? Am I guilty of some great sin? No! Not so! I take refuge in your righteousness. I glory in your justice. I gloat in your vindication. You know my mind and my heart. You know that I am upright in heart. Be my shield in my distress; you will not let me be ripped apart, trampled to death. Do not let me be disillusioned. Do not let me fall into a pit. I will give thanks to the Lord because of his righteousness; I will sing the praises of the name of the LORD Most High.

How do you respond when your heart is in torment?

How can you rest on God's righteousness and not be overwhelmed by guilt?

Dear Jesus: Even you, Lord, sweated blood and asked for the cup to be taken away from you. You know how it feels to be this way, to feel as if every man's hand is against you. You know. Help me to rest in the arms of the Father and to be obedient to the Word and respond to the urgings of the Spirit. Thank you that you said that everything would work out for those who love the Lord. I believe. Help my unbelief. Amen.

155. A TRIPTYCH: PSALM 8

Bible Reference: "Lord, our Lord, how majestic is your name in all the earth!" (Psalm 8:1).

Meditation: You remind me where it all began. You remind me that you are the Creator of everything, that everything that is belongs to you. You remind me that you gave me that everything, put everything under my feet. You remind me that I am your image bearer on earth. Despite my insignificance compared with your majesty, you nonetheless give me significance, make me a little lower than the angels, give me dominion, give me blessed work to accomplish for your glory.

And you remind me that I have an even more blessed position. As a leader in a Christian school, I am surrounded by children, even infants, whose praise gives me a stronghold against the Satan. Stockbrokers can't say that on Wall Street! Diplomats can't say that in their embassies! But I am given a stronghold in my school every time my children sing your praise and confess your name.

You made the expanses of the universe and I feel tiny thinking about it. You put the moon and the stars in the sky to give light in darkness and I want to be like them. I am amazed that you can do such great things and still pay attention to me. More than that, you have given me dominion! Let me use it wisely. You have given me power over others! Let me be humble. You have put everything under my feet! Let me tread carefully.

O Lord, our Lord, how majestic is your name in all the earth. What a privilege to be able to say "our Lord"! I praise you for your humility in allowing me to be part of you and your intention for the world. I am awed by your humility in coming to earth and becoming fully man to die on my behalf. O Lord, our Lord, how majestic is your name in all the earth!

Have I stopped surrounding myself with the sound of God's praise?

What are ways in which my leadership can reflect the strength of the children I serve?

Dear Jesus: You remind me that I have to become a little child to enter the kingdom of heaven. Through this psalm you remind me why. Help me to become a little child again and always sing your praise. Help me to carry out my God-given tasks to your glory. Thank you for making me a new Adam through your sacrifice. Amen.
(Matthew 18:3)

156.   A TRIPTYCH: PSALM 9

Bible Reference: "I will give thanks to you, Lord, with all my heart; I will tell of all your wonderful deeds" (Psalm 9:1).

Meditation: Lord, you made a covenant with Noah; you made a covenant with Abraham; to fulfill that covenant, you led the children of Israel out of bondage in Egypt; you came and were present in Solomon's Temple; you brought them back to the land of milk and honey from the captivity of Babylon; you wept for them as they disobeyed you and followed other gods; you came and became present for us in your life, death, and resurrection; you asked us to be a temple in our own bodies for you.

I thank you, Lord, for everything that you have given me, nothing of my own deserving. Yes, many things are challenges in my leadership. Through them all shines the reality of you as righteous judge, as our God who never forsakes his children, as someone who lifts me up from the gates of death. You are my life and in you I am never forgotten.

And I am astonished that I, a breath, mere decades of living, am considered so valuable that you know even the hairs of my head, that you love me to the extent of sending your only Son, that you pay attention to my thoughts and prayers. I give thanks to you with my whole heart. I give thanks to you with my whole heart. I give thanks to you with my whole heart. I give thanks to you with my whole heart.

Do my followers (as a Christian leader) know that I am thankful? How would they know?

In what ways do I acknowledge the beauty of God's presence in my community and bring my community through to thankfulness?

Dear Jesus: Thank you. Thank you. Thank you. Amen.

157. GOD HONORS ME!

Bible Reference: "I will deliver him and honor him" (Psalm 91:15).

Meditation: It's truly amazing what happened this year. We, God and I, we accomplished a lot. I know that because I can see it with my own eyes. I know I acknowledged God's name. And God answered me when I called upon him; he is with me in trouble; he honored me. The Psalmist is right. Again.

At the last game, a parent came up to me and praised my leadership. I thank you, Lord. You honor me.

After a chapel where I spoke, a student came and thanked me and said my words had touched him. I thank you, Lord. You honor me.

Just sitting in my office one day, an email popped up from a family saying that they were re-enrolling their children, and what a blessing the school was in their lives. I thank you, Lord. You honor me.

Another student came and sat next to me at lunch and told me about the college she was going to and how she was going to praise the Lord for his leading. I thank you, Lord. You honor me.

At a leadership meeting, we went around the room and spoke aloud something amazing that had happened in each person's area. It was humbling to hear. I thank you, Lord. You honor me.

I visited a donor couple in their house. We sat and had coffee. They told me that they could think of no better place to invest their money. I thank you, Lord. You honor me.

I am amazed that when I make the Most High my dwelling place, when I acknowledge his name, God shows me my salvation.

Can I be amazed on a daily basis?

How can each person on campus feel the blessing of the Lord?

Dear Jesus: By your death and resurrection, you made possible everything that happens in my school. Be at my side and help me to stay faithful. When I doubt, move my heart. When I speak unbelief, touch my lips. When I act unfaithfully, stay faithful with me. Thank you for your steadfastness through the times of trouble that you had. I honor you; I love you; I follow you. Amen.

158. WHO DESERVES WHAT?

Bible Reference: "Take your pay and go. I want to give the man who was hired last the same as I gave you" (Matthew 20:14).

Meditation: I know this parable is about salvation. It challenges me today to think that the new hire has the same value for you as I do. It challenges me to think that the brigand on the cross will be with you for eternity. If I have to translate it into everyday life, it almost feels worse. How do I lead with that in mind?

Are my parents all of equal value? The family that just made the transformational lead gift to the campaign as much as the couple that struggled to make the last tuition payment? The 15-year volunteer who is now on the Board as much as the new parent who just showed up in my office to complain about lunch?

And the new teacher I must think of having equal value with my 25-year veteran star? And act on that thought?

And for the students? You can't mean that the 4.0 quarterback with the dazzling grin has the same value as the 2.2 kid who leaves immediately after school and rarely cracks a smile? You want me to value the Ivy League student in the same way as I value the kid who graduates and goes to work as a mechanic?

Leadership in this way can only be disastrous, surely! That's not the way the world works. Unless I have the wrong idea about leadership entirely.

Maybe, instead of paying lip service to being a servant leader, I should actually take it seriously. I know you were called the suffering servant and you are the greatest leader of all time. You wanted all to be in Paradise with you today. I have to do the same.

How have my values been affected by the values of the world and its leader – Satan?

How can I value people in the way Jesus did?

Dear Jesus: You came not to lord it over everyone but to serve. You told your disciples that the first shall be last and the last shall be first. You spoke this parable about God's generous love. Help me to be just as generous in my own leadership. Help me to take to heart your example of servant leadership. Strengthen me to continuously study your Word to fill me with God's wisdom. Thank you for all kinds of adults and children around me. Thank you for the infinite value you have placed on them through your death and resurrection. Amen.

159. WASTING PEOPLE

Bible Reference: "Because no one has hired us" (Matthew 20:6).

Meditation: It's easy to get into a rut when you think about the people around you. They "ARE" a certain way and you know them well. In fact, some of them you've known for a very long time, even decades. Is it possible that your thinking about them has not progressed as fast as they have?

I come across this problem routinely in dealing with my children. They came into the world as precious, helpless, dependent infants who moved toward me at every opportunity. It's easy for me to hang onto that picture of them as they travel through their various developmental stages. I listen to people talking about adolescence as if it is a terrible stage and they can't wait for their children to move through it. Why? Because they are no longer cute, and we prefer them that way. They are no longer dependent, and we enjoyed that feeling. They are no longer always moving toward us, and we sense a loss.

When my children, who were in university, came home over Christmas, they were independent, thoughtful, argumentative; they were themselves. I had to train myself to enjoy this because years of doing <u>for</u> them trained my brain to think about them in a way that is no longer close to being true.

Are you "seeing" the people around you as the same as when you first met? I find people in the marketplace that were not hired so fascinating. They were there in plain sight all day long, yet they were not seen. They were willing to work if someone hired them. When they were hired, they immediately set to work even though there was little time left in the day. Those people exist in our school. Am I seeing them? Can I update who I think they were to who they really are today? That's as true for my students as the adults!

What skills, aptitudes, possibilities, capacities are hiding in plain sight around you?

What are the factors that might stop you recognizing people's growth and development?

Dear Jesus: You continually push us to grow and move from "milk" to "meat." You expect that we will mature and develop and lead in better and better ways. Help me to see that in those around me. Help me expect that teachers and staff members and colleagues and Board members and children will all grow and change – help me enjoy those changes and put them to good use. Thank you that you are using my talents to serve you. Amen.

160. THE STARS ARE SHINING – IT'S TIME FOR A WALK!

Bible Reference: "Praise him, sun and moon; praise him, all you shining stars" (Psalm 148:3).

Meditation: You've come home from the school and are ready to settle in for the night. Supper is eaten; the family has done the dishes; the children are doing homework or reading or playing a video game; the sofa beckons with its own book, snacks, hot chocolate laid out.

Leave them for an hour. Don't sit down. The stars are shining! Go for a walk!

Praising God is something we do in church, in study groups, in daylight. Of course, that's good. Try a different perspective. Genesis says: "He also made the stars" (1:16). God showed Abram the stars and promised that his descendants would be as numerous as they were. That star promise was repeated to Abraham, Isaac, Israel, and David. Moses held God accountable to it at the time of the golden calf. It inspired those who returned from exile to build the 2nd Temple. The Psalmist says that God has given each and every star a name and knows each one! (Psalm 147:4). The magi followed a star to Jesus. The light of the stars will be covered up at the 2nd coming of Jesus. Go walk under the stars.

Reflect on God's greatness in the glory of creation. Consider his promises to his people. Think about the glory of God coming to earth by the sign of a star. Remember the signs in the heavens, among the stars, that will presage his glorious return to earth. Give thanks to God for the stars that give light at night and that reflect the goodness and the wisdom of God. Like anything that has been made, they are not to be worshipped but seen to reflect the One whom we should worship, the Creator of all.

And stand amazed that as you look up at them, they praise God as well, singing a cosmic song of joy and blessing: "Let them praise the name of the Lord, for his name alone is exalted; his splendor is above the earth and the heavens. And he has raised up for his people a horn, the praise of all his faithful servants, of Israel, the people close to his heart" (Psalm 148:13-14).

Do you know, really know, that the whole of creation praises God, that you are just one voice among cosmic trillions?

In what ways does your leadership point to the blessing of creation and its praise of its Creator?

Dear Jesus: You created everything from nothing. Man often worships the creation. Yet creation itself witnesses to the Creator with its own cosmic song. Help me to stand often in the midst of what you have created and worship together with it. Thank you for the witness of sun and moon and stars. Amen.

161. HAD A CONVERSATION WITH ME RECENTLY?

Bible Reference: "Just then, the disciples returned and were surprised to find him talking with a woman" (John 4:27).

Meditation: One commentary says of this passage telling the story of the Samaritan woman: "We can scarcely believe that the evangelist did not mean for us to contrast the unsatisfactory faith of the Jews (John 2: 23-25) based on a superficial admiration of miracles with the deeper faith of the Samaritans based on the Word of Jesus" (bible.org). Let's take it one step further. Let's contrast it with the story, just one chapter previously, about Nicodemus who comes at night. While the Samaritan woman and her people believed in Jesus, Scripture does not say that Nicodemus does. Indeed, the interlude between the two stories has John the Baptist making that very point – whoever believes will have eternal life; whoever rejects the Son will not see life.

What about you? A Christian leader? A representative of Jesus in your school and in your community? Who have you talked to recently? Think about it! I mean, really think about it!

It's easy to get into a pattern of talking with people who like you, whom you trust, with whom you agree. Of course. It's understandable. First, it's efficient. Being with people who agree with you or say yes to you takes a lot less time than talking with the opposite. Second, it affirms you in who you are and what you believe. Third, it sort of makes sense since trust is key to taking advice. Why talk to people you don't know and / or don't trust?

But you are a leader not just in, but *of* a school, of a community. You are the leader of all of them, not just the ones you like and who like you. Will you walk out of your office today and find someone you have never talked to and have a conversation? It might be an adult, a Board member, a child, a teenager. They are all Samaritan women at the well. They need you as much or even more than your friends do. Go talk with them! Talk with one every day.

With how many people in your school / community have you actually had a real conversation?

Is Jesus just too hard an act to follow?

Dear Jesus: You talked with everyone, it seems. You talked with Samaritans, Roman officers, tax collectors, real rotten scumbags, religious opponents. Your objective was always to be the light of the world to them. Help me to grow in my leadership so that I can also talk with everyone, the loveable as well as the unlovable. Thank you that you love me. Amen.

162. DO YOU HAVE TO SHOUT TO BE NOTICED?

Bible Reference: "Many rebuked him and told him to be quiet, but he shouted all the more" (Mark 10:48).

Meditation: When I was growing up, it was clear who the "in people" were. The kids in sports were almost always the top dogs. After all, they were athletic and thus good-looking, they had some confidence based on their team exploits, they were encouraged to act and not sit back, they were strong. And they were male. The female athletes didn't command the same respect. Nor did the male or female actors, although they were not despised either in my school. And to be in the madrigal group was a feather in your cap since the music teacher was maybe the most popular teacher in school. There were lots of groups and, depending on the group, determined where you sat and how you walked down the corridor.

The blind man was part of a group too. It's not just that he was blind, but that, because of that blindness, he was not a full part of the community. Jesus' healing of him was not just a good thing physically, but far more important, a radical thing in terms of his family, his village, his synagogue, the nation of Israel. He could not only see, he could think of himself as part of the covenant again and look forward to God's kingdom. He was whole physically, and his community would accept him as whole spiritually.

Leadership in our schools can be complex when we start to consider who is getting the "mission" full-bore and who is only accessing a piece of it. Not everyone in a school feels a full citizen. They are not equally picked to be part of the in group. They are not even all thought of when possibilities come up. Some are invisible. We would like to imagine that our community is different, that everyone is equally a member. The blind man reminds us that this is not so.

When was the last time that we had a good leadership conversation about the invisible members of our community?

What about those who are not highly regarded?

Dear Jesus: Your purpose was to bring forgiveness of sins and the restoration of your kingdom to all nations, to everybody. Help me lead in a school where everyone can be a part of the community, where everyone can walk down the center of the corridor. Thank you for giving me the leadership role that gives me the power to ask questions and interrogate answers. Amen.

163. DON'T WORRY – GOD LOVES MORE THAN WE DO

Bible Reference: "Tremble, earth, at the presence of the Lord, at the presence of the God of Jacob, who turned the rock into a pool, the hard rock into springs of water" (Psalm 114:8).

Meditation: How do I love like God? I go through Good Friday and Easter Sunday and am overwhelmed by the magnificent and outrageous love of God for me. I am most of the way through another school year that has made painfully clear how lacking my own love is for God and for my neighbor. The demand of God that I love seems too much. I tremble at the presence of the Lord.

But Jesus is "the pioneer and perfecter of our faith" (Hebrews 12:2). Jesus "loves us and has freed us from our sins by his blood" (Revelation 1:5). In my school, there is "neither Jew nor Gentile, neither slave nor free, nor is there male and female, for (we) are all one in Christ Jesus" (Galatians 3:8). I, my colleagues, my students, my parents, my Board Trustees, all of us can lay claim to "the incomparable riches of his grace, expressed in his kindness to us in Christ Jesus" (Ephesians 2:7). I am a "prisoner of Christ Jesus" (Philemon 1:9). In Jesus, I am freed to love.

I cannot love like God – he is Love. But I can be grateful that God loves me and loves me perfectly. His presence turns the hardness of accusation and the rock of judgment into pools of living water. Jesus tells us that in the springs of water we enter the kingdom of God (John 3:5), that the pool is living water that gives eternal life (John 4:10), that through Jesus I can also be a source of living water (John 7:38). I cannot be Love; but I can love – and that is good enough.

Can I get over feeling inadequate and start doing some "skipping"?

In what ways do I reflect the love of God?

Dear Jesus: You know me and you know my imperfections. Yet, the Psalmist declares that you made me wonderfully. Help me to acknowledge what God has done for me and rejoice that he has done great things for me. Help me to love fully without worrying about how much. Thank you for your love for me shown through your life, death, and resurrection. Amen.
Psalm 139:14

164. FRIENDSHIP AND BEING A FRIEND

Bible Reference: "Who is this? He commands even the winds and the water, and they obey him" (Luke 8:25).

Meditation: Spring is a time of thunderstorms, and last night was a great example of it. The rain lashed the house where I was staying, the wind whipped the trees back and forth, and the roll of thunder with answering flashes searing across the sky was an awesome backdrop. On the one hand I wanted to run out into the middle of the storm and feel the rain coursing through my hair, and on the other hand I felt a great urge to kneel and pray for deliverance.

Thunderstorms seem to parallel the disciples' encounters with Jesus. On the one hand, Jesus was the good guy who turned water into wine (amazing but fun!), who healed and gave them power to heal (they seemed to get quite a kick out of that). On the other hand, Jesus could seem like, well, the Son of God – he commanded the storm to stop, he walked on water, he walked through crowds as if they weren't there, he bantered with the intellectuals of the day, handling them so easily they eventually gave up.

He obviously didn't want to be an austere, distant part of their lives. This is what he said one time: "I no longer call you servants, because a servant does not know his master's business. Instead, I have called you friends, for everything that I learned from my Father I have made known to you" (John 15:15). How does the Christ, the Messiah, **be** a friend? Can we believe that? In the midst of that thunderstorm on Lake Galilee, he is our friend. In the midst of death and the amazement of resurrection, he is our Friend. What does that even mean?

Can we be friends with those around us? If Jesus is our Friend, what does that imply about our students, our sisters and brothers in ministry? It's terrifying. God embraces us. We are to embrace each other. In the storm as much as in the fellowship meal.

Does Christian leadership mean that I am to call everyone "friend"?

If someone is not my "friend," what is she? What is he?

Dear Jesus: You were scary in the eyes of your disciples. You are scary to me as well. You call me a friend. That's seems too much to handle. Help me to be "with" those in my school. Whether the school is in the eye of the storm or whether it is sailing along in clear weather, help me to lead with the assurance and confidence that you are my Friend, and that those I lead are my 'friends'. Thank you for your desire to be close to me. Thank you for your love and for your friendship. Amen.

165. DISCIPLING AND LEADERSHIP

Bible Reference: "If every one of them were written down, I suppose that even the whole world would not have room for the books that would be written" (John 21:25).

Meditation: We call the Bible inerrant. We call it the Word of God. And we are right to do so. But think about it. There are only 4 Gospels, and they tell us about the life and death and resurrection of Jesus. There could have been hundreds of Gospels written about the life of Jesus – just the last three years of that life! Even if we acknowledge some poetic hyperbole by St. John, clearly the evangelists only wrote down the most, most, most important events and sayings of Jesus while on this earth. We can study the Gospels for years and read thousands of books about them. It's amazing to think that there could have been thousands of Gospels!

Would it be wrong to be grateful that there are only 4? It's like a good teacher. When you walk into the classroom and see all those expectant faces waiting for a year of wonder and exploration (at least I hope that's what happens at your school), do you give them a university-level deluge of concept and content? Of course you don't. You tell them a story. You start slowly. You develop their understanding over time and allow their knowledge and understanding to grow.

Thank God that he didn't want to deluge us either. The first 37 books of the Bible are a fantastic story. Can you imagine 37 books of Paul? Or 37 books of Jesus telling parables? No, God was gracious and gave us just enough to chew on and grow in faith in him. As a Christian leader, there might be a lesson for us in that. Discipling should follow God's example. Four short books is plenty. The child, the colleague, the new recruit, the person we meet at a conference, they need to be invited into God's kingdom, not overwhelmed by it.

When is less more?

How can I be a better leader of disciples?

Dear Jesus: You told the disciples and the crowds who followed you interesting stories. You discipled in bits and bites, by example and demonstration. Help me to be a better leader with less "preaching" and more ways of communicating, as you did. Help me to know when to speak, when to listen, and when to walk away. Thank you that you have given us the Gospels to instruct us in discipleship. Amen.

REFLECTION

It is time to take a break and think about the journey you are on. Use this page to reflect on how you can accelerate your impact as a Christian school leader.

_____
_____
_____
_____
_____
_____
_____
_____
_____
_____
_____
_____
_____
_____
_____
_____
_____
_____
_____
_____
_____
_____
_____
_____
_____
_____
_____
_____
_____
_____
_____

166. THE SUMMER'S ABOUT PRUNING AND GROWING – PART 1

Bible Reference: "Every branch that bears fruit, he prunes to make it bear more fruit" (John 15:2).

Meditation: The end of the school year is a funny time, in my experience. It was always great to celebrate what had been accomplished. It was wonderful to see students who had struggled so hard reap the rewards of their work. I loved acknowledging student leaders in a variety of ways. There was always a lot of focus on the students, but I sometimes struggled with what to say to faculty. "Great job, folks! See you next year!" Sounds okay but seems a bit flat.

It helped me to remember that the Christian teacher is on a journey. Since I usually taught, myself, I could reflect on my journey too. That journey didn't stop just because summer was there. It's certainly a time for holiday, for relaxing, enjoying family, hitting the mountains or the beach, throwing a ball for the dog, playing in the garden. It's lovely to have a more relaxed pace and not have so many meetings. But if that's all it is, then the time is not well spent.

What if the summer was a time for pruning? During the year, a teacher is working hard just to stay above water. It's all about doing, and evaluating, and discussing children, and attending events, and preparing events, and putting together lesson plans, and collaborating on the fly. There are certainly moments in the year when reflection and planning can happen. But that's not the norm. During the year is when we "bear fruit."

During the summer though, there is time to get better at what we do. Jesus talks about God pruning so that we can bear even more fruit. Each year, it seems, God expects us to get better and better. We may think it's unfortunate (!), but the implication is clear that growing is a godly expectation. To grow, we have to cut away the things that impede us. Pruning trees requires the removal of 20% to 30% of the foliage. Can we imagine pruning 20% of who we are in order to really grow?

What does the faculty meeting look like where you lead the growth conversation?

How can you support teachers in pruning and growing over the summer?

Dear Jesus: I know pruning is not intended to be judgmental. Help me to use words carefully so that I come across to my teachers as supportive. Help me to have a clean heart to provide a firm foundation for our conversation. Imbue me with your Spirit so that I can listen and learn from my teachers in order to support them. Keep me humble and don't let me jump to conclusions. Thank you that I have been cleansed and pruned by your Word. Amen.

167. THE SUMMER'S ABOUT PRUNING AND GROWING – PART 2

Bible Reference: "Every branch that bears fruit he prunes to make it bear more fruit" (John 15:2).

Meditation: Pruning is a dangerous activity. One website noted that overpruning causes *excessive wounds that must be healed, reduced food storage, increased interior sprouting, decreased tip growth, increased end weight on limbs, increased chances of sunscald/sun injury, increased maintenance expense, increased chances of wind or ice damage, AN UGLY TREE!* (http://www.arborilogical.com/tree-knowledge-articles-publications/dangers-of-over-pruning/). Ouch!

This is maybe the toughest test of leadership. When you prune, you must be judicious because each cut is a wound that must have time to heal. Too many cuts and you will kill the plant you are trying to help. Not enough and the plant will become diseased and unhealthy. With people, the parallels are uncanny. We must discern what season the person is in, which of those improvements are necessary now, and which can wait till later. We need to be humble so that our followers can't point at the "plank" in our own eyes (Matthew 7:3-5) and call us judgmental. We need to be communicators (cf. Colossians 4:6) who can speak so our followers can hear us. If you prune too hard, you can damage the person!

Of course, it is best if your followers can be self-aware and able to plan their own pruning and growth pattern. Pruning is best done during the dormant season which is why the summer is such a great time for it. It's not that change can't happen, and sometimes has to happen, during the year. But during the dormant season (cf. Ecclesiastes 3:1), it can be thoughtful, measured, not carried out in haste, pondered over, fine-tuned, adjusted. Sometimes you have to step back and let your followers think it through themselves without your "brilliant" advice. Other times, they seek your wisdom and you must share it. At other times still, you must direct because they lack experience, or the courage to self-examine, or the knowledge.

Pruning is not an option. It is a leadership responsibility. Take it on.

Is summer purposeful at your school?

Which of your followers needs subtle pruning and which needs heavy pruning?

Dear Jesus: It is rather scary to think of myself as a pruner. It would be much easier to leave it all to you. Help me to take on my leadership responsibility. I know that if I don't do it, my school can't move ahead. Give me inspirational words so that each person hears the call of God to grow. Give me wisdom and discernment in my individual conversations. I thank you that you are the vine and your Father is the vine-grower. Amen.

168. THE SUMMER'S ABOUT PRUNING AND GROWING – PART 3

Bible Reference: "Every branch that bears fruit he prunes to make it bear more fruit" (John 15:2).

Meditation: I don't find the leadership activity of pruning others an easy one. When I begin to apply it to myself, it is terrifying. Each part of who I am seems so key to my identity. I can't imagine getting rid of anything. I know I am not perfect, but when I have to look at what the imperfections are, they don't seem so bad after all.

What does your summer look like? Some Principals I talk to have their summer all planned out: a 2-week vacation with the family to relax; working in the office from 9 to 4; continuing to do admission tours and interviews; a couple of planning meetings; thinking about the beginning of the year, what the theme will be, what the faculty retreat will look like, how to start with a bang! All sounds pretty good – except for pruning. There's no pruning in there.

Can you add it in? Can you make it a key part of your summer? Can you take three hours every day to prune and grow? Maybe you identify key leadership knowledge deficits and put together a reading program; or you recognize that you are lacking in spiritual understanding and you read, spend time with a spiritual mentor, or even go on a spiritual retreat; or you ask your Board President and 2 or 3 leaders in the school to come in and do a 1-on-1 reflection to you as to where you need to grow; or you ask your spouse or best friend to identify your worst leadership habit and implement a plan to curb it.

Terrifying, right?

Remember that God has chosen you and appointed you to "bear much fruit" (vse. 16). God doesn't seem to have much time for mediocrity. He's big into "much." In this chapter alone, John uses the words "much" and "more" 3 times, and adds the phrase "bear fruit, fruit that will last." God is ambitious for your life. Are you ambitious too?

Who do you know who would be totally honest, in love, about where you need pruning?

Can you be as ambitious as God is for your life?

Dear Jesus: I am too much in love with myself. While you have helped me grow in so many ways, I know that you are urging me to continue that throughout my life. Give me the courage not to stop growing. Give me the wisdom to listen to my friends' insights. Give me the desire to become a better and better leader. Let me abide in you and bear much fruit that will last. Amen.

169. THE SUMMER IS FOR RE-CREATION

Bible Reference: "My soul rests in God alone, from whom comes my salvation" (Psalm 62:2).

Meditation: The end of the school year is a joyful time for the entire school community. Newly minted graduates are embarking on new paths, students anxiously await a slower pace and fewer commitments in the summer, as do faculty and staff. Central to this celebratory season is the concept of rest. Resting is essential for our well-being and sanity. The coming summer months provide us with the opportunity to rest and recharge – routinely. This time allows us to recreate, returning us to a state of physical and mental health. But what about our spiritual health? Have we sought ways to rest our spirit and make it strong? Unfortunately, we often neglect our spirit and fail to take care of it, especially when our regular workload becomes easier.

One year, the school's ex-officio chaplain, Fr. Tom Tavella, a Paulist priest, gave a homily at the year's closing mass to faculty and staff that many of us still talk about to this day. He made a play on the word "recreate" in the summer, reminding us this word can and should also be read as "re-create." Fr. Tom reminded us that God created our wonderful earth in 6 days and rested on the 7th. And, upon that day of rest but not before, he understood it to be *good*.

Fully realizing our good work requires rest and separation to change our perspective.

We should finish the school year exhausted for having poured ourselves into our students. As the year winds down, we should also feel both deeply satisfied and desperately desiring to rest. The summer months provide us with the opportunity to "re-create" ourselves spiritually, physically, and mentally, so that we return the following school year full and whole, prepared to expend ourselves again to build God's kingdom.

In what ways do I need to "re-create" myself over the summer?

How can Jesus accompany me on my recreational activities?

Heavenly Father, you invite me to rest in you, which is the best medicine for my weary soul and tired body. You modeled that in your earthly life when you rested many times. Sometimes it didn't work out because people wanted to feed from you. But you knew it was important and you took the time to do it. Help me to understand the power of restoration. Thank you for the Sabbath as a weekly reminder. Amen.

170. FINAL REFLECTIONS ON EXCELLENCE

Bible Reference: "Everyone brings out the choice wine first and then the cheaper wine after the guests have had too much to drink; but you have saved the best till now" (John 2:10).

Meditation: This is an amazing story – one of seven miracles that St. John talks about in his Gospel. But we are going to go in a different and pretty simple direction. The master of the banquet almost accuses the bridegroom of bringing out the best wine when many would not be able to appreciate it. It seems that Jesus cannot do anything except the best – the undertones in the story of the creation of the world in 6 days by just the Word, and it was all good, emphasize this reality. Jesus acts and can only act in an excellent manner.

As you reflect on the year that has almost come to an end, as you sit with your leadership team, as you review the year with your support group or sit at lunch with your Board President, consider those moments of the year that were truly excellent. You cannot aspire to the constancy of Jesus' excellence, but you can celebrate those times where the school really rose to the peak of its potential.

Was it at a detail level where individual students made breakthroughs in their learning? Was it the underperforming team that suddenly became inspired and fulfilled its potential? Was it the new teacher who became a leader over the course of the year? Or the veteran who once again, as she has for several years now, was a force in the classroom and an innovator with her colleagues? Was it an intervention that you personally had with a family that was under stress? Or your coaching of a faculty leader that led to significant growth? Or the implementation of a strategic item that gave the Board confidence and optimism about other initiatives?

Reflect on these examples of excellence in your school this year and give thanks.

Why is it easier to remember all the errors than celebrate what my leadership has resulted in?

Thinking about all these examples of excellence, how have I grown as a leader this year?

Dear Jesus: It is easy to be downcast by acknowledging my failures. Help me to truly see your hand at work in my life through the successes, and through the opportunities to grow that any failures provided me. Let me aspire to excellence every day, as you did. Thank you for your presence with me in those times of "triumph." Let me honor them and thus give you glory. Amen.

For Jesus; Through Mission; With Students

171. I GIVE THANKS TO THE LORD FOR HIS UNFAILING LOVE

Bible Reference: "Let them give thanks to the Lord for his unfailing love and his wonderful deeds for mankind" (Psalm 107:8, 15, 21, 31).

Meditation: It is the last day of the school year. Think back on the year. Pray now in three ways.

First, pray in desolation for the times you wandered, for when your soul fainted; for the times when you were sitting in darkness and gloom, when you were rebellious; for the times when you were sick in your sins, for your own self-loathing; for the times when you were at your wit's end, staggering and reeling like drunkards; for the times when you were thirsty and hungry and refused to eat good food and drink from the springs of living water.

Second, pray in thanks for the love of the Lord; for his leading along straight paths and finding of friends and neighbors who helped us; for his steadfast love and his gifts of food and drink, bread and wine, body and blood; for his guiding light in times of darkness and advocacy, giving us the victory in understanding and wisdom; for his healing of our flesh and spirit, even when we did not know how deep the wounds were; for being the Creator and Sustainer of our lives in every part.

Third, pray in joy for his wonderful deeds; for the miracle of new birth in the lives of children, and especially in the lives of *(add in the names of children who have grown so much this year)*; for his wonderful works in being true to his covenant with you; for his promise fulfilled in Jesus that he made to Abraham, Isaac, and Jacob, to Sara, Rebecca, and Leah; for that being true in the resurrection life you have experienced this year in your leadership.

Read Psalm 107 all the way through and repeat the last line 3 times: "Let those who are wise give heed to these things and consider the steadfast love of the Lord" (vse. 43).

Then say, Amen. Amen. Amen. Praise the Lord! And go into your summer with a blithe spirit, knowing that the Lord is with you from everlasting to everlasting.

Dear Jesus: Thank you for this year that has passed. Thank you for encouraging me to work in your harvest field. Thank you for being by my side. Thank you for being my strength in times of hardship. Thank you for your forgiveness so undeserved. Thank you for your salvation so freely given. Thank you for the victories and triumphs, some quiet and some exultantly loud. Thank you for the hope you give me. Bless me this summer. Amen. Praise the Lord!

WHERE IS MY JOURNEY HEADED NOW?

If I look back 10 years from now, what are the most important things that will have happened in my spiritual journey?

___

What do I have to do next?

___

CONCLUSION

You've made it through a year's journey. Hopefully, the devotions will continue to be inspiring to you as you continue on.

If you were to have a T-shirt made now, what words would you want to put on it?

If you are a member of CSM, contact us at christianschoolmanagement@gmail.com. We'll get it made for you and ship it to you at your school! If you are not a member, consider joining, and then ask us for your T-shirt.

If you really enjoyed this journey, tell us. If you would like another devotional similar to this, encourage us to write it. Maybe you would like to contribute 5 or 10 or 20 devotions to it!

We wish you every blessing as you continue on your journey. We leave you with Jesus, as we started.

"I have revealed you to those whom you gave me out of the world. They were yours; you gave them to me and they have obeyed your word. Now they know that everything you have given me comes from you. For I gave them the words you gave me and they accepted them. They knew with certainty that I came from you, and they believed that you sent me.

I pray for them. I am not praying for the world, but for those you have given me, for they are yours. All I have is yours, and all you have is mine. And glory has come to me through them. I will remain in the world no longer, but they are still in the world, and I am coming to you. Holy Father, protect them by the power of your name, the name you gave me, so that they may be one as we are one.

While I was with them, I protected them and kept them safe by that name you gave me. None has been lost except the one doomed to destruction so that Scripture would be fulfilled. I am coming to you now, but I say these things while I am still in the world, so that they may have the full measure of my joy within them.

I have given them your word and the world has hated them, for they are not of the world any more than I am of the world. My prayer is not that you take them out of the world but that you protect them from the evil one. They are not of the world, even as I am not of it. Sanctify them by the truth; your word is truth. As you sent me into the world, I have sent them into the world. For them I sanctify myself, that they too may be truly sanctified.

My prayer is not for them alone. I pray also for those who will believe in me through their message, that all of them may be one, Father, just as you are in me and I am in you. May they also be in us so that the world may believe that you have sent me. I have given them the glory that you gave me, that they may be one as we are one – I in them and you in me – so that they may be brought to complete unity. Then the world will know that you sent me and have loved them even as you have loved me" (John 17:6-23).

APPENDIX 1:
GOVERNANCE – THE CORD PRINCIPLE

Ecclesiastes 4:12 (NIV)
"A cord of three strands is not quickly broken."

The Christian school includes 3 organizational partners who work in service to the school's students:

1. The Board establishes the mission, hires the Head of School, holds the Head accountable for full classrooms, plans for the future, and provides the resources (money and facilities) needed for that plan to succeed.

2. The Administration, led by the Head, determines the vision, fills the school, carries out the Board's plan, and supports the faculty to success.

3. The faculty serve the children, deliver the mission, witness to the action of God in the lives of children, and act collaboratively as a professional learning community. The staff support both Administration and faculty by engaging with resources and planning for their effective deployment.

In the same way, the Christian school includes 3 human partners who cooperate in service to the child:

1. The parent(s) to whom God gives the responsibility of unity (the "two shall be one," reflecting the unity of God) within which the child grows safely, and through which the child, known by God from before the womb, can fully develop God's intent for her or his life.

2. The teacher, who is the intersect (the relationship-in-action) of the school's mission with the child and who is fundamentally concerned with empowering the child's agency in interaction with the school's mission.

3. The Head, who stands as the guardian of the child's healthy development, the proactive partner with the parent, and the sustainer of the teacher's Godly genius.

These 2 sets of 3 strands (organizational and human) form the Cord Principle created by Christian School Management (CSM). Together, they are effective, and the school operates harmoniously.

In conflict, or where the parts do not lift up each other's sphere, the school is in disarray and mission delivery is endangered. Let us discuss each of these in turn.

The Board of Trustees: This entity (sometimes also called the Board of Directors or Governing Board) has clear responsibilities and clear boundaries. *BoardSource* (Ten Basic Responsibilities of Nonprofit Boards, 2015) writes that "strong Board leadership is fundamental to a strong and effective organization" (p. 11). This strong leadership is often construed as running the school. Nothing could be further from the truth or more destructive. We encounter far too many Christian schools where the Board continuously interferes with the operations side of the fence, directing school employees and negating the authority of the Head. This has also led the Board to arbitrarily dismiss the Head, even in the middle of a contract, and assume the Head's responsibilities at the Board level. The Cord Principle is emphatic that the Board's sphere is strategic: establishing the school's mission and using it "as the first frame of reference when making decisions" (p. 21); hiring the Head, who is the Board's ONLY employee, who must then be supported and evaluated (ch. 3); setting the school's "strategic direction" together with the Head and using that direction "for budgeting and other priorities" (p. 39).

There is one other major consideration for the Board – in holding the Head accountable, a key metric is enrollment. This does not imply that there is a good and a bad enrollment in terms of school size. Good schools exist at 100 students and at 1,000. No, the metric is whether the school is full, whether there are empty seats. This is a key metric for which the Board holds the Head accountable.

There are, of course, other considerations for the Board – but if it can focus and do these 4 things brilliantly, the Board members can sleep easily at night. These tasks constitute the strategic function of the Board and can be contrasted with the operations function, which the Board is incompetent to carry out. This is an important understanding for individual Board members and the Board as a whole – as volunteers from many walks of life, the perspectives each brings to the collective table are invaluable. However, none is actually skilled in running a school and in running THIS school.

To avoid the "blind leading the blind" (Luke 6:39), the Board, for example, approves the budget, but the Head spends it; the Board identifies strategic priorities, but the Head executes them; the Board approves construction, but the construction company builds the building. The Board cord is both a strength and a potential noose – wise Board leadership understands the strategic / operations difference and leads strategically. This makes it a healthy organizational partner and allows it to contribute meaningfully to a strong and healthy school.

The second organizational partner is the Administration. It doesn't matter how small or large your school is and thus how many people are in the Administration. In some very small schools, it might be the Head, an admission / marketing part-time person, and a bookkeeper. In very large schools, the Administration might include the Head, a Chief Financial Officer, a Division Head or Principal of each division, an Admission Director, a Marketing Director, a Director of Development, an Athletics Director, and a Director of Guidance and College Counseling.

Wherever your school is, the Administration's task is as well defined as the Board's: deliver the mission with excellence, fill the school, carry out the strategic plan together with its financial framework, be disciplined around the budget, maintain a safe school. And it is clear how this works – the Board determines the budget (and thus sets tuition) while the Administration spends the budget; the Board creates the strategic plan and the budget to support it while the Administration implements; the Board creates and / or affirms the mission while the Administration interprets the mission in the light of everyday realities and uses it to guide and direct conversation and decision making. The Administration must be competent to run the school and, because no one was born with the skills to do such a complex thing, the Administration must also be committed to continuous improvement, thinking about administrative duties along spiritual, financial, organizational, curricular, and human resource lines and seeking to learn every day.

Note that the second task, after delivering the mission with excellence, is filling the school. This is not the same thing as balancing the budget. The latter is, of course, a good thing. But it is not a holy thing. It is merely practical. The holy thing is ensuring that no seat is empty for the Satan to sit on. Once you determine what size of school you are to have under grace, the Administration is bound to expend every effort to achieve enrollment success – a full school.

This is excellent modeling for the third organizational partner, the faculty and staff. Their primary task is to deliver the mission directly to the students / children of the school. This is sometimes lost on administrators who, being student-centered (cf. The Child Principle) think that they are also carrying out that task. Well, to some extent they are right. But they are not the Kindergarten teacher rolling on the floor all day with 5-year-olds or the music teacher working with choirs of 60 or 160 children in preparation for a worship service or a Christmas celebration. No, it is the teachers and the front-line staff (the assistants and the janitors and the lunch folks) who interact on a daily and minute-to-minute basis with the school's reason-for-existence, the children. Neither the Board nor the Administration can do those jobs, which are incredibly taxing and not always well compensated. We thus consider this partner the most *important* of the 3. The other 2 partners, Board and Administration, therefore have as their focus the support of the faculty and staff, and all they do is geared to that end.

The responsibility placed on the faculty and staff is glorious and also daunting: "The student is not above the teacher, but everyone who is fully trained will be like their teacher" (Luke 6:40). Their character and expertise must be beyond reproach. The science teacher, for example, must understand and really know science as well as be a Godly person. The 2 aspects of character and expertise must be constantly sought for and, as for all the partners, must be expanded through continuous professional renewal of body, soul, mind, and heart.

At the same time, to 'do' is not enough for a faculty member. The witness to the mission's action, what we would hopefully describe as the Spirit's action in the life of each child is a key responsibility. This communication from teacher to student is a reflective communication, enabling the child to understand the working of God's Spirit within them, and the outcome of their cooperation in this faithful living through their effort using God's good gifts. The communication from teacher to parent is an awakening communication, particularly in these days of emotional distance. For the parent to know and understand how their very own flesh and blood is progressing, growing, maturing within and through God's love expressed in the teacher's actions is to appreciate, enjoy, and be with their own child as together they witness in the world as a family.

The 3 human partners form a cord within and around the 3 organizational partners and, of course, there is overlap. While these principles are primarily focused on the excellent operations of Christian schools, we must always remember that the students come to school, but they belong to their families. At the same time, this is a complicated relationship because the government has mandated that the child be educated, although that can happen in a variety of ways – home schooling, public and private schooling, to identify the basic methods. So the government mandates, the parent chooses, and the student goes to school. What is the importance then of the parent, and how does the parent fit into the cord?

There have been many learned books and articles written about this, and we make no effort to replicate or compete with them. We take a very practical stance. Parents are responsible for their children: "Children, obey your parents in the Lord for this is right" (Ephesians 6:1). And they are distinct from them: "Parents are not to be put to death for their children, nor children put to death for their parents; each will die for their own sin" (Deuteronomy 24:16). The school is responsible for the children through the contract that is signed and because it takes on legal responsibilities. For example, Garcia v. City of New York (1996) held that schools, once they take over physical custody and control of children, effectively take the place of their parents and guardians to both control and protect them. But schools have responsibilities beyond the parent because they act as representatives of the state. In this relationship, the Head takes a leadership role for her or his faculty and staff and has responsibility for mission delivery.

We would thus say that the parents' task is to choose a school that is consistent with their ambition for their child(ren). This is usually epitomized by the school's mission and values, and felt through the sense of community the Christian school has. Once that choice is made, the parent does not relinquish responsibility to support the school to effectively educate the child. At the same time, the parent must now submit to the school's authority, given to it both by the parent and the state: "Have confidence in your leaders and submit to their authority, because they keep watch over you as those who must give an account. Do this so that their work will be a joy, not a burden, for that would be of no benefit to you" (Hebrews 13:17).

That authority is localized in the Head, who has been appointed by the Board of Trustees and who has the power to both accept and reject a student. This authority is not unlimited, however, because at the end of each day the school gives the child back to the parent. This is why it is the Cord Principle – the 3 cords cannot be untangled without causing great harm to the child. The 3 cords must cooperate on the basis of mission and the Child Principle. When such cooperation exists, we typically experience the most powerful outcomes in the child's life.

APPENDIX 2: THE CHRISTIAN SCHOOL – THE CHILD PRINCIPLE

Matthew 19:14
"Jesus said, 'Let the little children come to me, and do not hinder them, for the kingdom of heaven belongs to such as these.'"

Mark 10:14
"When Jesus saw this, he was indignant. He said to them, 'Let the little children come to me, and do not hinder them, for the kingdom of God belongs to such as these.'"

Luke 18:16
"But Jesus called the children to him and said, 'Let the little children come to me, and do not hinder them, for the kingdom of God belongs to such as these.'"

Matthew 18:3-5
"And he said: 'Truly I tell you, unless you change and become like little children, you will never enter the kingdom of heaven. Therefore, whoever takes the lowly position of this child is the greatest in the kingdom of heaven. And whoever welcomes one such child in my name welcomes me.'"

As the Christian school strives to implement the Child Principle, it recognizes that all 3 of the Synoptic Gospels tell adults to stop getting in the child's way. The Child Principle, as defined by Christian School Management (CSM), requires the Christian school to:

- Put the child first (be student-centered).
- Instruct adults to meet the child where the child is first, before requiring the child to meet the adult where the adult is.
- Recognize that authority is there to serve the child, not to lord it over the child.

We need to be clear that child-centeredness is operating with the child at the center under the authority of God. Being child-centered should never be considered outside of the context of God's love and grace. First comes the recognition that we believe in God and that knowledge of God is primary: "Only be careful, and watch yourselves closely so that you do not forget the things your eyes have seen or let them fade from your heart as long as you live. Teach them to your children and to their children after them" (Deuteronomy 4:9). The cry to not forget is key to our status as a religion that is embedded in a teleological history centered in incarnation and resurrection.

But when we think of the child within the context of the Christian school, we quickly recognize that adults create school often to their own benefit, not to the primary benefit of the child. Let's think of a couple of actual examples:

- We create schedules that fit the convenience of teachers and administrators rather than the clear needs of the child.
- We teach in a way that is comfortable for me and reflects my particular style rather than fitting and meeting each child's unique needs and style.
- We allocate time to meet bureaucratic requirements and arbitrary rules (such as the 120-hour Carnegie Unit) rather than considering how much time – more or less – makes sense from the child's point of view.

We must remember that school is a mandatory place for children but an optional place for adults; it is a place where children have little or no power and adults have much. Children continually move through and have no necessary sense of permanence, while adults might stay for an entire career / vocation. It can be a place where well-meaning disciples "hinder" the children from coming to the Father.

Being child-centered makes us sensitive to our adult self-centeredness. Indeed, it is only within the context of God's love and grace that leaving the self-centeredness of adults behind makes any sense and, indeed, is possible. When we are able to stop being self-centered as adults, we are freed to become immersed in the lives of our children. Then, we can "teach (the laws) to your children, talking about them when you sit at home and when you walk along the road, when you lie down and when you get up" (Deuteronomy 11:19). This all-encompassing embrace of the teaching life is what turns it from mere career into vocation.

Of course, God takes the same approach, considering us his children, embracing us and being with us (Emmanuel) through the indwelling of the Holy Spirit, through the law written on our hearts, through the reality of knowing we are created beings, and teaching us (Psalms 25: 4-5; 27:11; 32:8; 86:11; 94:10; 119). He was with us at the beginning of time teaching the man (Genesis 2:16) while in Eden and apprenticing the man and woman in the making of clothing (Genesis 3:21). He came to us in Jesus, a child teaching in the Temple (Luke 2:46) and a man teaching the multitudes. In our schools we must note that God came to Adam and Eve within his creation and Jesus comes to us within the context of our lives. This is our model of how we should approach children – within the context of their own lives, teaching them where they are and in the way they can understand.

Child-centeredness thus asks us to leave behind our own adult selfishness (which scripturally is always attached to ambition, cf. 2 Corinthians 12:20; Galatians 5:20; Philippians 2:3; James 3:14). It asks us to come towards the child within the child's own context and in a way that makes sense to the child. And it asks us to exercise authority in order to serve the child, not to dominate the child.

We are reminded in our speaking of authority that Jesus remarked that we should receive the kingdom of God "like a child" (Mark 10:15) or not enter in. His last evening with his disciples was spent teaching them about foot washing. "Do you understand what I have done for you?" he asked them. "You call me 'Teacher' and 'Lord,' and rightly so, for that is what I am. Now that I, your Lord and Teacher, have washed your feet, you also should wash one another's feet" (John 13:12-14). Our authority is then to serve, a paradox in any age but no less in our own – where authority means to lord it over others and exercise privilege.

None of this is to take away the difference between an adult and a child, the person who has been trained and the one who has not, the administrator who has been promoted and the one who has not. All these reflect our talents and gifts (given to us) and their developmental growth. It is not to take away the authority that has the sense of judgment – there are plenty of places to go in Scripture to demonstrate the validity of that. But in our schools, the dominant impulse is always to look at education from the child's point of view, through the child's eyes, and with the child's best interests at heart. The dominant impulse is, thus, to love.

In our schools, that means actually paying deep attention to what we say we are doing and what we are actually doing; to recognizing our missions as being almost exclusively and correctly about helping the child; to asking children their thoughts, fears, dreams, aspirations and finding them of value and acting on them; to beginning each conversation with the admonition to keep the child at the center; to coming to decisions and asking the question as to whom the decision primarily benefits; to running meetings that focus on mission delivery to the child, whatever the topic of conversation.

Schools with children at the center are fun, happy, high achieving, extraordinary places. Adults in them are vocation driven, selfless, wise, pure. James warns against being a teacher, noting how many pitfalls there are. But for those who know that is their calling, he also encourages in James 3:13, "Who is wise and understanding among you? Let them show it by their good life, by deeds done in the humility that comes from wisdom. But if you harbor bitter envy and selfish ambition in your hearts, do not boast about it or deny the truth. But the wisdom that comes from heaven is first of all pure; then peace-loving, considerate, submissive, full of mercy and good fruit, impartial and sincere." That is the Child Principle.

APPENDIX 3:
CHRISTIAN MANAGEMENT / LEADERSHIP – THE SERVANT LEADER PRINCIPLE

"Jesus knew that the Father had put all things under his power, and that he had come from God and was returning to God; so he got up from the meal, took off his outer clothing, and wrapped a towel around his waist. … When he had finished washing their feet, he put on his clothes and returned to his place. 'Do you understand what I have done for you?' he asked them" (John 13:3-4, 12).

Christian school leaders are servant leaders. They have the following obligations:

- Serve the mission of the school – everything else is a subset of this.
- Serve the children of the school as the primary client.
- Recruit and support faculty and staff to:
  - provide resources,
  - be present for them and know each one,
  - be in an ongoing conversation with them,
  - help them grow throughout their careers,
  - hold them accountable, and
  - let them go when they are unable to fulfill their task with excellence.
- Partner with the Board for effective planning.
- Execute the plan with diligence and efficiency.

Authority and service seem to always be in tension. If I am in authority, how can I at the same time be in service? As the Head of School or Division Leader or Business Manager, where is authority and where is service? How do they link?

Authority is not to be denied. It is there for 3 important purposes: to know and do a job in such a way that people follow; to hold others accountable; to bring a key perspective to conversations and thus enrich decision making. Each of these purposes is part of leadership.

To be obvious, you can't be a leader unless you have followers. Gaining followers happens in a variety of ways, as history shows: the "strong" individual, the mystic, the rich person, the visionary, the person of power, and so on. Most of these are not servant leaders. It is important to know that – servant leadership is only 1 of many ways to lead. Christian School Management (CSM) considers it to be the highest form of leadership.

In a school, servant leadership operates at every level. The teacher needs to lead children from being subordinates to becoming followers as quickly as possible and does that through building relationships, demonstrating competence, teaching with passion, and having an expansive vision of where each child can go. The administrator optimally serves followers who are similarly committed to the mission of the school, are supported in their growing competence, trust in the leader, are held accountable, and contribute to the whole as members of a productive team. The Head serves the team by optimizing and expanding its strengths. Gallup, the polling organization, found that the 4 needs of followers were trust, compassion, stability, hope. In the Christian school, these words have resonance as well. Still, we might rewrite them in this form:

Gallup	Christian School
Trust	Competence and making and keeping promises
Compassion	Love – desiring always the best for the other
Stability	Knowing that Jesus is the Rock and standing securely there
Hope	Mission, planning, execution

Leadership does not always operate according to the organization chart. Formal leadership is often supported by informal leadership in the organization – the exemplary teacher who leads conversations, presents at conferences, and chairs committees has an authority far beyond her title. Informal leadership is the place where we discover those who have the servant's heart. While we may hire those who already have titles and / or reputations, we see in the everyday interactions of each person much more clearly what his or her impulse to action is – whether to power or to service.

Robert Greenleaf of the Greenleaf Center for Servant Leadership wrote: "The servant-leader is servant first ... It begins with the natural feeling that one wants to serve, to serve first. Then conscious choice brings one to aspire to lead. That person is sharply different from one who is leader first, perhaps because of the need to assuage an unusual power drive or to acquire material possessions ... The leader-first and the servant-first are 2 extreme types. Between them there are shadings and blends that are part of the infinite variety of human nature. The difference manifests itself in the care taken by the servant-first to make sure that other people's highest priority needs are being served. The best test, and one that is difficult to administer, is: Do those served grow as persons? Do they, while being served, become healthier, wiser, freer, more autonomous, more likely themselves to become servants? And, what is the effect on the least privileged in society? Will they benefit or at least not be further deprived?"

This leads to the key observation that for the Christian school, servant leadership has an objective that is clear and non-negotiable. At the heart of the word "service" is the person of the child. We are not in our schools to serve everyone equally. Far from it. First is the child, who is the reason for the school, its mission outcome, and the most vulnerable person in the school community. Servant leadership is thus not even-handed. Within the context of the school, each servant leader serves first the student. Both the adult leader and the adult follower must know that their contract obligation to fulfill their responsibilities in return for various benefits is the legal mirror for their moral obligation to deliver the mission to the student.

The practical issues that arise are difficult in practice, while clear in theory. What happens if adults do not do their jobs well? How do we hold adults accountable for that mission delivery, irrespective of whether that is in the Business Office, in the classroom, on the playing fields, on field trips or in the Advancement Office? What about that beloved member of the church community who happens to be a mediocre teacher or administrator? Does servant leadership imply that we place adult community as the prime concern? Is rocking the boat being a servant? Should we overlook adult misconduct because we genuinely do care for every member of the school?

This would suggest that "servant" is a soft term with no substance. To the contrary – when we recognize that the center of our attention is the child, to serve the child implies that we are all accountable in the most demanding ways, both personally and collectively. In that collective sense, it is the school that takes on the responsibility for mission delivery to each child. Thus, the school must corporately take on the characteristic of servant leader to fully develop each child's God-given gifts and fulfill God's purpose in each child's life. Adults thus operate in 2 ways. The first is as an individual where the servant leader seeks to deliver the mission to the child and support, enhance, and develop the skills of each employee. The second is as a school body exhibiting corporately the servant leader disposition. Here, the requirement that each individual be a contributing element to that corporate identity is key.

If we are committed as servant leaders merely to the individual employee, it would be possible to imagine the needs of the adult becoming, as often happens in our schools, equivalent to or even greater than the needs of the child. Where, however, we are committed as servant leaders institutionally to the child, now each adult has a critical role to play and for which to be held accountable. Being a servant leader is thus not just an individual but a corporate responsibility. Note that 1 Corinthians 12 is implacable that we all play a part in the body of Christ and, implicitly, in whatever station of life we have been led to. "Even so the body is not made up of one part but of many" (v. 14).

The Head as servant leader primarily for the child must therefore root out adult incompetence and ensure that the child receives the best mission-centered education. Similarly, the Board of Trustees must hold the Head accountable. Once the highest needs of the child have been taken care of, and in order to achieve that goal, the adult is also nurtured and fed. Accountability is thus a key element of being a servant leader.

"Jesus called them together and said, 'You know that the rulers of the Gentiles lord it over them, and their high officials exercise authority over them. Not so with you. Instead, whoever wants to become great among you must be your servant, and whoever wants to be first must be your slave—just as the Son of Man did not come to be served, but to serve, and to give his life as a ransom for many'" (Matthew 20:25-28).

The Christian school is an exemplar of servant leadership. We give our lives as a school body to deliver the mission to the student. We are held accountable for the excellence of that delivery. I individually deliver the mission and am held individually accountable. When the Christian school functions in this healthy way, it can achieve excellence.

APPENDIX 4:
THE CHRISTIAN SCHOOL –
THE KINGDOM PRINCIPLE

Matthew 6:10
"Our Father in heaven, hallowed be your name, your kingdom come, your will be done, on earth as it is in heaven."

Matthew 22:36-39 (NIV)
"Teacher, which is the greatest commandment in the Law? Jesus replied: 'Love the Lord your God with all your heart and with all your soul and with all your mind.' This is the first and greatest commandment. And the second is like it: 'Love your neighbor as yourself.' All the Law and the Prophets hang on these two commandments."

The Christian school is one that:

- intends for its children to bring God's kingdom "on earth as it is in heaven" (the Christian School Management motto)
- creates its mission carefully and delivers it with excellence, and
- recognizes Jesus as the Master Teacher.

In its simplest terms, the Kingdom Principle states that God gives us good work to do right here and now. This work is not menial nor does it merely fill in time until we go to be with the Father. Rather, God intends for us to do his will on earth, which has many rich possibilities and is individual to each one of us in our schools. Many scholars believe that "on earth as it is in heaven" applies to each of the 3 preceding phrases, i.e., hallowed be your name, your kingdom come, your will be done.

In a Christian school, this principle is made concrete through the mission of the school. Certainly, theologically, from a church perspective, we could discuss the beautiful implications and applications of this prayer given to us by Jesus as the paradigm of prayers (including the injunction not to "babble like the pagans"!). But we are not theologians and our interest is in what this means in the life of a Christian school.

God's holiness, God's kingdom, God's will are made manifest in the Christian school through its mission. Don't be overwhelmed; within that context, the Christian school's role is to carry out its mission – and that is enough. The Christian school should not harbor ambitions that make the mission too bold. The mission should have authority, and it should be humble. The mission articulates clearly the purpose of the school and the purpose must be limited because we have limited money, people, facilities, land, students. We cannot do everything, and we are not called to do everything. We are called as a Christian school to do our mission.

Consider these slightly edited examples from real schools:

1. The mission of XXXX Day School is to assist the Christian family by providing an education marked by a biblical worldview and academic excellence so that students are equipped to be salt and light for God's glory.
2. XXXXXX Academy empowers students for leadership and service in our global society.
3. Within an atmosphere of love, concern, and mutual respect, XXXXXXX Preparatory School is committed to instilling Christian values, to developing future leaders, and to preparing students for college and lifetime learning through academically challenging programs and affirming competitive experiences.
4. XXXXXXXXX School develops in students a love of learning, respect for self and others, faith in God, and a sense of service to the world community.
5. The purpose of XXXX School is to enlighten the understanding, shape the character, form the habits of discipline, and prepare young men and women to fulfill their God-given potential.

We note here that CSM does not judge the mission of a school. We recognize it as the human attempt of each school to bring God's kingdom into the lives of children here on earth, we respect it as such, and we hold the school accountable to do what it does to a standard of excellence.

We can see that these missions are very different from one another. Based on the school's founding history, its journey to this point, the challenges it sees and wishes to address, the children it wishes to serve, and its resources, the Christian school makes – and must make – a determination about its mission by both being bold and far-seeing in its vision and humble and limited in its reach.

It's hard to imagine the Christian school committing to a standard of mediocrity. But we have to understand that truly doing our mission at a standard of excellence comes with significant investment. Let's consider that by turning parts of the above mission statements into questions.

- How do we invest in "academic excellence"? Our children work hard in class and devote hours to further study. Our teachers provide engaging, faith-filled, relevant, practical, meaningful lessons – the work of a lifetime of application and study. Buildings that nurture the mind in a healthy environment conducive to imaginative and creative study can cost millions.

- What is the investment in "empowering students for leadership and service"? Leadership is not easily learned. It must be practiced in many situations, reflected upon, mentored by those who themselves understand and exemplify leadership. There can be significant risks that must be accepted in order for children to take on these tasks – loss of control, imperfect outcomes, mistakes. Service requires resources that could be devoted to "academic excellence"! If we are committed to service, those resources cannot be shifted to some other worthy objective.
- How do we invest in "an atmosphere of love, concern, and mutual respect"? At the least, it requires consistent and persistent modeling by people whose actions are authentic and grounded in a firm understanding of the love of Jesus. Students must be trained to put aside their natural self-centeredness and practice a different way.
- What is the investment that empowers children "to fulfill their God-given potential"? This might mean a willingness to explore and understand yourself and to discover what gifts God has given you. It means hiring teachers who delight and continually expand their own potential. It means the school's willingness for the child to fulfill a potential that was not in the school's plan, and maybe in a way that was not in the teacher's plan.

These are not simple things to talk about, let alone do. CSM has worked with schools that think of their mission statement as words rather than as God's call to bring his kingdom. We urge the Christian school to:

1. Prayerfully examine its mission and ensure that it truly represents the school's witness in the world.
2. Believe that the mission is sufficient, i.e., that the school cannot and is not responsible for everything.
3. Understand the mission in the light of the Kingdom Principle.
4. Ensure that the mission is embedded in the daily life and practice of the school.

When the Christian school takes its mission seriously, commits to its fulfillment at a level of excellence, and makes it meaningful daily, it will be in the best position possible to provide God's children with a glimpse of his kingdom.

APPENDIX 5:
CHRISTIAN TEACHERS:
THE LOVE PRINCIPLE

1 Corinthians 13:4-8a (NIV)
"Love is patient, love is kind. It does not envy, it does not boast, it is not proud. It does not dishonor others, it is not self-seeking, it is not easily angered, it keeps no record of wrongs. Love does not delight in evil but rejoices with the truth. It always protects, always trusts, always hopes, always perseveres. Love never fails."

Zechariah 7:8-10
"And the word of the Lord came again to Zechariah: "This is what the Lord Almighty said: 'Administer true justice; show mercy and compassion to one another. Do not oppress the widow or the fatherless, the foreigner or the poor. Do not plot evil against each other.'""

Christian teachers provide an environment for their students that is loving and just:

- Just – not arbitrary or capricious – fair: allows the students to meet each interaction with an adult with certainty because the response to behavior or performance (good or bad) can be predicted irrespective of time or place; it is "Always."
- Loving – student-centered, not judgmental: goes to where the student is; assures the student that, whatever the circumstances, the adult has the student's best interests at heart and will do whatever is needed for the student to be successful; it is Love incarnate.

It is good to remember the admonition of James that is, maybe, not spoken enough: "Not many of you should become teachers, my fellow believers, because you know that we who teach will be judged more strictly. We all stumble in many ways. Anyone who is never at fault in what they say is perfect, able to keep their whole body in check (ch. 3)."

That is not to say that James (and Paul in many other passages using δνιδάσκω) is talking about teaching in a Christian school! This is not a statement of theology. It is to say that we must seek hints as to the appropriate relationship between a child and teacher. James provides a significant insight that we can all associate with – the task of teaching is carried out with words and actions, and the way in which we use words and interact with children has enormous significance.

Today we think of that truism not just as the overt use of criticism or praise with the power to motivate or demotivate, but in elements of incredible subtlety. Consider the use of vocabulary that includes or excludes; the way words are supported – or contradicted – by body language; the exercise of authority versus power; communication preferences; communication methods, including technology; the giving and taking of responsibility; rewards and sanctions. Placing the student at the center of the conversation, i.e., focusing on the way in which students can benefit from our words and actions, leads to asking how completely a child can trust us. Here, we are not talking about truth and deceit (which are obviously important) but rather about the just and loving nature of our words and actions.

The Love Principle, at its heart, is about establishing a trust relationship. The writer of Titus says: "In your teaching show integrity, seriousness and soundness of speech that cannot be condemned, so that those who oppose you may be ashamed because they have nothing bad to say about us ... but to show that they [the teachers] can be fully trusted, so that in every way they will make the teaching about God our Savior attractive" (Titus 2:6-7).

It is important that we always recognize that the teacher in a Christian school not only wants the child to do well in an academic sense, thus securing a hopeful secular future, but also to be open to the Word of God and thus to have that secular future imbued with and infused with God's love, giving it meaning and eternal significance. We will not think of this as a biblical worldview (although that can be a useful phrase) but rather as the presence of God personally in the child's learning experience. The Love Principle brings the presence of God into the presence of the child. The teacher's trustworthiness is a model of God's trustworthiness.

God's trustworthiness can be thought of in this context as providing 2 feedback loops:

- offering a true assessment of who we are – dead in our sins, and
- providing the way through – making us alive.

As Paul says in Colossians 2:13: "When you were dead in your sins and in the uncircumcision of your flesh, God made you alive with Christ." We trust God because we know in ourselves that his assessment of us is accurate (we are dead in our sins) AND that he did whatever needed to be done (died and rose again) and told us how we needed to respond (your faith in the working of God – vse. 12). It is this essential trustworthiness of God that the teacher echoes as a faint shadow in every interaction with a child. The teacher speaks truth in love (Ephesians 4:15) so that the child can mature. The teacher provides a true assessment and a solution at the same time.

Too many schools are far too individualistic in creating this environment of trust, one that consistently reinforces for students that ALL teachers are just / fair and loving / committed to students' success. The way individual teachers put these ideas into practice can vary so significantly that the environment is not empowering from the students' point of view. Instead, it may seem contradictory, even capricious.

The Love Principle, therefore, also supports the Christian Professional Learning Community. Through this approach, being just and being loving becomes systemic through the best practices of communities of teachers. In such a community:

- The student's development is the key measure of success, and the community's commitment to that is primary.
- Each faculty member's commitment to his or her own development is palpable.
- The willingness to engage in professional conversations as a norm of professional practice, unbounded by time or place, is endemic to the faculty culture.
- There is a common and unquestioned commitment to the mission of the school. There is generative conversation about the translation of that mission to every area of school life and to every developmental stage of the students.
- Study of the research and improvements in the practice of learning and teaching are valued. Best practice should imply a journey, not an ending!
- The faculty collaborate to ensure that their own improving practice is aligned (not identical) and that it is clear what is meant by curriculum, assessment, and standards.
- Faculty examine practice in their own classrooms and those of their colleagues, critique on the basis of student learning, and implement on the basis of continual improvement.

The Love Principle is both individual and corporate. It certainly is individual. Each faculty member is just (accurate and fair), while always supporting the student through thick and thin. As Jesus identified the failings of those around him, so he also drew people to himself so that they could be healed. While we are not so grandiose, nonetheless, we are an important echo of his ministry in the lives of our students. Through us, they will have a glimpse of the eternal. This principle is also corporate. We cannot do this on our own. Together with our colleagues (and assuredly with study and prayer), we must become a Christian Professional Learning Community where being just and loving is encoded in everyday practice, an environment in which learning becomes not just possible but profound for each student.

And that is the final point of this principle. It is not enough for us to do this for some, most, or even almost all students. As families are called to our mission and students enter our hallways, so our measure of success individually and corporately is 100%. Outside of circumstances where the student or family must be counseled out, our measure of success is absolute – all "100" students must be met, nurtured, and brought to a place of success. "What do you think? If a man owns a hundred sheep, and one of them wanders away, will he not leave the ninety-nine on the hills and go to look for the one that wandered off?" (Matthew 18:12).

The Love Principle looks easier than it actually is. To be just and loving every minute of every day of every week of every month of every year can only be accomplished through personal and corporate commitment to the task. "Finally, brothers and sisters, rejoice! Strive for full restoration, encourage one another, be of one mind, live in peace. And the God of love and peace will be with you" (2 Corinthians 13:11).

APPENDIX 6:
CHRISTIAN PHILANTHROPY –
THE MARY PRINCIPLE

Luke 8: 3
"Mary (called Magdalene) from whom seven demons had come out; Joanna the wife of Chuza, the manager of Herod's household; Susanna; and many others. These women were helping to support them out of their own means."

Christian schools need supporters who will give of their abundance (at whatever level that indicates) in order to further the work of the school. While parents can be expected to pay tuition and fees for the services they receive, that money typically does not purchase property, build facilities, or provide items that are over and above normal everyday expenses. It is thus very important that Christian schools:

- raise money over and above operating income,
- treat donors honorably and respectfully, and
- follow the highest ethical standards.

From our perspective at Christian School Management (CSM), it is no casual statement to call this the Mary Principle. The women mentioned in Luke's Gospel had been "cured of evil spirits and diseases" (vse. 2). They had experienced an astonishing change in their circumstances and were giving, we might assume, out of gratitude for deliverance. We can assume that these women were also the same ones who, in Luke 23 and 24, gave Jesus' body its final ministrations and were the first at the tomb the next day. Certainly, having someone as wealthy as Joanna in the ranks would have been enormously important in order to cover the expenses of this work.

Mary Magdalene is so important that she is mentioned at least 12 times, more than many of the apostles, and mentioned in connection with the key events of Jesus' life. These women were not just appurtenances, but key and vital members of Jesus' work with characteristics that one might find in other passages such as Proverbs 31. Connecting philanthropy to these women is to establish important points about the work of raising money for Christian schools. There are 5 operating principles that the Lukan narrative identifies:

1. Giving is in gratitude for what has been done.
2. Giving is done by people who are intimately involved with the action.

3. Giving includes involvement, not just the act of giving itself.
4. Giving galvanizes possibilities that otherwise could not be imagined.
5. Giving is recognized and honored.

We don't know if these women were asked to give or if they initiated the conversation. We can imagine, however, that once someone like Joanna had been healed, she asked in what way she could be part of what was going on with Jesus. There was obviously some kind of organizational structure to Jesus' ministry such that when he arrived at a place, there had been some preparations: food bought for the road, fresh clothing to replace what was wearing out, new sandals on occasion, even transportation such as the special time that Jesus told his disciples to seek out the ass for his entrance into Jerusalem. It can't have been a simple thing for 13 men and other followers to travel around the countryside living a peripatetic lifestyle. Joanna would have been gratefully welcomed into the company of donors who kept things on an even keel. Maybe she asked; maybe she was asked. What we do know is that she and others (many others) were thought important enough to be specifically honored through Luke's narrative.

Giving for Christian education needs to follow these 5 principles. Unfortunately, caring for the money of others has not been a strong practice on the part of Christian schools. Christian donors often (very often) become disillusioned because their money, given thoughtfully and hopefully, vanishes into a black hole that has these characteristics:

- It is not well accounted for or accountable – how was it spent and what was it used for.
- It does not solve problems; in fact, it merely papers over the problems the school fails to address. The consequence is that the need for the donation recurs.
- It does not move the school forward. It does not create space for creative solutions or visionary possibilities. Far from opening up opportunities, it reaffirms the school in thinking that its "faithful prayer" has been answered. The future is not a new day of creativity but only the present day repeated.
- It does not support building capacity in the administration, faculty, and staff of the school. The gift is used to cover deficits in the current budget. It does not fund "moving forward" items such as significant professional development, the use of consulting services, professionalization of operations, technology systems to collect and manage data.

Thus, Christian schools must manage and think about gifts in a different way. Even the manna in the desert enabled the Jewish people to move towards the Promised Land! Christian schools must know how to look after the gift legally and ethically. Christian schools must know how to use the gift in a way that moves the school from the present into the future. Gifts that only serve the present, by definition, mask underlying management and leadership problems that the Board of Trustees and Principal are not addressing effectively. Gifts are about the future and about vision and about direction.

Interestingly, Christian schools have trouble asking people for money. It would seem that Jesus and his disciples were not shy about it. Mary, Joanna, and many others supported their work. The Mary Principle suggests that many want to support the work of Jesus in the Christian school. Penelope Burk in her research into giving says that, for example, "9 to 10 percent of people say they have put bequests in their wills, but more than 30 percent say they would definitely do it or take under serious consideration if asked."

It is clear that our schools do not have the confidence, or they do not think it is right, to ask their potential supporters for money. There is sometimes the thought that these people SHOULD give and we shouldn't have to ask them. We do not take a position on that. What we do know is that if the school does not ask them, many who would give will not. After all, they ARE being asked by many other organizations and individuals, sometimes on a weekly basis, to contribute to many worthy causes.

The Christian school needs philanthropic dollars. It is not a "love of money" that leads to asking for investment into the lives of children in the school. It is an appreciation of the need to serve the children of the school and carry out its mission. It is because the school can clearly and authentically identify a future-oriented need. It is done with complete integrity and open accountability. It is done transparently and without embarrassment. It is done with the operating budget taken care of – it is not a replacement for good daily management and accounting practices.

From the donor's perspective, the gift is given because it has been asked for. Donors feel that their philanthropy is an excellent investment in the future. They equally feel that they are honored in their giving – first, by being asked within the context of a plan; second, by being included appropriately in the conversation; third, by being thanked, told that their gift was used as asked, and given evidence that children benefited. Finally, the donor is treated in a way that makes him or her want to be equally or more generous the following year. A "tired" donor is typically someone for whom these things have not happened.

The Mary Principle is built on the Ox Principle. A school that balances its budget, limits its debt, compensates its employees professionally, and has a reserve is a school that is positioned to succeed in raising money optimally. The school that manages its budget poorly, fails to charge tuition that pays the bills, goes into debt, and asks its employees to work "sacrificially," i.e., without sufficient income to raise their families, is positioned to fail in any meaningful fund-raising. These 2 principles work hand in hand.

Every Christian family that is involved with a Christian school wants to support it. The Mary Principle, and the Ox Principle that underlies it, gives them every opportunity to do so. They will be eager and excited to see the miracles of what God has given them translate into the miracles that God will perform through their school.

APPENDIX 7: CHRISTIAN FINANCES – THE OX PRINCIPLE

1 Timothy 6:17
"Do not muzzle an ox while it is treading out the grain."

Numbers 18:21 (NIV)
"I give to the Levites all the tithes in Israel as their inheritance in return for the work they do while serving at the tent of meeting."

1 Timothy 6:8
"Anyone who does not provide for their relatives, and especially for their own household, has denied the faith and is worse than an unbeliever."

Proverbs 22:7
"The rich rule over the poor, and the borrower is slave to the lender."

Exodus 41:33-36
"And now let Pharaoh look for a discerning and wise man and put him in charge of the land of Egypt. Let Pharaoh appoint commissioners over the land to take a fifth of the harvest of Egypt during the seven years of abundance. They should collect all the food of these good years that are coming and store up the grain under the authority of Pharaoh, to be kept in the cities for food. This food should be held in reserve for the country, to be used during the seven years of famine that will come upon Egypt, so that the country may not be ruined by the famine."

The Christian school thinks about money a lot. It enjoys the thought that God provides richly for his people. It wants to have the best resources it can to serve its children. It is neither embarrassed nor ashamed to talk about God's gift of money. The school has an obligation to:

- provide resources that allow it to deliver the mission with excellence,
- balance its budget,
- compensate its employees honorably and respectfully,
- provide a safe and optimal learning environment,
- minimize / eliminate debt, and
- maintain a reserve.

Let's start with the last item first: maintain a reserve. The Minnesota Council of Non-Profits discovered that "nonprofits with minimal or no reserves were more likely to have cut budgets, eliminated staff positions, reduced wages and benefits. They were also less likely to have been able to increase services to respond to growing demand." That is, if your school has no cash reserves, it is in a constantly unstable situation, whether it needs to deal with economic hard times in a healthy way or to respond to economic good times by being able to take advantage of opportunities.

And there is no justification in the Christian school for taking the attitude that the Lord will provide. Certainly, there are times when the widow's jar of oil stays miraculously full. And we rejoice in the goodness of our God. At the same time, it is clear that trust can often (often!) be a misnomer for poor management, with the result that our schools go out of business because they lacked the cardinal virtue of prudence. Aristotle defined prudence as *recta ratio agibilium*, "right reason applied to practice." And St. Thomas Aquinas considered it the first of the virtues.

When we apply prudence with the guidance of the Holy Spirit, it may well lead us to take steps that may appear foolish from a worldly point of view – but that does not include the lack of foresight. Our God is a God of planning. Jeremiah 29:10 says, "For I know the plans I have for you," declares the Lord, "plans to prosper you and not to harm you, plans to give you hope and a future." Indeed, it is the ungodly who fail to plan: "Let us eat and drink ... for tomorrow we die" (Isaiah 22:13).

Interestingly, that planning often meant that the great Christian leaders have often had to operate by faith that the plan would come to pass and not in their own lifetimes. So it is with our schools. Reserves are one of the ways in which the Christian school exercises prudence and foresight in order to ensure that the school will still be here for the next generation. Whether used or not in "my" time of service, they will provide Joseph's sustenance in the time of famine.

With that in mind, we can turn to the issue of the school's budget. Talking about money for the Christian school always begins with the school's mission. Many commentators have said that we should begin with the end in mind, and it is good advice. At Christian School Management (CSM), we would take it one step further and say that the "end" of the Christian school – its mission – is what dictates its budget.

Let there be no error here. Budget for many Christian schools means eking out a painful existence on the backs of poorly paid workers and badly maintained buildings. We don't have to go to the prosperity preachers to know that this is bad economics of body, mind, and spirit. There is no Christian character in being paid below the poverty level or not having the resources to teach with the right materials or passing the buck by deferring the upkeep of buildings and grounds.

For Jesus; Through Mission; With Students

The question thus becomes whether we believe in delivering the mission at a level of excellence and what that means. CSM believes that we are called to excellence, and that we witness that to our own people / community as well as to those who are watching us from the outside. "But you are a chosen race, a royal priesthood, a holy nation, a people for his own possession, that you may proclaim the excellencies of him who called you out of darkness into his marvelous light" (1 Peter 2:9). Witnessing to excellence means exemplifying excellence in our own financial practices. There are then very clear steps to take in thinking about the budget:

1. Understand your own mission statement – what does it mean when we apply the standard of "excellence" to each of its words and think about the investment that is necessary to make that happen? (cf. the CSM Kingdom Principle)
2. Don't assume that the budget you have had for so many years is, de facto, the best budget. In fact, assume that there are deficits that you want to improve over time. As school leaders, be aware that our followers (employees) will want to act sacrificially in order to support the mission of the school and to help as many students as possible. Applaud that and appreciate it. However, don't let it stop the conversation about supporting them appropriately in their mission delivery.
3. Unless the school is new, debt is typically the wrong way to raise money.
   - This includes lines of credit required because there is not enough money to get through the year. Budgets must be balanced, and balanced by ensuring that the families who want this education cover the cost through their tuition.
   - When building improvements and new construction are needed, the money should be raised through fundraising.
   - Debt payments are a tax on tuition and degrade the school's budget.
4. The issue of compensation is important. It is just wrong not to compensate Christian workers professionally. The notion that they should be "underpaid" because it is a ministry fails to honor them. Certainly, it is a ministry. We will not try to define a fair wage. But we do know this: When our workers are paid at a level that does not allow them to raise a family, or that forces the them to rely on income from a spouse who works in a "secular" occupation, or that results in them not having benefits or any kind of retirement opportunities, then our budget lacks a moral foundation. We can go further and say that in order to attract and retain the best teachers and staff, we will pay them competitively, recognizing their value and honoring it.

A note about fundraising: CSM believes that the school's operational expenses must be paid for through tuition and fees. Fundraising is the gift of the heart that invests in the future of the school and to the direct benefit of the children. God has made us generous people. It is part of the way in which we are created. The school should joyfully ask its supporters for their gifts, given because of God's generosity to us (cf. the CSM Mary Principle).

We are committed to being great stewards of the riches that God gives to us. We need to think of God as generous and thus that he will meet our needs. We have a responsibility to express those needs in such a way that we exemplify excellence in our mission delivery, professionally pay and provide benefits to our people, maintain prudence in our reserves and debt management, and balance the budget. That is the Ox Principle.

APPENDIX 8: THE CHURCH YEAR

In our daily lives we keep track of our activities and special events with a calendar. The church throughout the centuries has also "kept track" of days and seasons and commemorating special occasions with a calendar.

The Christian church has continued to follow the example set in the Old Testament of structuring the year around the marvelous acts of salvation that God completed for us in his Son, Christ. We call this structure the Church Year.

The church year calendar is organized into 3 sections: Sundays and seasons, feasts and festivals, and commemorations. The seasons of the church year are marked by specific liturgical colors to give us a visual reminder.

Found here are the Sundays and seasons in the cycles of the Church's liturgical calendar: Christmas/Epiphany, Good Friday/Easter, and Pentecost, followed by the Season after Pentecost that includes Creation Time. You may find them helpful as you think about your own structure of the academic year and how that relates to the amazing story of redemption.

APPENDIX 9: THE MARKETING PAGE

Okay, you're still reading. But remember, I warned you – this is a marketing page!

If you are a real leader, you never stop learning. Becoming a CSM member for only $7.87 a month (christianschoolmanagement.org) gives you access to advice that is different from all other advice. It is:

- Specific to schools
- Rooted in Scripture
- Steeped in experience
- Filled with practical, doable advice
- Backed up by research in many fields
- Tested in schools every year
- Always updated when our faith understanding, the practical application, and/or research findings dictate

It also gives you access to CSM consultants for advice and counsel – fill in a form and, voila, responses provide you with options for you to consider.

Finally, membership makes you a partner to help schools like yours across the United States and Canada as we work to help schools grow enrollment and make a Christian education available to every child everywhere.

Consider how we might help you at your school through our consulting services, provided by Christian school leaders who are integrated into CSM thinking and CSM Principles. We never lose you money! If we were to boast, we would tell you that when we come to your school, you can expect an intellectual return on investment, a financial return on investment, and a spiritual return on investment. Talk to school leaders we have served and find out for yourself whether that's true. Our client schools are on our website.

We also have publications – currently 3 including this one. Think about buying them for yourself, your Board, and for your own school leaders for their professional growth.

1. *A Call to Authentic Christian School Trusteeship: The Christian School Trustee Handbook* (2017)

2. *Stewards of Transformation: The Board President / Head of School Partnership in Christian Schools* (2018)

Finally, consider whether you are called to join with CSM in its mission. Call us if you feel God's tug on your heart at 519-401-2351, or email us at christianschoolmanagement@gmail.com.

APPENDIX 10: INDEX OF BIBLE PASSAGES

You can also pick devotions based on the scriptures we have used as home bases. Listed below are all the theme scriptures quoted from the Psalms and the Gospels and the number of devotion where you will find them.

Psalms	Devotion
2: 12	10
3: 6	49
7: 1	154
9: 1	105
11: 3	96
15: 1-3	51
18: 35-40	136
20: 4	27
22: 30-31	41
27: 1	137
27: 14	32
30: 5	47
33: 11	64
35: 4	104
37: 1-2	75
37: 3-4	98
37: 24	31
40: 1	13
40: 3	4
42: 8	1
60: 12	43
62: 2	169
67: 1-2	126
70: 5	151
73: 6-7	128
73: 13-14	127
73: 16-17	129
77: 11	138
78: 72	30
90: 12	58
90: 12	74
90: 17	28
91: 15	157
96: 12	35
97: 1	33
107: 2-3	86
107: 26	76
107	171
114: 8	163
117	122
119: 6	25
119: 9	102
124: 1	147
126: 2	42
126: 2	59
127: 3-5	135
130: 4	6
133: 1	80
133: 1	101
139: 8	134
139: 14-15	94
145: 15-19	20
145: 18	8
147: 1	123
147: 3	7
147: 7-8	124
148: 1	52
148: 3	160
150: 4-5	121

Matthew	Devotion
1: 5	11
1: 19	48
1: 24-25	22
2: 1	63
5: 14	2
5: 14-16	150
5: 20	9
5: 37	15
6: 21	142
6: 22-23	115
6: 28-29	87
6: 33	19
6: 33	29
6: 33	148
7: 1-3	44
8: 11	69
8: 23-26	141
9: 4	21
11: 28-30	45
11: 29	107
14: 32	97
16: 1	46
16: 3	112
16: 24	73
19: 8	3
20: 6	159
20: 14	158
20: 16	34
20: 30-33	106
22: 34-37	54
23: 23	16
24: 4	56
25: 27	79
26: 42	125
28: 16-20	89

Mark	Devotion
1: 1	39
1: 16-18	108
1: 17	144
2: 16	85
2: 17	153
2: 21	110
3: 16-18	24
3: 24	116
3: 33	91
5: 30	82
5: 35-36	90
6: 31	68
8: 1	155
8: 33	36
8: 34-35	145
9: 1	156
9: 32	71

		John	Devotion
9: 39	146	1: 14	114
10: 14-16	57	2: 10	170
10: 21	77	4: 27	161
10: 48	162	4: 35	61
12: 43	103	6: 5-6	65
15: 27	53	6: 9	120
16: 33	38	6: 68	50
19: 30	26	7: 63	5
Luke	**Devotion**	8: 12	70
1: 8-9	23	13: 27	111
1: 46-49	131	14: 23	66
8: 25	164	14: 26	93
2: 1	40	14: 26	139
2: 1	62	15: 1-2	55
2: 40	117	15: 2	166
3: 4	143	15: 2	167
3: 8	88	15: 2	168
6: 40	100	15: 10	67
7: 9	60	18: 38	113
8: 1-3	14	19: 25	152
9: 38	118	20: 22	130
10: 27	72	21: 16	132
10: 30	18	21: 25	165
10: 30	78		
11: 39-40	140		
10: 36	84		
10: 38	81		
11: 13	12		
11: 18	17		
11: 52	109		
14: 11	95		
14: 28-30	99		
14: 34	37		
15: 9	149		
18: 13	92		
18: 39	83		
24: 10-11	119		

CPSIA information can be obtained
at www.ICGtesting.com
Printed in the USA
LVHW062120160719
624322LV00004B/7/P

9 781545 667927